The Radical Imagination
of Black Women

The Radical Imagination of Black Women

Ambition, Politics, and Power

PEARL K. FORD DOWE

OXFORD
UNIVERSITY PRESS

OXFORD
UNIVERSITY PRESS

Oxford University Press is a department of the University of Oxford. It furthers the University's objective of excellence in research, scholarship, and education by publishing worldwide. Oxford is a registered trade mark of Oxford University Press in the UK and certain other countries.

Published in the United States of America by Oxford University Press
198 Madison Avenue, New York, NY 10016, United States of America.

© Pearl K. Ford Dowe 2023

All rights reserved. No part of this publication may be reproduced, stored in a retrieval system, or transmitted, in any form or by any means, without the prior permission in writing of Oxford University Press, or as expressly permitted by law, by license, or under terms agreed with the appropriate reproduction rights organization. Inquiries concerning reproduction outside the scope of the above should be sent to the Rights Department, Oxford University Press, at the address above.

You must not circulate this work in any other form
and you must impose this same condition on any acquirer.

Library of Congress Cataloging-in-Publication Data
Names: Ford, Pearl K., 1972-, author.
Title: The radical imagination of Black women : ambition, politics, and power / Pearl K. Ford Dowe.
Other titles: Ambition, politics, and power
Description: New York, NY : Oxford University Press, [2023] |
Includes bibliographical references and index.
Identifiers: LCCN 2023014253 (print) | LCCN 2023014254 (ebook) |
ISBN 9780197650790 (hardback) | ISBN 9780197650806 (paperback) |
ISBN 9780197650820 (epub)
Subjects: LCSH: African American women—Political activity. |
African Americans—Politics and government.
Classification: LCC E185.86 .F648 2024 (print) | LCC E185.86 (ebook) |
DDC 305.48/896073—dc23/eng/20230428
LC record available at https://lccn.loc.gov/2023014253
LC ebook record available at https://lccn.loc.gov/2023014254

DOI: 10.1093/oso/9780197650790.001.0001

Paperback printed by Marquis Book Printing, Canada
Hardback printed by Bridgeport National Bindery, Inc., United States of America

For Karen,
May your radical imagination soar

Contents

Acknowledgments	ix
Introduction	1
1. The Radical Imagination of Black Women's Ambition	7
2. Black Women and Ambition: A Community Decision	42
3. An Ambition That Resists Marginalization	82
4. Black Women's Leadership: Connecting Socialization, and Careers	116
5. What Do Black Women Need from Black Women Elected Officials?	145
6. Conclusion	163
Appendix A: List of Interviewees	169
Appendix B: Interview Questions	171
Appendix C: Focus Group Questions	173
Notes	175
Bibliography	179
Index	201

Acknowledgments

This book has been a long time coming! Since I began conceptualizing this project over eight years ago I have gone through several transitions, and I'm blessed to say that they have been positive. During times of career advancement, family growth, and relocation to a new university in my home state, this book has stayed with me. My time working on the book has ebbed and flowed. There were periods in which I was able to give considerable time to researching and writing, and others in which other responsibilities pulled me away, and I could only hope for free time to write. I can't recall all the many pages I marked up and rewrote, the books and articles I studied, and the ideas I had about what this book could become. However, I remember the people and resources provided that assisted with making this book a reality.

First, I am sincerely indebted to the women who granted me a portion of their precious time to talk extensively about their careers and opinions. I appreciate the trust you bestowed upon me and the candor with which you told me your stories. I hope that you feel that these pages honor your voices and journeys.

Conducting a qualitative research project of this kind requires significant support. I was fortunate that at every phase of the research resources were made available to me. I am grateful for the support provided by the American Political Science Association's Centennial Center, the SEC Faculty Travel Program, the Provost's Office of the University of Arkansas, and the Diane D. Blair Center of Southern Politics and Society. This support allowed me to travel to conduct focus groups and several interviews.

I am likewise grateful to my hosts, in particular to Elsie Scott and Howard University's Ronald Walters Leadership and Public Policy Center. Elsie, your belief in my project provided me with the opportunity for extensive visits to the Washington, DC area and introduced me to the network of Black women political activists and organizers who assisted my understanding of the Black political woman. Thank you also to my dear friend Keesha Middlemass for opening your home to me. The focus group participants you introduced me to were critical to my data collection and analysis. They also shaped how I thought about the voices of young Black women.

I have been fortunate to have worked with colleagues who are not only outstanding scholars but also amazing people whom I am fortunate to call friends. The University of Arkansas provided a space for me to grow as a scholar and academic leader. Thank you to my former department chairs, Margaret Reid and John Gaber, for your support, and to my former Dean and forever friend Todd Shields. Todd, I still have your notes from our conversation about how to structure this book and disentangle the numerous research questions I had at the time. While at Arkansas, I worked with colleagues who provided feedback and gave me a much-needed sense of community. Thank you, Angie Maxwell, Xavier Medina Vidal, Yvette Murphy-Erby, Raphael Jimeno, and Shirin Saiedi. I also had the distinct pleasure of spending time writing with Shauna Morimoto and working with Lisa Corrigan to secure grant funding. Some amazing graduate students assisted me at various stages of the writing process. Dara Gaines, Briana Hyman, and Monica Cooper: thank you for keeping me on track and moving forward. I owe a special thanks to Briana; you came through to assist in the middle of drafting your dissertation. I cannot thank you enough for helping bring this book to fruition.

In 2019 I moved to Emory University. Thank you to Andra Gillespie for recruiting me and welcoming me into a new intellectual home. The people and resources available to me contributed to the completion of this book. I am indebted to the Center for Faculty Development and Excellence and the funding it provided to hire Jane Jones as a developmental editor and coach. Jane, you are a phenomenal developmental editor. Your guidance and support forced me to think differently and more effectively about how I did my day job and approached this book. Without those conversations I'm not sure if I would have kept writing. Thank you to my division chair, Ken Carter. Your vision for our division gave me access to Ulrike Guthrie. Ulrike, you are an amazing editor, and your keen eye and thoughtful critiques helped me fill in gaps and structure a book that I hope readers will enjoy. I am grateful to the African American Studies Department at Emory, which provided funding for scholars Wendy Smooth and Kira Sanbonmatsu to review the manuscript. Wendy and Kira: your insight and necessary suggestions surely helped bring forth a finalized book.

So many of you have meant so much to me over the years. Your encouragement, friendship, kind words, willingness to read pages and talk through ideas has meant the world to me. Thank you to Nikol Alexander-Floyd, Carol Anderson, Sharon Wright Austin, Najja Baptist, Ray Block, Nadia Brown, Khalilah Brown-Dean, Randy Burnside, Tameka Cage-Conley, Kesicia Dickson, Kelly Dittmar, Janeria Easley, Andra Gillespie, Keneshia Grant, Julia Jordan- Zachery, Tonja Simmons Lee, Molly McGehee, Charles Menifield, David Montague, Melanye Price, Elsie Scott, Jamil Scott, Valeria Sinclair-Chapman, Artemesia Stanberry, Dianne Stewart, Jessica Stewart, Carl Suddler, and to my National Conference of Black Political Scientists (NCOBPS) family: thank you for providing the space to receive feedback and encouragement.

Much of the joy that I have experienced as an academic and woman has come in spaces with other Black women. First, I want to thank the Sisters of Fulbright. This group of Black women faculty and graduate students at my college in Arkansas came together at a pivotal time for me. My book club Sister Circle: oh, what a blessing! Our once-a-month meetings were a respite from Saturday morning grading and writing. Our shared love of literature, culture, politics, and good food constantly refueled me and brought joy to my soul. Thanks also to my sister scholars, Wendy Smooth, Keesha Middlemass, Christina Greer, Niambi Carter, and Shalya Nunnally. We came together in a text message following a conference, and we have been together ever since. The random jokes, celebrations, and candid chats have been soft spaces to land when everything around me was going awry.

I owe the deepest appreciation and love to my family. Thank you to mama, April, and Virgil. You have always been my cheerleaders and have had a steadfast belief that I could achieve anything. To Alfred and Karen: I am so grateful to have a husband and daughter who yielded hours of time to allow me to complete this book. Your love and support of me is amazing and inspiring. I look forward to giving back to you what you have unconditionally given to me.

Introduction

> You can pray until you faint, but unless you get up and try to do something, God is not going to put it in your lap.
> —Fannie Lou Hamer

The idea for this project came to me one day in 2014 while reading online news articles. Two articles argued that white women candidates were critical to potential Democratic victories in Republican-led southern legislatures. My research on Black politics and electoral politics prompted me to question that premise. I knew that Black women were more likely to be victorious in their campaign efforts than white women and that that nationwide white women were more likely to vote Republican, not only in the South. Both my knowledge and the flaws in these articles led me to think more deeply about Black women who seek office and those already serving.

Who were the Black women who had run for elective office? Why did they run? And, how did they win? I reflected upon my own experiences and observations of Black political women. Growing up in Savannah, Georgia, in a working-class family and a neighborhood of both Black working- and middle-class families, I was immersed in Black culture and the ways that Black people understood and did politics. I found politics interesting, and during election cycles often observed Black candidates (men and women) and community members on the news advocating for issues relevant to the Black community.

The women who ran for office were similar to the circle of Black women I knew. Many of these women were engaged in and spoke highly of the organizations and churches to which they belonged. Members and even non-members respected those organizational affiliations. For example, as high school students do, I, along with my peers, casually complained about teachers we considered too hard or exams that seemed too difficult. One day my group walked into our biology class complaining about the math exam we had just taken. Our biology teacher, whom we considered one of the cooler teachers, stopped us short. Her coolness turned to harshness. She was not, she said, going to stand by and let us speak ill of her sorority sister. Her response ignited my curiosity about what a sorority is and why our cool teacher was so serious about it.

Women like my biology teacher were not only proud sorority women but were also members of other organizations. Some of these women could be referred to as "super joiners," as they not only were members of Black sororities but also were actively engaged in other organizations, such as the Links Incorporated, Top Ladies of Distinction Incorporated, and Jack and Jill of America, whose membership is made up of professional, college-educated, middle-class Black women. These same women often boast about their Historically Black College and University (HBCU) alma mater(s) during homecoming season. This included the local HBCU, Savannah State, which would become my alma mater. The local Black newspapers often featured these women for their church and civic engagement. These were the women who ran for office and won.

Due to my sorority affiliation and HBCU alumni status, I often engaged with Black women elites who were similar to the women I knew and witnessed growing up. These Black women were entrenched in a network of civic and social organizations and community networks that were sometimes linked to churches and HBCUs. I observed when a member of these networks ran for office, she often could rely on fellow network members to campaign on her behalf. After much contemplation, I knew I had a project. It took several years of reading, writing, and pondering the best approach to this project before I realized that I needed to tell the story of how Black women make the decision to run for office and how they win. Eventually, I came to realize that for many Black women the resources located within their communities and networks motivated their decision-making process and provided opportunities that led to their electoral success.

The central argument of *The Radical Imagination of Black Women: Ambition, Politics, and Power* is that elite Black women have a unique political ambition that compels them to move beyond service to seek office. Black women's unique experience of being Black and a woman has shaped their worldview, commitment to community, and how they address and understand their position within society. The literature on political ambition has largely overlooked Black women's political engagement. Why? Because social science in general and political science in particular often neglect the unique and abiding dynamics of Black political culture, a culture that cultivates public opinion and offers resources for potential candidates (Ford 2010). But as well as filling in that gap, I also seek to move the extant literature beyond the premise that the political ambition of Black women is less than white women or men. It appears so because political science approaches political participation very narrowly.

Other than voting, political science tends to disregard mechanisms through which Black women politically engage, such as community and civic engagement. Black women political scientists such as Mae King, Mamie Locke, and Jewel Prestage were the first to chronicle the positionality of Black women in society and politics. Their work showed us that these Black women were strategic, deliberate, and constantly engaged in American politics. Others' efforts have shown that Black women's political organizing and work have traditionally been in service to improving political and economic conditions for the Black community (Giddings 1984) and that Black women are significant actors as both voters and candidates (Brown and Dowe 2020; Tate 1991; Simien 2006; Smooth 2008).

To expand our understanding of how Black women decide to run for office and the resources that they are able to access, it is necessary to explore the source of those resources and how Black women are socialized to function politically. Black women have long robustly participated in the political process, and researchers have shown that they participate at higher rates than their white female and male counterparts (Cole and Stewart 1996; Harris, Sinclair-Chapman, and McKenzie 2005; Burns, Schlozman, and Verba 2001). This behavior has puzzled scholars because they have tended to rely on scholarship about women's political participation, specifically on Verba, Schlozman, and Brady's (1995) resource model. However, Black women don't fit neatly into a paradigm in which money, time, and civic skills predict high levels of political participation that influences candidate emergence (Gamble 2010; Smooth 2014).

Why not? Because such resources have not always been accessible to Black people. Instead, they find resources in community institutions that assist with political mobilization, teach democratic norms, and cultivate political activity among members (Morris 1986; Calhoun-Brown 1996; Robnett 1997; Brown and Lemi 2021). Although Black women are less likely to have resources typically associated with increased political participation (Burns, Schlozman, and Verba 2001; Verba and Nie 1972), they do in fact participate in numerous political activities at high rates (Junn 1997; Tate 1991; Gay and Tate 1998; Alex-Assenshoh and Stanford 1997; Smooth 2014).

My framework of *ambition on the margins* allows me to argue that Black women make conscious decisions about the offices they seek based on their assessment of which office enables the greatest community impact and how they can best navigate a marginalizing political structure that offers them limited resources or support in seeking political office. I observed this phenomenon in the various cities in which I lived. I saw Black women running for office and winning, and yet choosing not to pursue higher office in spite of their strong experience and popularity in their districts. By exploring not only women's motivation to run and what resources are available to them but also their decision to stay in a particular seat, I advance our knowledge about how Black female elites maintain their community-based interests even as they ascend to power. Three factors are important for such a holistic understanding of Black women and their political ambition: their political socialization, their gendered and racial identity, and their networks. The political socialization of Black women shapes their opinions of themselves and their identity and sense of agency, and it provides mechanisms to navigate the world as a Black girl child and later as a Black woman. Battling both racism and sexism, they experience the world differently from those who are not Black and female. Black women use their enormous community social capital and access to resources via social, civic, and community organizations to fundraise, mobilize voters, and gain access to potential voters.

While this framework is confirmed by women across the country—those that not only represent majority Black districts but also those who reside in districts and municipalities where Black voters make up a small percentage of the voting population—I am aware that my framework means that I focus on a particular type of Black woman candidate. The politicians I interviewed for this book are middle-class, college-educated professionals who have the means to pay membership dues and the time to participate in activities outside of work and home. I am also aware that although Black women are indeed motivated by community, they are also ambitious and have personal goals to ascend in politics. There are numerous Black women who are career politicians who engage in politics for power. However, due to the communities upon which they rely for votes, these women don't deviate very far from opportunities for community engagement.

Outline of the Book

Chapter 1 introduces the reader to the ways Black women's political work has affected community development, electoral outcomes, and public policy. I explore the limitations of the present literature on political ambition, including the negation of the unique political resources that the communities of Black women offer. The chapter introduces the theoretical framework that provides a roadmap for the book. Chapter 2 challenges existing research by showing that Black women (political) elites maintain their community-based interests even when they ascend to power; they never lose sight of the intersectional challenges they faced as they moved up the ranks. Their community's needs drive their interests, their rise, their agendas, and where they serve. This sense of community is fostered by the racialized, gendered socialization process and the network of community organizations and volunteer work that elevates the standing of Black women in their communities.

Chapter 3 moves further into the theoretical framework to explore the facets of the marginalization of Black women. It explores how stereotypes that have long attempted to define and limit opportunities for Black women shape perceptions of potential voters, media, and political parties about Black women candidates. This limits the political strength and advancement of Black women, and how Black female political and social networks resist and respond to those tactics and succeed in advancing their agendas for empowerment and justice for themselves and society. Chapter 4 takes a look at how Black women learn to lead. Political ambition theory has argued women are more inclined to decide to run for office if they are in certain professional careers, but for Black women this is not applicable as they have often found themselves in the government or nonprofit sector. The majority of the women in my sample not only had careers outside of private industry, but they also had transferrable skills they gained from community engagement that they carried into their careers. While in their careers, these women enhanced their leadership skills by coupling their understanding of societal injustices and disparities with their experiences in policy development and implementation. That chapter also explores the challenges and strategies Black women elected officials employ to implement policy preferences on behalf of their constituents.

Chapter 5 offers an exploration of how Black women voters view policies and Black women as political leaders. Central to my theoretical argument is that Black women elected officials are invested in their communities. Therefore, it is important to understand the expectations community members have of Black women politicians. Knowing what those possible expectations are can help us understand how Black women present themselves as candidates and elected officials.

The concluding chapter summarizes the rich data presented. Despite their impressive levels of participation, Black women still face many challenges in implementing their own and their community's policy preferences. As well as enumerating these, Chapter 6 also raises questions that still need to be addressed about Black women seeking office.

1
The Radical Imagination of Black Women's Ambition

> This may only be a dream of mine, but I think I can make it real.
>
> —Ella Baker

> I'd like to be remembered as a person who wanted to be free and wanted other people to be also free.
>
> —Rosa Parks

In 2020 an unprecedented number of Black women sought political office, were at the forefront of voter mobilization efforts, and worked at high levels of campaign management on national campaigns.[1] This robust political participation was particularly noteworthy given American's long history of disenfranchising, neglecting, and ostracizing Black women (Collins 2000; Jones 2020; Berry and Gross 2020). This political work began as women organized and fought for freedom from slavery to seeking the right to vote (Brown 1994; Dittmar 2015; Jones 1985; Jones 2020). Black women were instrumental in passing the Voting Rights Act of 1965 and today are engaged in activism to change restrictive voter identification laws in numerous states that make it more difficult for some individuals—especially Black and Latino voters, women and men with low incomes, and young and older individuals—to vote (Gaskins and Iyer 2012; Jones 2020; Lockhart 2020). In addition, as of 2016, Black women have been the most active group of voters in the country.

Speaking on the campaign trail in Iowa as she sought the Democratic nomination for president in 2019, Senator Kamala Harris stated, "I have faith in the American people to know that we will never be burdened by the assumptions of who can do what, based on who historically has done it."[2] The words of then senator and currently Vice President Harris echo the belief that, despite the mistreatment Black women have faced, they hold on to a radical faith that their vision for change through leadership is of value and will be accepted by communities outside of their own.

Women such as these envisioned and still envision a more just world in which their resistance matters and benefits both those who look like them and society as a whole. Professor Robin D. G. Kelley referred to this imagination as way to propose "a different way out of our [social, economic and political] constriction" (2003, p. xiii). Kelley stated, "Visionary dreams of a new society don't come from little think tanks of smart people.... Revolutionary dreams erupt [out] of political engagement; collective social movements are incubators of new knowledge" (p. 8). For Black women, these visionary dreams formed a "culture of resistance" that formulated a legacy of struggle for family and community and an ethic of caring (Collins 1990). I refer to this type of social vision as *a radical imagination* that propels ambitious elite Black women despite adversity and marginalization to translate their vision of justice, equality, access, and freedom into social action. Black women's radical imagination convinces them that individually and collectively they can change a world that tells them they are less than. They express this radical imagination through the tangible work of networks and activism that motivates Black women to seek office for a more equitable society. In short, this radical imagination combined with community support often champions and resources Black women's political ambitions.

The Case of Stacey Abrams

In 2018, a historic number of women ran for office. Of those,[3] Stacey Abrams not only campaigned to become the first Black female governor in the nation, she also worked to raise awareness and develop a network of advocacy to address voter suppression. Her example echoes the history of Black women's political ambition that is and has so often been activated not only by personal ambition but also by the desire to advance the interests and needs of the Black community and other communities that have been underserved and marginalized.

Abrams is not an anomaly. Along with women such as Sojourner Truth, Harriet Tubman, Mary Church Terrell, Anna Julia Cooper, Ida B. Wells, Pauli Murray, Constance Baker Motley, Ella Baker, Septima Clark, Jo Ann Robinson, Fannie Lou Hamer, Shirley Chisholm, Florynce Kennedy, Barbara Jordan, Alicia Garza, and many more, Abrams stands in a long line of Black women who dared to use their bodies, minds, and talents to oppose violence, discriminatory laws, social norms, culture, and the possibility of death not only to make their own voices heard but also to implement a liberatory form of politics that not only meets the needs of Black women and the Black community but also society more broadly (Robnett 1997; Gilkes 2001; Cooper 2017).

Abrams, a native of Gulfport, Mississippi, earned an undergraduate degree from Spelman College, a Historically Black College for women.[4] She subsequently earned advanced degrees from the University of Texas at Austin and Yale Law School, and in 2011 she became the first woman and person of color to lead the Georgia House of Representatives as House minority leader. Abrams served as such during one of the lowest points of the Democratic Party in Georgia. By 2010 Democrats had become unable to win any statewide race, and in 2012 the State Senate fell to a Republican supermajority. Abrams used her position to connect with both Democrats and likely Democratic voters throughout the state in an effort to understand why the Democratic Party was performing so dismally. She concluded that the changing demographics in the state along with Democrats shoring up their infrastructure, developing a clear message, and clearly delineating how they were different from Republicans would connect not only with tried-and-true Democrats but also those who were disconnected from politics, which could translate into Democratic wins in the future.

Similar to the history of Black women organizing that sought to not only advance their own communities but to also extend the promise of equality for society, Abrams embarked on a political project that imagined greater access to voting that extended beyond a racial construct. She would embark on a 10-year journey to cultivate new political strategists who reflected the diversity of the state and consolidated the multiple long-standing voter registration and mobilization efforts throughout the state into the New Georgia Project—which in a span of two years registered over 200,000 voters of color. It is important to note that these long-standing efforts had been led by Black women such as Helen Butler of the Georgia Coalition for the People's Agenda, Tameika Atkins of Pro Georgia, and Deborah Scott of Georgia Stand Up who laid the foundation for much of what the New Georgia Project would be able to achieve. By bringing together the multiple efforts throughout the state momentum increased and Democrats started to win elections.

Abrams' gubernatorial run is largely remembered for her losing by a mere 1.4 percent, or 55,000 votes, to her opponent Brian Kemp, who was the sitting secretary of state, the state's chief election officer. During the election cycle, Kemp faced public pressure to resign from his position due to conflict of interest: he oversaw the election process in which he was involved. Former President Jimmy Carter, who had extensive experience monitoring elections abroad, spoke out about this conflict of interest, saying it ran "counter to the most fundamental principle of democratic elections—that the electoral process be managed by an independent and impartial election authority."[5]

In addition to questionable ethics of Kemp, the 2018 gubernatorial election was impacted by the 2013 *Shelby v. Holder* case that ended protections southern voters, in particular Black southern voters, found in the Voting Rights Act.[6] With the Department of Justice no longer having the authority to approve changes to voting laws in Georgia, Kemp approached the secretary of state's role as an opportunity to apply strict guidelines to voting access. In short, Kemp used his office to hinder the Georgians' voter registration efforts by rejecting or delaying registration of 35,000 Georgians from 2013 to 2016. This he did by using the "exact match" screening process, which meant the state accepts new registrants only if their information precisely matches information in other state databases, including hyphens, accents, and typos. He also used his authority to challenge voter registration efforts by organizations that targeted potential Democratic voters and the New Georgia Project in particular (Niesse 2018). He publicly referred to the voter registration cards that arrived at the secretary of state's office as possibly fraudulent while acknowledging privately that Democrats were working hard to register voters and that their efforts could lead to wins (Anderson 2018).

Kemp had also purged more than 1.5 million voters from rolls, eliminating 10.6 percent of voters from the registered electorate between 2016 and 2018 alone. In the election year itself, he removed nearly 700,000—or 10 percent of the registered electorate—from the rolls. The purge was not due to persons relocating out of state or dying—which would have been valid reasons—rather, it was persons who had opted not to vote in previous elections (Caputo, Hing, and Kauffman 2020). Kemp also placed 53,000 voter registrations in electoral limbo a month prior to the election. The Associated Press estimated that 70 percent of those were Black voters. Kemp closed more than 200 polling places across the state, the majority of which were in communities that were African American and had consistently voted Democrat (Nadler 2018). During the election, voters reported long lines, malfunctioning voting machines, and other problems that delayed or thwarted voting in those areas. *The Atlanta Journal-Constitution* found that precinct closures and longer distances to polling locations likely prevented an estimated 54,000 to 85,000 voters from casting ballots on Election Day. The impact of this was that Black voters were 20 percent less likely to vote than usual due to long distances to voting locations (Niesse and Thieme 2019).

Abrams's response to the defeat amplifies the idea of Black women's radical imagination. She did not leave politics; instead, she concluded that her defeat was not due to her vision for the state or her political acumen, rather, her razor-thin loss was due to the oppressive efforts that targeted mostly Black communities and potential Democratic voters (Galloway 2018). This led her to expand the mission of the New Georgia Project. She said it was important not only for building a broad coalition of voters through coordinated voter registration and mobilization efforts but also to educate voters about efforts to suppress their voting strength. Abrams would subsequently form a new organization called Fair Fight, which continues and expands upon the work of the New Georgia Project to increase voter participation along with voter education about elections and voter rights. Not only that, she, along with the Abrams campaign and its allies, registered more than 200,000 new voters in the run-up to the 2018 election. When Fair Fight and the New Georgia Project tried again in 2020, they quadrupled those results, registering more than 800,000 new voters. This effort had a significant impact: it put Democratic candidate for President Joe Biden over the top and paved the way for Kamala Harris to serve as vice president, the first Black woman ever to do so.

The work of Abrams exemplifies the radical imagination of Black women who have faced failures but find an opportunity to relaunch their vision. Despite considerable challenges, in particular a voter suppression effort that expanded beyond Georgia, Abrams cultivated a vision for success and believed that her success would empower marginalized communities and society more broadly. Her loss is not as important as the impact of her political work that placed vision into action.

Ambition on the Margins, the Radical Imagination at Work

Black women have long understood that political engagement enhances their lives and the lives of their community members. In spite of the marginalization that is evident by continued pay discrimination, sexism, public shaming, and isolation, Black women use political engagement strategically to undermine that marginalization by sustaining ambition and fostering a socialization process that fosters both independence and collective identity through families, organizations, and religious institutions. This marginalization is exhibited in the fact that Black women's contributions to American society and economy has been undervalued and undercompensated. Black women often are among other women of color with the highest labor force participation rate in the nation among women, but at all educational levels Black women are concentrated in lower paying jobs than most other groups of workers (DuMonthier, Childers, Milli 2017). These same women played an integral role in the fight to desegregate public schools in the 1950s and 1960s, the passage of the Voting Rights Act of 1965, and multiple movements to ensure equal treatment for

Black and brown women and men, and currently they are critical community leaders and organizers in the fight against police brutality and racial inequality.

Through interviews with 36 Black women of various backgrounds from across the country, the character of the radical imagination is consistent across different political and social environments. This leads me to suggest that the radical imagination is evident in the political works and processes for empowerment created by Black women. This includes networks of indigenous organizations, political mobilization, and seeking office.

This process has long nurtured and developed a leadership cadre of Black women who uplift not only their communities but also themselves to resist marginalization. The agency and collective action that springs forth from this imagination is ably summarized in the 1997 movie *Soul Food* by the "Big Momma" character (the matriarch of an African American family): "One finger pointing the blame don't make no impact. But if you ball all of them fingers up into a mighty fist you can strike a mighty blow!"

Shirley Chisholm exemplified this radical imagination with her 1972 campaign for president. She stated:

> If I decided to run, I could serve to give a voice to the people the major candidates were ignoring as usual. Although I could not win, I still might help all the people who were offering me support, by increasing their influence on the decision about who would be the Democratic nominee. That did not seem an impossible goal; difficult, but not impossible. (Chisholm, 1973, p. 44)

Although Chisholm did not win the Democratic nomination, her vision for her campaign exemplifies how the radical imagination of Black women's political ambition also takes shape once Black women are elected. The consequence of Black women in the electorate has demonstrated their significant role not only in increasing descriptive representation of Blacks but also in increasing substantive representation. Once in office, Black women champion the interests of Blacks and underrepresented populations, supporting progressive agendas more than their male and female counterparts do (Bratton et al. 2007;

Smooth 2006; Brown 2014). This legislative behavior is consistent with the level of community activism the group uses to address gendered and racial challenges. Collins argues that "African American women embrace a form of identity politics [and have] developed a worldview that sees lived Black experiences as important to creating a critical Black consciousness and crafting political strategies" (2000, p. 219).

The radical imagination is central to my theoretical framework in *Ambition on the Margins*, which I employ as a way to explore why Black women decide to run for office and engage politically, and what resources they have at their disposal that are indigenous to their identity and community. Much of the recent work on the political ambition of women concentrates on white women and often negates the lens through which Black women view themselves—namely their political agency and how they navigate political choices, opportunities, and obstacles. By exploring not only the motivations of these women but also the resources available to them, I demonstrate how Black female elites maintain their community-based interests even as they ascend to power.

Our understanding of how ambition influences the motivations of Black women has not been fully explored (Brown 2014). In fact, scholars have debated if ambition theory is an adequate way to understand how individuals decide to run (Carroll and Sanbonmatsu 2013; Hardy-Fanta, Pinderhughes, and Sierra 2016; Bernhard et al. 2019). This strand of literature offers an explanation grounded in structural factors about the decision to run and for which office to run for. I contend that for elite Black women that ambition is not only about a personal desire to hold a position, but it is a motivation that is also fueled by a vision for a broader, more impactful democracy that not only impacts the lives of Black women but is also beneficial to society broadly. This ambition is also cultivated by collective experiences within the communities in which these women reside along with the day-to-day challenges Black women face in a gendered and racialized America.

I find that the community-based interest of Black women is critical to the cultivation and expression of Black women's political influence. For Black elite women, their community provides unique opportunities for leadership development, a base for potential voters, and a separate power resource that is distinctive and often removed from larger institutions, such as political parties, that are challenged with structural and discriminatory practices that hinder the success of Black political women.

The Electoral Strength of Black Women

Largely due to Black women voting and seeking office themselves, since 1990 there has been a significant increase in the number of Black elected officials nationwide. During this same period, Black women exceeded the number of Black male elected officials (Hardy-Fanta et al. 2007; Orey et al. 2007; Smooth 2014). Early on, many Black officials found electoral success in majority Black districts, but recently Black women have found success in majority-minority districts as a result of the upsurge following the round of redistricting in 1990 that sent a significant number of Blacks to Congress which included Black women (Tate 2003; Scola 2007; Smooth 2014), and they have also shown the potential to be successful in non-majority-minority districts, which presents the possibility of increased Black women's representation.[7] African American women are also more likely to be politically ambitious than their white counterparts (Darcy and Hadley 1988; Frederick 2013; Holman and Schneider 2018), which is evident in the fact that African American women account for a greater proportion of Black elected officials than white women do of white elected officials (Williams 2001; Reflective Democracy Campaign 2020).

Black women have also made strides within state legislatures. As of September 2021, 354 (351 Democrat, 3 Republican) Black women serve as state legislators nationwide, comprising 15.5 percent of all women in state legislatures (Dittmar 2021). In 2020, Black women mayors led eight of the 100 cities with the largest populations in the U.S. The demographics and location of the cities vary from large to small Black populations and from coast to coast. The increased presence of Black female elected officials, especially at the mayoral level, is no surprise considering the level of civic engagement of Black women in traditional political behavior and nontraditional forms of participation, such as organizational and club memberships, talking about politics, and participating in religious institutions (Smooth 2018; Austin 2022). The most recent trend of increased representation of Black women at the local level began in 2017 with a series of victories across the nation, ranging from small to major cities (Austin 2022).

Those women included Yvonne Spicer, who was elected as the first mayor in the 317-year history of Framingham, Massachusetts;[8] Vi Lyles, who became the first Black female mayor of Charlotte, North Carolina, having served as a city administrator for 30 years before running for office; Mary Parham-Copeland, who became the first Black mayor of Milledgeville, Georgia; and Andrea Jenkins, the first openly transgender Black woman elected to office, who won a seat on the Minneapolis City Council. And in one of the most high-profile mayoral races of 2017, Keisha Lance Bottoms became the second Black woman to serve as mayor of Atlanta. In 2018 LaToya Cantrell became the first Black female mayor of New Orleans, and London Breed became the first Black woman elected as mayor in San Francisco. In 2021, Kim Janey became acting mayor of Boston, and Tishaura Jones became the first Black woman elected mayor of St. Louis.

Following the 2018 election cycle, a record number of women ran for and were elected to Congress. In total, 476 women (incumbents and non-incumbents) filed as candidates, a fourfold increase of any other year between 1992 and 2016. In what came to be referred to as the Blue Wave, of the 80 Black women who ran for the House, 41 won nominations and 22 won their seats (including five incumbents). To explain why this happened at that moment, most news outlets invoked women's emotive nature and their anger about the outcome of the 2016 presidential election and the policy agenda of the Trump administration. Yet Dittmar (2020) shows that Black women who ran in 2018 were less likely than white women to describe themselves as motivated by anger, which suggests that anger was not the only feeling or motivation, nor was it a new motivation (given their history and the tendency for Black women not to express their emotions fully so as not to be accused of racist tropes such as being "angry Black women"). In short, their motivations and public discussions were different from those of white women. To claim only anger as a motivator overlooks and dismisses the long history of Black women using political behavior to resist oppression and efforts to silence their voices.[9]

The continued increase of Black women seeking office was evident in the record number of Black women running for Congress in 2020. A total of 117 Black women (89 Democrats and 28 Republicans) ran for Congress, meaning they were 20.1 percent of all women House candidates and 5.8 percent of all House candidates in 2020. Of these, 61 went on to become the Democratic nominee in their respective race. Black women numbered 25 percent of all Democratic women candidates and 9.4 percent of all Democratic candidates for the House (Dittmar 2021). Twenty-five of them won, including three nonincumbents. Among the latter was Cori Bush, who became the first Black woman to represent Missouri in Congress. Bush, who is a registered nurse, has been active in the Black Lives Matter movement since 2014. She first ran for office in 2018 against long-term Congressman William Lacy Clay and finally defeated him in 2020. Former Senator Kamala Harris (D-CA) served until ascending to the vice presidency on January 20, 2020; that move left no Black women serving in the U.S. Senate. Former Congresswoman Marcia Fudge (D-OH) served until she was confirmed as secretary of housing and urban development. The increasing number of Black women running for each electoral level confirms that Black women are not only engaged as voters but also have ambition that should be studied.

Ambition

The radical imagination of Black women indeed informs not only their dreams but also their actions. This imagination fuels ambition and empowers Black women to engage politically in various arenas, such as community work, voting, and seeking office. Unfortunately, this type of work is often misunderstood as signifying *lack* of ambition because it is less individual and more communal. Such work is rarely included in how we understand the motivations of Black women seeking public office. The literature consequently limits ambition to running and moving up the political ladder, preparing to seek the next level of office.

In contrast, I suggest that the political ambition of elite Black women has something broader in view: not just seeking office but the desire to affect and implement the radical imagination for a more equitable society and service to community. Previous research has shown that women as elected officials spend more time compared to men on tasks that fulfill communal goals (Duerst-Lahti and Johnson 1991; Kathlene 1989; LangTakac and Osterweil 1992; Tilly and Gurin 1990; Schneider et al. 2016). Similarly, Black women's actions once in office are not only influenced by communal goals, but the desire to seek office is often also motivated by community. Thus, although structural factors undoubtedly affect and determine which political offices women seek, another consideration is what political venue or office will make and allow for the most impact on their communities. In some cases, this means staying in a position at the local level or in a state legislature although a woman may have the political wherewithal to seek higher office. An excellent example of this is recently retired Tennessee State Senator Brenda Gilmore. Gilmore, an extremely popular politician who was a part of Nashville politics for over 20 years. She began her career as a member of the Metro Nashville Council where she served for eight years before winning a seat in the state house that she held for 12 years. The last four years of her career she spent as a state senator. Throughout her career, Gilmore was often approached about running for Congress when it appeared she could likely win and when it seemed she would have a tough fight. She informed me that she declined because she enjoyed "staying local" and having a direct impact on the citizens of Nashville. Despite a consideration for the community, Black women in fact hold higher levels of political ambition compared to other racial or ethnic groups of women (Holman and Schneider 2018).

The body of work known as ambition theory has neglected this sense of community that leads Black women to engage in a unique type of political work. The foundational book on political ambition—Schlesinger's *Ambition and Politics* (1966)—argues that political careers depend on the structural conditions of the political system and political opportunity. Black (1972) reframed this theory within the rational choice model and argued more explicitly that candidates evaluate and calculate their decision to run for office by weighing the benefit of attaining that office, the probability of attaining that office, and the costs required to run a campaign. According to Black, politicians make decisions based on their judgement to run for higher office or keep their current seat while determining whether political conditions such as potential competition and voter demographics are likely to help them succeed. The concept of political conditions has expanded to include incumbency, stereotypes, partisanship, and electoral systems (Darcy, Welch, and Clark 1994; Holman et al. 2011; Schneider and Bos 2014; Hayes and Lawless 2015, 2016). Structural factors undoubtedly affect and determine which political offices women seek. All candidates face obstacles such as incumbency, partisanship, and the structure of the electoral system (Herrick and Moore 1993); these, along with institutional support and party recruitment, predict ambition (Maestas et al. 2006).

Gamble (2010) has shown that Black women likewise weigh these rational, structural, and strategic elements before running, yet they also consider personal factors. Gamble's findings expose a gap in the literature's understanding of how and why Black women come to the decision to run for office. Part of the reason that the experiences and political paths of women of color are not accounted for in current discussions of the candidate emergence process is that to date the majority of women included in studies have been white women from professions such as law and business, which have been regarded as the only appropriate stepping stones or pipelines to elected office (Carroll and Sanbonmatsu 2013). For example, Lawless and Fox (2005) defined "potential candidates" for their Citizen Political Ambition Study as men and women who have backgrounds in law, business, education, or political activism. These categories typically exclude women with backgrounds in, say, community activism who are not necessarily involved in party politics. And yet Moore (2005) shows that women who identify as community activists express higher levels of political ambition than those from traditional "pipeline" professions to public office.

The extant literature that does consider why women become candidates (Sanbonmatsu 2002; Crowder-Meyer 2013; Carroll and Sanbonmatsu 2013) has focused on the value and necessity of candidate recruitment and a willingness to run. In recent years scholars have pushed to explore how and why Black women become candidates and engage in politics. This has led to an increasingly intersectional approach to studying women in politics. For example, it is clear that race and gender have a significant role to play in one's political ambition

(Phillips 2017). For Black women in particular, their marginalized position in the American political space not only informs their approach to politics but also motivates their interest to run for office (Dowe 2020). Scholars in the area of women of color in politics have argued that the unique positionality of Black women and women of color creates not only unique daily experiences but also unique political experiences (Crenshaw 2013; Hancock 2007; Davis 2008). These identities influence opportunities and experiences that are in turn shaped by structures that influence political preferences (Collins and Bilge 2020; Jordan-Zachery 2007; Brown 2014). For example, one's relationship to structures of power, privilege, and marginalization shapes one's orientation to politics (Smooth 2011; Locke 1990) and one's access to political resources (Nash 2017; Montoya 2019).

Politicians and parties typically look at potential candidates' education, occupation, and income when they are considering asking them to run for office. These traditional assumptions do not make it impossible for Black women to win, but they do limit the number of Black women who are considered eligible (Gamble 2010). One clear concern is that these women might not have the ability to raise a considerable amount of funds or do not have a sufficiently broad network to secure the necessary votes. If parties focus on traditional careers for an eligibility pool, it is likely to have fewer Black women than white women. Black women who have careers in fields that are not considered stepping stones to politics (in short, careers in fields other than business and law) find themselves underrepresented and are greatly underpaid in comparison to both white men and women (Conrad 2008; Ortiz and Roscingo 2009; Roux 2021). Black women in professional fields also find themselves disadvantaged due to being shut out of professional networks that could assist with career advancement and ultimately support a political career (Bell and Nkomo 2003).

The continued discriminatory practices that hinder the professional growth of Black women possibly hinders the development of professional networks and financial security to build a campaign. Previous scholarship has noted that Black candidates often raise less money (Carroll and Sanbonmatsu 2013)—not through lack of ability, but because their constituents typically make smaller donations, therefore pushing such candidates to seek donations from outside of their districts (Singh 1998; Wilhite and Thielmann 1989). A more recent study by Bryner and Haley (2019) reveals a clear disadvantage in Black women candidates' fundraising efforts in particular in securing large donations, a disadvantage perceived to be a result of their race and gender.

Scholars note that Black women's electoral successes defy expectations (Darcy and Hadley 1988; Smooth 2018) therefore proving them to be more politically ambitious than their white counterparts and to have had greater success in seeking, local, legislative, and congressional offices than white women throughout the 1970s and 1980s. This success comes from Black women's abilities to draw support from and engage with multiple communities of voters as a result of their gender, race, and life experiences that resonate with potential voters from different backgrounds (Philpot and Walton 2007; Smooth 2014). Like their male counterparts, Black women have historically found success in majority-minority districts (Scola 2007) and show the potential to be successful in non-majority-minority districts, which itself suggests the value of increased Black women's representation. Indeed, there has recently been a significant shift in the outcomes of Black women in majority-minority districts, which increases the likelihood of their future recruitment and support. This is evidenced by four of the five non-incumbent women elected to Congress in 2018 coming from majority-minority districts: Ilhan Omar of Minnesota, Lucy McBath of Georgia, Lauren Underwood of Illinois, and Jahana Hayes of Connecticut.

I mentioned earlier that much of the research on political ambition and women has focused primarily on the political fate of white women. By ignoring Black women, the literature does not recognize the unique ways Black women develop networks and desire to engage in activities that advance their communities, especially how they are situated within the world as Black women. This limited perspective prompts a series of questions: What marks the path to Black women's political ambition? It is a path not only about attainment of an office but also about a desire to serve one's communities. Such a path is often driven by women's vision for their communities. How do Black women overcome political marginalization with resources from their communities? What does a Black woman's leadership development look like if she endeavors to serve in political leadership roles in a long-term capacity?

Given the dearth of research examining the forces that shape Black women's experiences serving in elected positions, given that in proportion to the population as a whole Black women remain underrepresented in political leadership, and given that Black women continue to be subjected to numerous social and attitudinal barriers that prevent them from seeking and succeeding in leadership contexts traditionally controlled by white men, I suggest that there are three key factors that should feature in a holistic understanding of elite Black women and political ambition: their gendered racial identity, their political socialization, and their participation in and use of networks. I address each of these in turn.

Gendered Racial Identity

Ambition theorists argue that gender socialization significantly affects women's political ambition, and it unfortunately does so by lowering women's confidence in their leadership capacities, inflating men's confidence, and leaving women to shoulder the majority of household and caregiving responsibilities (Lawless and Fox 2005; Fox and Lawless 2010; Frederick 2013). However, these studies do not consider the significant variations of gender and racial identity and their impact on ambition. For Black women, race and gender are interwoven; race constructs how Black women experience gender, and gender constructs how Black women experience race (Mansbridge and Tate 1992; Gay and Tate 1998; Simien 2005). The failure to study the complexity of multiple identities has contributed to the invisibility of African Americans and women (King 1988; Crenshaw 2013; Giddings 1984; Collins 2000; hooks 2000; Cohen and Carroll 2003; Hancock 2007; Junn and Brown 2008). It is high time for scholars to recognize the importance of taking an intersectional approach to the influence of identity (Gay and Tate 1998; Simien and Clawson 2004; Smooth 2006; Jordan-Zachery 2007; Philpot and Walton 2017; Simien 2005; Brown 2014). Why? To understand what challenges Black women encounter when seeking office, the decision-making processes involved, and the resources available to them.

Baxter and Lansing contend that Black women have come to see themselves as "a special interest group fighting to overcome the twin barriers of racial and gender discrimination" (1983, p 108), both within and outside their own communities. Battling both racism and sexism, they experience the world differently from those who are not Black and female. Patricia Hill Collins (1990) argues that Black women viewing the world through such a lens of racism and sexism consider the various forms of oppression to be "one overarching structure of domination." This unique perspective of Black women and their resistance to racial and gender oppression, say Baxter and Lansing, accounts for their higher rate of political participation.

Such resistance to oppression has a long-standing history among Black women. Black women understood at the inception of the U.S. Constitution and of state and local laws that the rights of property owners and the dominant social, economic, and political structures would not afford Black women the protections extended to white women (Locke 1990). Black women resisted such oppression by creating nontraditional spaces of women's activism, such as literary circles, temperance organizations, educational groups, and antislavery groups. After Emancipation, these spaces evolved into church auxiliaries and women's conventions, clubs, and civic organizations (Brown 1994; Giddings 1984; Hine and Thompson 1999; Sterling 1997; Higginbotham 1994; Terborg-Penn 1998; Simien 2012; Cooper 2017; Jones 2020; Daniels 2021). The spaces and organizing in which Black women engaged functioned at the periphery of Black indigenous institutions such as the Black church and Historical Black Colleges and Universities (HBCUs), both of which fostered skills for political participation (Brown and Dowe 2020; Harris-Lacewell 2004; McDaniel 2013; Simpson 1998; Calhoun-Brown 1996). These institutions have been critical to Black women's political socialization due to their ability to cultivate political activity, foster political mobilization, and teach democratic norms (Calhoun-Brown 1996). These activities and spaces existed outside of formal politics due to oppressive systems of exclusion, and, as a result, a Black elite formed from engagement within these spaces. These spaces provided access to other Black elites while supplying resources and support for political careers (Scott et al. 2021).

Due to the distinctive experiences that Black women face as Black and as female, their status is often referred to as "doubly bound" (Gay and Tate 1998), as posing a "double jeopardy" (Beale 1970), or as existing in "multiple jeopardy" (King 1988). While these terms speak to the lived experiences of Black women and to how both gender and racial discrimination create barriers to women's election, this vantage point does not fully address how they respond and resist those interlocking oppressions and find political success. More recent research on Latinas and women of color analyzed the resources that having multiple identities afford women seeking office. Fraga et al. 2005 show that women of color have "more opportunities to 'soften' their ethnicity by [positioning] themselves as women, mothers and community advocates in ways that limit race-based white backlash" (p. 1). In fact, Bejarano (2013) presents findings that show that intersecting identities of gender and race/ethnicity do not automatically create a double disadvantage but can instead provide opportunities for multiple sources of electoral support.

My interest in this book is furthering the conversation about the unique mechanisms Black women have at their disposal and the means to cultivate the multiple resources of which Bejarano speaks. It has, after all, been established that Black women have a robust political participation that incorporates organizing, activism, voting, and running for office, and that they engage in this at high rates (Junn 1997; Tate 1991; Gay and Tate 1998; Alex-Assensoh and Stanford 1997; Brown 2014). This participation happens in spite of Black women being less likely to have the resources that tend to be markers of increased political participation (Burns, Schlozman, and Verba 2001; Verba and Nie 1987). In addition to high levels of participation within their own cohort, Black women participate at higher levels than their white female and Black male counterparts (Cole and Stewart 1996; Harris, Sinclair-Chapman, and McKenzie 2005; Burns, Schlozman, and Verba 2001).

Why? And what moves Black women from organizing, to voting, and to seeking office? I suggest that just as important as tangible resources such as income, education, and class resources that encourage voting and political engagement are psychological resources such as trust, political efficacy, and sense of civic duty (Aldrich 1993; Avery 2006; Brady, Verba, and Schlozman 1995; Nunnally 2012). The community efforts in which Black women have historically engaged, according to Gilkes, "focus on changing ideas, stereotypes and images that keep a group perpetually stigmatized," and it "consists of everything that people do to address oppression in their own lives, suffering in the lives of others and their sense of solidarity or group kinship" (2001, p. 17). This community work is political participation that provides social capital for Black women (Farris and Holman 2014) and develops networks that, among other things, help such women cultivate political mobilization. The political work in communities provides Black women with "levels of prestige and influence" (Gilkes 2001, p. 19) that can be used to shape community consensus and support for larger social movements and political engagement (Robnett 1997). It also helps them to cultivate political skills that are essential for political candidacy (Smooth 2001).

The unique juxtaposition between gender and race was evident when Black women found themselves marginalized by both the Black and female struggle for equality (King 1975). During the suffrage movement, Black women navigated the sexism of Black men and the racism of white women who saw Blacks as inherently inferior (hooks 2000; Locke 1990; Walton, Smith, and Wallace 2017; Jones-Branch 2021; Giddings 1984). Even organizations within the Black community have been controlled mostly by male leadership and historically have been less than responsive to gender issues of concern to Black women. Black women also found themselves outside of the mainstream formal leadership during the Civil Rights Movement. Tiyi Morris (2015) notes that Black women's position at the intersection of race, gender, and class oppressions resulted in multiple forms of subjugation while giving them significant insight into the intersectionality of their oppression.

Thus, Black women's leadership status was not the result of their ineffectiveness but of gender roles, power, and expectations in the Black community. Yet Black women were a critical part of framing the efforts of the movement in grassroots roles—which Robnett (1997) calls "bridge leadership," that is, they fostered the ties between the movement and the community in which they were highly engaged.

Furthermore, the literature on the social history of African American women notes that they are important intergenerational resources for their communities (Collins 1991; Giddings 1984; Gilkes 1988; Sudarkasa 1998; Berry and Gross 2020). These women not only provide valuable economic stability as a result of their labor (Roux 2021) but also have been looked to function as mothers, wives, and caregivers who also seek to resist racism and benefit or preserve the Black community (Barnes 2015). As intergenerational resources, they provide racial socialization for their children (Thornton et al. 1990), which Nunnally defines as "the process by which African Americans learn about and identify with the influence of race on their social status, culture and group history in the United States" (2012, P. 58). Educator, activist, and Black feminist Anna Julia Cooper more specifically identifies the unique role that Black women hold as "the fundamental agency under God in the regeneration . . . of the race, as well as the [initiator of the] groundwork and starting point of its progress upward" (Giddings 1984, p. 81).

The race and gender status of African American women strongly influences how they define family and community and determines which political strategies are best suited to meet the needs of Black women, their families, and the race (Gilkes 1988; Hine 1999; Morgen 1988; Morgen and Bookman 1988; Naples 1991, 1992; Gay and Tate 1998). This therefore also suggests which strategies and causes they might participate in most effectively. Historically, African American women have viewed political participation as a means to achieve full equality and improve the status of Blacks, more specifically Black women and a society in which they are often excluded (Shingles 1981; Giddings 1984; Tate 1991; Collins 2000; Barker, Jones, and Tate 1999; Simien 2012; Jones 2020). In a nation transitioning to a population that is becoming less white, this perspective is relevant to the discussion of policy preferences, potential coalition development, and the advancement of African Americans as a group.

I suggest that in addition to the unique social capital within their communities that Black women have cultivated—work that functions as political work—the spaces in which Black women conducted these endeavors and their racialized gendered identity helped and helps them develop a unique consciousness that distinguishes them from

Black men and white women. This consciousness, which shapes the radical imagination, motivates Black women's community work and political engagement. It is this continuous thread of community that propels these women to sustain high levels of voter participation, engage in political organizing, and ultimately seek political office.

Efforts to exclude Black women from formal political participation such as voting prompted them to develop nontraditional forms of engagement informed by their political, economic, and social conditions (Giddings 1984, 1988; Jones 2021). Examples of such engagement are the heightened level of community work and internal networks that middle-class Black women developed via clubs, sororities, civic organizations, and religious auxiliaries. For Black women in general, these networks increase their social capital. For those seeking office, they also provide access to potential voters and donors and facilitate candidate recruitment, fundraising, and voter mobilization. These networks are often fostered in spaces within academic institutions such as Black Greek letter organizations and Black female civic groups (Daniels 2021). Both also provide opportunities for Black women to cultivate community and develop strategies for social change within their organizations and professions.

Political Socialization

Central to my argument is that Black women's ambition is shaped differently and performed differently than their white counterparts on whom much of the literature focuses. What cultivates this radical imagination of Black women is their socialization to serve rather than only to achieve. The very service that Black women provide as individuals and within groups of other Black women is ultimately what releases the resources to support the women deciding whether to run for public office and is therefore what helps them overcome challenges to running. Black women are typically more likely to be discouraged from running for political positions than their white counterparts and are also less likely to be recruited. Ambition theory posits that ambition is shaped by access to careers that allow potential candidates to access resources to seek office and that demand and cultivate skills also useful for navigating a political environment. Along with career access, traditional gender socialization perpetuates a culture in which women are least likely to run (Lawless and Fox 2005; Elder 2004). Women tend to disqualify themselves because they do not feel they have the political skills needed—though this is in fact largely because they do not see women being valued or promoted in public and political spheres (Eagly and Karau 2002; Huddy and Terkildsen 1993; Rosenwasser and Dean 1989).

According to the political ambition socialization model, women who enter politics are typically outliers. Yet recall that this model was developed during the 1970s, when women rarely worked in the legal or business professions, the two fields from which a significant number of politicians emerged (Welch 1977). As a result, scholars posited that socialization into certain careers reinforced structural obstacles and that the perpetuation of traditional gender roles both hindered the emergence of women candidates (Fowlkes, Perkins, and Tolleson Rinehart 1979) and promoted a masculine ethos in electoral politics (e.g., Carroll 1994; Enloe 2004). Flammang (1997) argues, for instance, that men's dominance of political institutions made it difficult for women to think of themselves as politicians. It became socially acceptable for men, especially those who are viewed as successful, to be confident, assertive, and self-promoting. These traits have been viewed as what makes a successful candidate (Huddy and Terkildsen 1993; Rosenwasser and Dean 1989). In women, such traits are perceived as aggressive, emasculating, and bitchy. Lawless and Fox found that women cited an aversion to the "masculine" components of campaigning (e.g., required extroversion, fundraising) as reasons they would not consider running for elected office. As a result, men develop a greater sense of efficacy as candidates, while women are typically less confident and often talk themselves out of running, *even if they are well qualified to seek office* (Thomas 2005; Lawless and Fox 2010). In combination with the small number of women candidates, the absence of women from campaigns reinforces the (mistaken) belief that women are not suited to political office.

Yet this (largely white) socialization model is not particularly applicable to Black women. Although Black women were indeed limited in their career options due to the combination of race and gender, the idea of a traditional woman/housewife has never fit most African American women (King, 1975; Stone 1979; King 1988; Guy-Sheftall 1995; Collins 2000; Simien 2005). For African American women have always played a compelling role in political socialization within their communities and have always contributed to their family's and community's economic stability (King 1988; Giddings 1984; Gay 2001). Furthermore, African American women are more likely than white women to be heads of household, have higher labor participation rates than white women, and typically have more autonomy and decision-making authority in their homes as parents and partners than do their white counterparts (King 1975; Prestage 1991; Guy-Sheftall 1995).

The autonomy they had in their homes and through their community work gave them significant social capital in Black communities (Prestage 1991; Guy-Sheftall 1995; Gilkes 2001; Simien 2012). It developed a culture that encouraged the pursuit of success and good careers, economic self-reliance, political activism, and value in effectively representing themselves to and for the Black community (Higginbotham 1994; Barnes 2015). The work in which Black women engaged in their communities placed them in prominent positions and gave them levels of prestige and influence unmatched in the lives of white women of similar class backgrounds (Gilkes 2001). Although the social class position of Black women comes with some gendered expectations, the identity of Black women within their communities brings about certain expectations that contribute to not only expectations of service but also an expectation that these women can do it, so they will. Thus, most educated African American women were raised in a culture that encouraged their pursuit of successful careers, their achievement of economic self-reliance, and their development as role models for the Black community (Higginbotham 2001; Shaw 1996; Barnes 2015; Dowe 2020). Barnes (2015) found that besides navigating career, marriage, motherhood, and extended family responsibilities, Black women have also long been concerned about representing the Black community. This unique race and gender status (Gay and Tate 1998; King 1988) strongly influenced how they defined family and community and resisted gender and racial oppression, and in turn led Black women to use political participation as a means to achieve full equality and improve the status of the group (Barker, Jones, and

Tate 1999; Simien 2005; Gilkes 1988; Gay and Tate 1998; Morris 2015; Cooper 2017).

Thus, still today political socialization shapes Black women's opinion of themselves, their identity, and their sense of agency. That socialization also provides mechanisms by which, first as a Black girl and later as a Black woman, they navigate the world. My theory of ambition on the margins, which operationalizes the radical imagination, helps us understand how socialization extends to the mechanisms that Black women use to transform their community influence into political careers, networks, and organizations.

Networks

Studies of political participation have consistently shown that persons who are educated and have above average incomes are more likely than others to engage politically (Brady, Verba, and Schlozman 1995). Social capital literature also argues that communities and individuals with lower socioeconomic status lack social capital, thereby limiting their political participation (McAdam, McCarthy, and Zald 1996; Berry, Portney, and Thompson 1993; Wilson 1978). However, for Black women the usual determinants of political participation (namely education and income) are not strong predictors of political participation (Baxter and Lansing 1980; Smooth 2014) or for the development of social capital. Black women's high level of officeholding and voting seems to be a "paradox of participation" that contradicts their material conditions (Smooth 2014). For in spite of their socioeconomic status, African American women are more likely than African American men to engage in both traditional forms of political participation and nontraditional forms of participation (such as belonging to organizations and clubs, attending church, and talking to people about politics).

What explains this? It seems that the exclusion of Black women from political participation because of gendered and racial discrimination actually prompted their development of nontraditional forms of engagement informed by their political, economic, and social conditions (Giddings 1984; Hine and Thompson 1998). This participation outside of the mainstream is evident in the internal networks that Black women have long developed. Elsa Barkley Brown (1994) describes the political participation of southern Black women already in the post–Civil War years as collective autonomy, as part of which women and men developed institutions and engaged in formal politics after emancipation.

It is through such nontraditional forms of participation that Black women have developed and continue to develop social capital. And it is their network of potential voters and fundraisers that enable Black females to achieve political success (Smooth 2014). These networks include institutions such as HBCUs, Black Greek letter organizations, and Black female civic groups such as The Links Inc. and Top Ladies. Like the Black church during the Civil Rights Movement, these organizations foster leadership development, promote voter education and civic empowerment, and, importantly, enable Black women to cultivate community. Many Black professional women have had to develop effective support systems for themselves to compensate for their marginalized status. The aforementioned networks and systems help them work through psychological injury, cultivate community within and across their immediate work contexts, and develop strategies for social change within their organizations and professions.

Regardless of class, Black women have structured their networks of support and activism in organizations. Gilkes (1982), in her work on Black women and "rebellious professionalism," notes that the racial and gendered identity of these women is a political socializing agent that ties these women to their communities. As a result, Black women's organizations, whether social, uplifting, or professional, have since the nineteenth century wedded community needs to those of the aspiration of Black professional women. This legacy of combined community and professional associations continues to this day.[10]

It is worth noting that of the 26 Black women who served at the beginning of the 117th Congress, 18 were members of Black sororities. Likewise, leaders of organizations focused on advancing the political and civic engagement of Black people and women tend to be Black sorority members and hold membership in other Black women civic-minded organizations. Among these are the President and CEO of the National Coalition on Black Civic Participation, the President of Higher Heights, and the President of the NAACP Legal Defense and the National Council of Negro Women. This is not coincidental. Many of these spaces make concerted efforts to foster political advocacy and engagement and activism by supporting Black women to run for office and by supporting Black politicians.

One of the earliest expressions of this was in 1925 when Delta Sigma Theta Sorority Inc. in an effort to expand its impact beyond college campuses and the immediate communities where these campuses resided, formed "The National Vigilance Committee." In addition to the purposes of addressing racial justice and the concerns of women and children, the committee was to "endorse the appointment of Negroes to policy making government positions" (Nelson 2013). In 1938, Alpha Kappa Alpha Sorority, Inc. established the Non-Partisan Lobby for Economic and Democratic Rights and hired a full-time representative to monitor and lobby for legislation that would address the needs of the African American community (Franklin and Collier-Thomas 2001). These organizations have shown that they are adept at meeting the political needs of Black women who aspire to seek office. As many members of these organizations have engaged as candidates and in the world of politics, organizations such as Alpha Kappa Sorority Inc. in 2018 formed IvyPAC to support the campaigns of sorority members for Congress, and in 2020 Delta Sigma Theta formed a 401c4 organization, D4Women in Action, to encourage, train, and support sorority members, Black women and women of color to seek office, and fundraise for candidates.

How else does such sorority membership and support manifest itself? During the 2020 election cycle, organizations of Black women received increased attention outside of the Black community. Vice President Kamala Harris gained significant media attention regarding her membership in Alpha Kappa Alpha Sorority (AKA), the oldest Black sorority and one with a membership of 300,000 women.[11] Other Black Greek letter sororities (Delta Sigma Theta, Sigma Gamma Rho, and Zeta Phi Beta) all engage in efforts to register voters and provide programming to inform the Black community about policy issues that affect them. During the election cycle, Black sorority members were critical in getting Democrats to consider an African American woman as the vice presidential candidate as well as conducting significant voter mobilization and education work that led to Senator Harris's win.

Marginalization

To learn about the factors that encourage Black women to run for office and provide resources for potential success, it is also important to understand the impact of the perception of their "doubly bound" identity and their communities. This doubly bound identity is an aspect of the dynamics of marginalization. As Cathy Cohen explains:

> A group is considered marginal to the extent that its members have historically been and continue to be denied access to dominant decision-making processes and institutions; stigmatized by their identification; isolated or segregated and generally excluded from control over the resources that shape the quality of their lives. Much of the material exclusion experienced by marginal groups is based on, or justified by, ideological processes that define these groups as "other." Thus, marginalization occurs, in part, when some observable characteristic or distinguishing behavior shared by a group of individuals is systematically used within the larger society to signal the inferior and subordinate status of the group. (Cohen 1999, 24)

Group members are evaluated through the stigma of marginalization. This stigmatized "mark" often becomes the primary identification by which group members are evaluated and how they experience the world. The available resources often lie in community networks of organizations and elite networks that help shape political strategies and perspective and group consciousness (Miller et al. 1981 and Dawson 2003; Harris-Lacewell 2004). Due to marginalization, there is often a distrust of the dominant institutions, and group members rely on community leaders, newspapers, organizations, and social networks for ways to understand and process their experiences (Dawson 2003; Nunnally 2012). Such leaders and institutions can encourage group members to view their deprived social position as a basis for mobilization. Richard Shingles (1981) notes:

> The realization that the reason for Black deprivation does not lie squarely on them has allowed many poor Blacks to transfer the responsibility for poverty from themselves to society and to the most

visible symbol of society, government. The result is a mentally healthier and politically more active Black citizenry. (p. 89)

Black women's resistance to marginalization informs us about the conditions that shape Black women and their political socialization, while ambition theory helps us understand what they do in response. Unfortunately, marginalized existence is often amplified by public actions that function within the boundaries of long-standing tropes that deem Black women as less than.

The Othering and Public Rebuke of Black Women

Indicative of their societal marginalization, when society has responded at all to the presence of Black women, it has tended to respond with discomfort, neglect, hostility, and expressions about the danger of Black women. This public dismissal of Black women is consistent with the broad marginalization that Black women have encountered politically. Calling such marginalization "a policy of invisibility," Mae King in 1973 explored how stereotypes, images, and myths result in the marginalization of Black women. She concluded that "although the stereotyped images of Black women are generally devoid of reality, this actually hardly diminishes their effectiveness in achieving the political power that they serve" (p. 22).

Since 2017, there has been increasing public hostility toward Black women. In April 2017, persons targeted the predominantly Black sorority Alpha Kappa Alpha (AKA) at American University by throwing throughout the campus bananas marked with the letters AKA. This incident occurred on the very day that Taylor Dumpson, a member of AKA, took office as the student government's first female Black president (Padilla 2019). Dumpson later received a $750,000 judgment against the neo-Nazi website that had targeted her and initiated the campus incident.[12]

As either journalists or politicians, Black women in the political arena have likewise faced public rebuke and been shamed by former President Donald Trump.[13] The women include Rep. Ilhan Omar, Rep. Maxine Waters, as well as journalists April Ryan and Yamiche

Alcindor. These interactions, whether via Twitter or during White House press events, attempt to demean these women as incompetent, unprofessional, and underserving of their position. These moments are not singular; in fact, when they happen, many people respond on social media. For example, Fox News Host Bill O'Reilly insulted 26-year veteran of the House, Congresswoman Maxine Waters (D-CA), about her speech on the house floor. He commented, "I didn't hear a word she said. I was looking at the James Brown wig. If we have picture of James Brown, it's the same wig." Both the comment and the reference in effect dismissed and disparaged her position and leadership in the House.

In 2018 leaders of the Democratic Party in the House and Senate received a scathing letter signed by over 200 Black women in response to the public rebuke of Rep. Maxine Waters. In June of that year, Waters urged opponents of President Trump to protest cabinet members wherever they encountered them because of the administration's zero-tolerance immigration policy that separates children from their parents at the southern border. Both House Minority Leader Nancy Pelosi and Senate Minority Leader Chuck Schumer distanced themselves from Waters.[14] The letter stated:

> We write to share our profound indignation and deep disappointment over your recent failure to protect Congresswoman Waters from unwarranted attacks from the Trump Administration and others in the GOP. That failure was further compounded by your decision to unfairly deride her as being "uncivil" and "un-American." In doing so, we believe this mischaracterizes her call to action for peaceful democratic assembly and the exercise of her constitutional rights to free speech in support of defenseless immigrant children and their families.

The efforts to embarrass Black women publicly continued during the 2020 election cycle (see Chapter 3). Upon Senator Harris's nomination, President Trump emphatically and deliberately mispronounced her name as a means of showing indifference and disrespect and to identify her as an "other." Trump also referred to Harris as incompetent and implied that she is possibly overbearing. If she were to become the first woman president, Trump stated, "You know what? People don't like her. Nobody likes her. She could never be the first woman president. She could never be. That would be an insult to our country" (Cathey 2020). In February 2022, Congresswoman Joyce Beatty (D-OH) who serves as chair of the Congressional Black Caucus, one of the most important and effective caucuses in Congress, recounted how her colleague poked her in her back and told her to kiss his ass after she asked him to put on a mask as part of the COVID protocols on Capitol Hill before boarding one of the congressional trains that transport congresspersons from building to building.

These examples of public efforts to dismiss or shame Black women are a function of the stereotypes formed to justify Black women's unpaid forced labor and abuse during enslavement, while white women were forbidden to work and were told they were fragile and deserved to be protected. The stereotypes that evolved also suggested that Black women lacked femininity and were overbearing and thus not deemed worthy of love, and they were deemed unintelligent and childlike and therefore needed to be controlled by more intelligent whites. These stereotypes did not remain merely in the imaginations of Americans but were actively used to restrict the mobility of Black women and to promote public policy that hindered economic development and access to better education and opportunities for career development. In the political sphere, such stereotypes function to negate the power of the offices that Black women hold, downgrade the influence their positions afford, and to diminish their very humanity. This effort to limit Black women's access to power is not limited to individual actions but are also evident by limited efforts by political parties to support Black women as political candidates.

Marginalization within Political Parties

In general, Black women are more likely to be discouraged from running for political positions than Black men and white persons, and they are less likely to be recruited by their white counterparts. The lack of recruitment has a substantial impact on political advancement. It is all the more impressive therefore when a Black female candidate succeeds, especially since few are sought out or helped by their political party (Carroll and Sanbonmatsu 2013). Political gatekeepers are consistently less likely to recruit women than men, and all the more so Black women (Fox and Lawless 2010). Particularly at the state level, parties are inconsistent and lacking in their recruitment of women (Sanbonmatsu 2006). This is due to the context in which state parties seek candidates; it is the groups and organizations they consult that largely determine who is recruited. Many of the networks and organizations in which viable Black female candidates engage are not a part of the larger candidate recruitment conversation.

Scholars have long noted the significance of party leadership in the candidate recruitment process (Aberback, Putnam, and Rockman 1981; Matthews 1984). Moncrief, Squire, and Jewell (2001) as well as Niven (2006) find that women officeholders and candidates are more likely than men to report that they were recruited by political gatekeepers which speaks to the value of candidate recruitment for women. Political parties have long been bastions of male dominance (Freeman 2000; Fowlkes, Perkins, and Tolleson Rinehart 1979) that act as gatekeepers in the candidate recruitment and nomination processes, especially at the state legislative and congressional levels (Aldrich 1993; Jewell and Morehouse 2001; Maestas et al. 2006). The irony of this process is that candidate recruitment does not always reflect who is voting for the party. This is evident in the challenges that Black women candidates face in receiving support from the Democratic Party (Brown and Dowe 2020; Brown and Lemi 2020).

Carroll and Sanbonmatsu argue that when it does happen, party recruitment of female candidates is more influential in the outcome of political success than it is for male candidates (Carroll and Sanbonmatsu 2013). Such hesitancy by party leaders reflects their limited idea of what type of candidate is electable (men, specifically white men, and certainly not Black women). Party leaders' doubts about candidate electability are problematic for Black women seeking election in majority white districts. This hesitancy makes it difficult to launch a successful campaign, not least due to the challenges in securing resources for a campaign without official party support (Sanbonmatsu 2006). Limited recruitment affects Black women's ability to secure campaign resources necessary to establish a viable campaign early on, especially resources from outside of their districts (Wilhite and Theilmann 1989). Consequently, we see that Black candidates tend to raise less money than white candidates, rely more heavily on small donations, and depend on donations outside of their districts (Sanbonmatsu 2006)—even if party leadership does not help them in doing the latter.

This exclusionary pattern is particularly evident in looking at Black women as candidates in the Democratic Party. Since the Civil Rights Movement, in which African Americans began to engage fully in the electoral process, the Democratic Party has often perceived the support of Black voters as a means to victory while also viewing them as a destabilizing force who push away white voters. However, Black voters were needed in order for Democrats to mount any type of viable campaign for all elections, particularly presidential elections (Frymer 2010).

The Democratic Party also needed African American voters to broaden the electoral base and increase the party's chances of winning presidential elections (Frymer 2010; Sonenshein 1990; Gamble 2012). This was most evident with the election of Barack Obama in 2008 and again during the 2020 presidential election cycle that saw former Vice President Joe Biden rise to become the 46th president (Eligon and Burch 2020).

The Democratic Party has long promoted its popularity and electoral strength among women, which, quite frankly, is largely the result of the staunch support of Black women and Latinas (Smooth 2006; Scruggs-Leftwich 2000). The scholarly study of the gender gap often focuses on gender-based differences and emphasizes the choices of white women (Carroll 1999; Simien 2005; Smooth 2006). However, further analysis of the gender gap reveals that Black women are more supportive of the Democratic Party and a progressive agenda than their white counterparts, as evidenced by white women gravitating to the Republican Party going back to 1952 (Junn 2017; Tien 2017) and that in 2016, 52 percent of white women voted for Donald Trump while over 90 percent of Black women cast their vote for Hillary Clinton.

With such data in mind, the inability of the Democratic Party to recognize the viability of Black women as candidates reflects the party's inability to address the political views and needs of its strongest voting bloc. Consequently, in May 2017, more than two dozen African American women, including political activists and elected officials, submitted an open letter to Democratic National Committee Chairman Tom Perez criticizing him for seeming to take for granted the party's most loyal base of support. In their letter, the women explained how frustrated this had made them, and, more specifically, they accused the party of neglecting Black women for party leadership positions. Their frustration grew following the 2016 election, when it transpired that the Democratic Party had attempted to solve its electoral problem by developing strategies to attract white voters who had left the party decades ago. In other words, instead of reaching out to Black women and applauding them for their loyal efforts, the party simply doubled down on seeking white voters. The letter stated: "We have voted and organized our communities with little support or investment from the Democratic Party for voter mobilization efforts. We have shown how Black women lead, yet the Party's leadership from Washington to the state parties have few or no Black women in leadership. More and more, Black women are running for office and winning elections—with scant support from [the] Democratic Party infrastructure" (NBC News 2017).

Black women have also begun to express their frustration in other places. According to responses to recent surveys by *Essence Magazine* and the Black Women's Roundtable, Black women's support for the Democratic Party is in decline.[15] Whereas in 2016, 85 percent of respondents felt that the Democratic Party best represented them, those numbers had dropped precipitously to 74 percent by 2017 and to 73 percent in 2018. According to the 2019 survey, only 45 percent of Black women ages 25 to 35 agreed that the Democratic Party best represented them. In my interview with Black Women's Roundtable member Dr. Elsie Scott, she explained: "Black women feel that they are being taken for granted. The Democratic Party seems to assume that Black women have no place else to go, but," she cautioned, "they can stay at home as many did in 2016. [The party should] stop taking Black women for granted. They can actively recruit Black women candidates and once they are recruited, support them with resources, including money."[16]

In spite of the lack of support by the Democratic Party, Black women have proven their electoral strength both as voters and candidates

(Gillespie and Brown 2019; Smooth 2014). However, as African American women aspire to move beyond the local level, they face greater challenges in winning office. In many ways, statewide offices are more difficult for African American women to secure. Without the sustained support of a political party, it is easy to understand why Black women face challenges in seeking office, particular for statewide positions and the U.S. Senate (Sanbonmatsu 2013).

No state has ever elected a Black woman as governor, and only 12 Black women have held statewide elected executive office. Though there is little research on the status of women of color and Black women in respect to seeking statewide office, anecdotal evidence suggests that women are overlooked by party leaders as candidates for statewide executive office—even in states such as Colorado and Maine, which have often led the nation in electing women to represent them at the state level (Sanbonmatsu 2006). The difficulties that women have faced in reaching high office, including the office of the governor, may stem from the challenges of building both party and donor support (Barbara Lee Family Foundation 2001).

Discussion

The election of several Black women to a multiplicity of local, state, and federal positions, as well as Kamala Harris's and Stacey Abrams's high-profile bids for the presidency and governorship of Georgia respectively, demonstrates that perhaps the Democratic Party is attempting to rectify its long-standing ambivalence toward Black women. Or perhaps it is the case that Black women's success is not dependent on the party at all. Perhaps this group is not waiting for the Democratic Party to embrace them but is taking it upon themselves to be the change they wish to see, with or without institutional support from their political party in which Black women ran against incumbents and not only won, but they also found themselves victorious when they did not receive support from the party apparatus that included high-profile endorsements.[17]

In any case, Black women have begun to take it upon themselves to increase their representation through the work of national organizations such as the Black Women's Roundtable, established by the National Coalition on Black Civic Engagement, and Higher Heights, which focuses on encouraging Black women not only to vote but also to seek political office. These efforts are means by which Black women are creating networks to influence the current system although they remain within the Democratic Party.

In spite of the neglect and pervasive functioning of stereotypes that influence media, voters, and political parties to address the needs and political ambition of Black women, the limited existing literature suggests that Black women's unique socialization, politicization, and life experiences make their political activity exceptional. Indeed, some scholars posit that the double discrimination that Black women face motivates their higher levels of participation—to combat the invisibility and hypervisibility of being a Black woman (Alex-Assensoh and Stanford 1997; Stokes-Brown and Dolan 2010; Brown 2014).

In the following chapters, I address radical imagination, ambition, and marginalization—the key variables that contribute to my theory of Black women's ambition on the margins. In the immediately following chapter, I explore the socialization process for Black women that is fostered through their navigation of gender and racial identities and the resources their communities offer them to develop esteem, efficacy, and support. These resources evolve in a constellation of institutions and organizations that allow these women to wield influence inside and outside the Black community.

2
Black Women and Ambition
A Community Decision

> When you're a Black woman, you seldom get to do what you just want to do; you always do what you have to do.
> —Dorothy I. Height

Black women have a long history of engaging with their communities to address a multitude of needs and shaping community consensus and support for larger social movements and political engagement through organizing, activism (Robnett 1997; Jones-Branch 2021), voting, and running for office (Junn 1997; Tate 1991; Gay and Tate 1998; Alex-Assensoh and Stanford 1997; Brown 2014). In spite of Black women being inherently less likely to have the typically assumed resources for political participation (Burns, Schlozman and Verba 2001; Verba and Nie 1987; Smooth 2014), their community work often gives them the necessary social capital (Farris and Holman 2014) that comes in the form of access to leadership development and political elites and increased influence among community members. This social capital enables networks to develop and cultivates both political mobilization and political skills that foster political ambitions (Scott et al. 2021) and candidate emergence.

In Leith Mullings' study of Black women across various classes in Harlem to understand and develop strategies to address inequalities that Black women found themselves assuming, that is, economic, household, and community responsibilities in the difficult conditions of discrimination and scarcity. However, Black women's responsiveness to these responsibilities, which played out heading households, working outside the home, and addressing community concerns, led to a "strategy for fostering the reproduction and continuity of the Black community . . . [and] throughout, African American women's individual and collective efforts on behalf of their community have facilitated group survival" (2005, p. 87). This unique positionality and responsibility therefore increase community members' leadership expectations of Black women by while elevating their status within the community. Because of the complexity of Black women's existence and their socialization, which includes the goals not only of achievement but also service, their "radical imagination" (Dowe 2020) sharpens their social vision of justice, equality, access, and freedom, and it is this that propels them to seek office. How do they cultivate that radical imagination?

My theoretical framework—ambition on the margins—helps us understand that Black women's radical imagination is cultivated in a layered socialization process that promotes service, excellence, and political engagement. This process encourages Black women's commitment to service, which in turn garners support from the communities where they are raised. The very service that Black women provide as individuals and within groups of other Black women is what ultimately releases the resources to support Black women as candidates and supply campaign resources. An invaluable resource possibly available to Black women through their engagement within their community is to be in proximity to indigenous political leaders and gatekeepers who can provide opportunities for political recruitment.

The extant literature does emphasize the importance of being asked to run on candidate emergence (Sanbonmatsu 2002; Crowder-Meyer 2013; Carroll and Sanbonmatsu 2013; Maestas and Sheperd 2019). Black women are typically more likely to be discouraged from running for political positions than their white counterparts and are also less likely to be recruited by political parties. Lack of recruitment has a sizeable impact on political advancement. Yet Carroll and Sanbonmatsu (2013) show that when recruitment does happen it is more influential in the outcome of political success for women than it is for male candidates.

How women are perceived, or in many cases misperceived, contributes to party leaders' hesitancy to recruit women and Black women in particular (Brown and Dowe 2020) and reflects the limited notion of what type of candidate is electable. Limited recruitment affects the ability of Black women to secure campaign resources, especially resources outside their districts (Sanbonmatsu 2006), that are necessary to establish a viable campaign early. Black candidates typically raise less money than others do (Bryner and Haley 2019), rely heavily on small donations, and depend on donations outside their districts (Sanbonmatsu 2006). This lack of resources to fund campaigns early often poses challenges in launching and running successful campaigns.[1] I find that the socialization and positionality of Black women offers them opportunities to navigate these structural factors that often hinder political ambition.

The Socialization Process That Produces the Radical Imagination

Racialized and gendered stereotypes challenge and often hinder Black women seeking office. The electorate uses a series of gender and racial stereotypes as heuristics while evaluating candidates. White women candidates are deemed competent, nurturing, and caring (Koenig et al. 2011), while Black women are perceived as controlling, angry, and tough (Littlefield 2008; Orey and Zhang 2019). Because of these stereotypes, Black women tend to be evaluated more negatively as political candidates, and consequently they tend to be less successful when running for political office. Exploring the mechanisms through which elite Black women engage in the world helps us understand how they overcome not only these hurdles but also the doubts and limited access to arenas that offer networks of support.

How Black women engage with the world has been shaped by a socialization forged by both race and gender and a unique desire to advance equality. The ethos of community care and support reinforces their pursuit of excellence (in this case seeking political office) and elevates their standing within the community (Robnett 1997; Collins 2000; Giddings 1984; Simien 2012; Barnes 2016). How Black women express this is also shaped significantly by class. During the late nineteenth and early twentieth centuries the Black community pushed young Black women to acquire an education to obtain jobs as teachers, lawyers, doctors and other professional positions that were removed from domestic work. These positions removed Black women from domestic labor and also had the purpose of racial and community uplift (Shaw 1996; Higginbotham and Weber 1992; Berry and Gross 2020).

During the turn of the twentieth century, the ideas of racial uplift and "saving" Black women converged with the development of a professional Black class (Barnes 2016). Tropes about womanhood and the idea of a "lady" articulated the gendered and class dynamic of racism (Higginbotham and Weber 1992). Being a lady was only applicable to white women with the exceptions of those who were poor, working class, or considered to be of limited character such as prostitutes. For Black women, it did not matter what level of education they had acquired, their marital status, or what examples of refinement they performed, they would never be considered a lady. Therefore, they could not expect societal protections from labor (working as a man) or physical or sexual violence. While the idea of being a "lady" restricted middle- and upper-class white women to their homes, Black women championed a commitment to family, community, and careers (Landry 2002; Giddings 1984; Cooper 2017).

Middle-class Black women formed their own institutions to uplift the community and developed a set of standards of behavior geared toward elevating the status of Black women and the entire race (Giddings 1984; Simien 2012; Cooper 2017; Jones 2020). The politics of respectability was deemed an elitist middle-class notion of culture that many believed did not dismantle the classist and sexist hegemony, rather, it only reinforced it (Gaines 1996; Cooper 2017; Higginbotham 1994). Lower income Black women, who were often not afforded the opportunity for higher education and financial security, developed their own strategies. They would be taught by mothers, female relatives, and community members to become independent; they could not depend on elitist practices or Black men to protect and support them due to discrimination and limited employment opportunities (Barnes 2015). As both groups of women sought ways to protect themselves and their families, their strategies for advancement would be shaped not only by their class but also by ideas promoted by leading men of the time, such as Booker T. Washington's call for self-determination; W. E. B. DuBois call for a talented tenth to access higher education and lead the community, and the liberatory ideas of Marcus Garvey's Back to Africa campaign (White 1999). These ideas all promoted a worldview that the identity of Blackness was not only cultural or a phenotype but also was relational, that is, it connected individuals to the larger group. As such the work of uplift and "saving" women incorporated the ideas of collective action, education, and independence, along with aspects of respectability, as necessary to address the needs of Black women and their communities.

The evolution of cultural expectations (Fordham and Ogbu 1986) and political ideology (Stewart, Settles, and Winter 1998) that promote excellence and participation are also tied to racialized socialization. The literature on the social history of African American women notes that Black women are important intergenerational resources for their communities (Collins 2000; Giddings 1984; Gilkes 1988; Berry and Gross 2020): they provide racial socialization for their children (Thornton et al. 1990), for example, which Nunnally defines as "the process by which African Americans learn about and identify with the influence of race on their social status, culture and group history in the United Sates" (Nunnally 2012, p. 58). Educator, activist, and Black feminist Anna Julia Cooper more specifically identifies the unique role that Black women hold as "the fundamental agency under God in the regeneration . . . of the race, as well as the [initiator of the] groundwork and starting point of its progress upward" (Giddings 1984, p. 81).

The socialization process that positions Black women in their unique role has a dual purpose: to transmit values, attitudes, and behaviors that prepare future generations for possible negative race-related experiences, and to cultivate a positive racial identity (Demo and Hughes 1990). The process of racial socialization links family, identity formation, and overall socialization. For example, gender roles are often learned in the context of race roles (McRae and Noumair 1997). Black women have a heightened sense of race identification derived from their uniquely disadvantaged status in the United States. Linda Williams (2001) suggests that both forms of group consciousness—race and gender—reinforce each other by increasing the rate of Black women's participation in the political process.

The race and gender status of African American women strongly influences how they define family and community, and it determines which political strategies are best suited to meet the needs of Black women, their families, and the race (Gilkes 1988; Hine 1990; Morgen and Bookman 1988; Naples 1991, 1992; Gay and Tate 1998), and therefore which strategies and causes they should participate in. Historically, African American women have viewed political participation as a means to achieve full equality and to improve the status of Blacks, more specifically Black women, and a society in which they are often excluded (Shingles 1981; Tate 1991; Barker, Jones, and Tate 1999; Simien 2005; Jones 2020).

Home Socialization

Literature that explores why women are unlikely to run for public office suggests that, along with career access, traditional gender socialization perpetuates a culture in which women are least likely to run (Lawless and Fox 2005; Elder 2004). According to the political ambition socialization model, women who enter politics are typically outliers. Yet this (largely white) socialization model is not particularly applicable to Black women. The limited existing literature suggests that Black women's unique socialization, politicization, and life experiences make their political activity exceptional, and some scholars posit that the double discrimination that Black women face in fact motivates their higher levels of participation—to combat the invisibility and hypervisibility of being a Black woman (Alex-Assensoh and Stanford 1997; Stokes-Brown and Dolan 2010; Brown 2014). Although Black women indeed had limited career options due to the combination of race and gender, being a traditional woman/housewife has never fit most African American women (King, 1975; Stone 1979; King 1988; Guy-Sheftall 1995; Collins 2000; Simien 2004).

African American women have always played a role in political socialization within their communities and have always contributed to their family's and community's economic stability (King 1988; Giddings 1984; Gay 2001). The economic conditions within the Black community made it difficult to begin or maintain a marital relationship if it did not provide enough economic support due to the employment challenges faced by both Black men and women. As a result, Black families developed different models that often incorporated networks in which Black families provided economically and socially for children (Stack 1974; Stack and Burton 1993). Mothers feel it is important for their daughters not to allow their gender and race to be barriers for identity development or for functioning as an adult (Thomas and King 2007). This is evident in how mothers praise excellence and achievement, promote the autonomy that African American women develop in their homes, and use the income and connections from their careers to give back to their communities.

As such, African American women are more likely than white women to be heads of household, have higher labor participation rates than white women, and typically have more autonomy and decision-making authority in their homes as parents and partners than their white counterparts (King 1975; Prestage 1991; Guy-Sheftall 1995). As Black women maintain their roles in the workforce, they also continue to value their roles as mothers. They see the survival of their family tied to the survival of the Black community.

Communal Socialization

As a result of the labor Black women have historically engaged in and the value they provide their communities, they found autonomy within their homes and through their community work that gave them significant social capital in Black communities (Prestage 1991; Guy-Sheftall 1995; Gilkes 2001; Simien 2012). The labor of Black women created a culture that encourages the pursuit of success and good careers, economic self-reliance, political activism, and value in effectively representing themselves to and for the Black community (Higginbotham 1994; Barnes 2016). Most educated African American women were raised in a culture that encouraged their pursuit of successful careers, their economic self-reliance, and their development as role models for the Black community (Higginbotham 2001).

This unique race and gender status (Gay and Tate 1998; King 1988) strongly influences how they define family and community and resist gender and racial oppression, which in turn leads Black women to use political participation as a means to achieve full equality and improve the status of the group (Barker, Jones, and Tate 1999; Simien 2005; Gilkes 1988; Gay and Tate 1998; Morris 2015; Cooper 2017). Barnes (2016) found that besides navigating career, marriage, motherhood, and extended family responsibilities, Black women have also long been concerned about representing the Black community. In addition Barnes informs us that Black professional women engage in "strategic mothering" to balance racism, sexism, career demands, and care for their communities. The continued work in which Black women engage in their communities places them in prominent positions and gives them levels of prestige and influence unmatched in the lives of white women of similar class backgrounds (Gilkes 2001).

Political Socialization

Smooth and Richardson (2019) show that the socialization process of Black girls shapes the development of leadership skills and political interests. The girls in their study stated that the persons they most admired were women who exhibited care for their communities and families who valued the collective and took risks on behalf of their communities. The researchers also found that Black girls are differently inspired to pursue leadership when they encounter Black women and girls leading and championing issues they care about, whether at the grassroots or public level. Black girls are also exposed to images of strength when they watch their mothers and grandmothers balance their jobs, family, and community work (Shorter-Gooden and Washington 1996). This strength is often considered to ensure survival and a means of protection against the challenges that gendered and racialized discrimination will bring. Recent studies about the lives of middle-class Black women bring forth a critique of the perpetuation of the idea of a "strong Black woman." While this image is often embraced, it has been viewed as a means to control Black women inside and outside the Black community (Collins 2000). For many Black women this image is seen as a badge of honor and is used as a strategy for resilience. However, for professional Black women, this image of a woman who not only manages but is also beholden to career, children, family, community, and spouse comes at a cost (Beauboeuf-Lafontant

2009; Harris-Perry 2011; Parks 2013). I will elaborate on this trope in Chapter 3 and its impact on political Black women.

In their study, Thomas and Speight (1999) demonstrate that African American girls are socialized differently than boys, specifically, boys tend to receive messages about egalitarianism and overcoming racial barriers. Girls receive more messages on racial pride, education, premarital sex and relationships with men, psychological and financial independence, and physical beauty. The socialization processes and subsequent identity development of African American girls is unique because of the particular interaction of racism and sexism and, hence, may be better conceptualized as gendered racial socialization. Ruth Nicole Brown advances our understanding of the importance and potential of this time period through her groundbreaking study of Black girlhood spaces. She contends that these spaces and this time period are not only for the process of socialization but also for the formation of creativity and relationships of accountability (Brown 2014). That, she contends, is how Black women gain an understanding of and value for relationships and community.

The Radical Imagination and Candidate Emergence

Past research on the development of political ambition has typically focused on why someone runs for office and, once they hold an office, whether they will express ambition to run again for their current seat or for a higher position (Schlesinger 1966; Black 1972). Such research assumed monolithic calculations about political opportunity and has limited applicability to Black women (Hardy-Fanta et al., 2007; Stout, Kretschmer, and Ruppaner 2017; Dittmar 2020; Bejarano et al., 2020). Most of the recent research has therefore focused on nascent ambition—the decision dynamics involved in moving from being a potential candidate to running and becoming an officeholder. Carroll and Sanbonmatsu (2013) found that direct recruitment and encouragement is more predictive of eventual candidacy for women than it is for men. Others have found that exposure to women officeholders might have a less direct but nonetheless encouraging effect on women's political ambition (Ladam, Harden, and Windett 2018; Sweet-Cushman

2018). Though these factors are undoubtedly critical to understanding the complexity of the decision-making process, I have found that for Black women, rather than there being a neat, linear, and upward process for many Black women, there tends to be a constellation of factors incorporated in an ambition on the margins.

My theory of ambition on the margins incorporates the idea of a radical imagination of Black women and their socialization cultivates political behaviors that Holloway Sparks calls "dissident citizenship" (Sparks 1997, p. 74) in which marginalized groups not only vote and lobby but also develop alternative spaces for engagement, such as protests and other ways to "address the state and the wider polity" (p. 75). This includes the development of community and civic organizations that disregard the limits broader society attempts to impose on Black women and their communities (Simien 2012; Giddings 1988; Jones 2020). The gendered and racial discrimination of Black women and their political, economic, and social conditions have long led them to develop nontraditional forms of engagement (Giddings 1984; Hine and Thompson 1999). Such engagement fosters in Black women the confidence to seek office, and through volunteer opportunities and networks gives them specific experiences and connections to enable their campaigning and pathway to office.

Often this radical imagination of Black women is primed and develops in alternative formal spaces, such as organizations or church auxiliaries, but it can also develop in intimate social spaces such as beauty shops, book clubs, and among friends (Collins 2000). These spaces cultivate women's talent and provide them with opportunities to engage and develop skills beneficial for a political campaign. Participation through organizations provides useful political capital and resources to political leaders who seek help in establishing consensus and promoting the deliberation process. It is necessary to note that the desire of Black women to carve out spaces of their own, as well as educate, mentor, and strategize among themselves, came from Black women not only seeking sisterhood but also the need to address exclusion from leadership positions in institutions within the Black community dominated by men. In fact Black women created parallel societies as a result of the sexist restrictions on their participation in educational, civic, and religious Black institutions (Higginbotham 1994; Cooper 2017; Berry and Gross 2020; Giddings 1988).

The type of engaged citizenship that Black women developed is perhaps most clearly expressed in the 1977 statement of the Combahee River Collective, a feminist organization composed of Black women from the United States' various social movements of the time. It begins as follows:

> Our politics initially sprang from the shared belief that Black women are inherently valuable, that our liberation is a necessity not as an adjunct to somebody else's [but] because of our need as human persons for autonomy.... We realize that the only people who care enough about us to work consistently for our liberation are us. Our politics evolve from a healthy love for ourselves, our sisters and our community which allows us to continue our struggle and work.

While this opening statement speaks from a voice of liberation, the statement also speaks to the rejection and pain that Black women feel when rejected from spaces that should be welcoming, such as spaces with feminists and organizations in the Black community that seek to address societal inequities. This acknowledgment of shared values, rejection and othering and self-edification also motivates the individual and organizational political work in which we see Black women engage today. This political engagement leads to the formation of organizations, networks and the joining of those networks and organizations to address issues of importance to Black women.

Historically, Black women have had to acquire leadership and power in nontraditional ways in comparison to their male counterparts, both Black and white. Despite that, Black women have played an integral role in race-based movements, although history often obscures their participation (Robnett 1997) because they rarely hold formal leadership roles (Giddings 1984; Dawson 2003; Ransby 2003; Jones 2020). I sat with Sharon Pratt, former Washington, DC mayor, as one of the 36 women I interviewed. She described the plight of Black women within the leadership structure of Black community to me this way: "Overwhelmingly the churches are male. Overwhelmingly civil rights organizations are male. When it is time to discuss the community and exercise power there, those positions have gone to me and other Black women." Every woman interviewed spoke of the value they placed on their community service. The majority of the women also spoke at length about how their community work put them close to the campaign process, enabled them to develop transferable skills, and helped them overcome their hesitancy to run for office.

The community networks cultivated by Black women mentor, recruit, and help Black women build campaigns and develop fundraising strategies among the respondents I interviewed. They also foster ambition. I discovered through interviews of Black women who serve or have served as elected officials that in addition to their unique social capital within their communities, the particular community spaces in which Black women conduct these endeavors, along with their racialized gendered identity, help them develop a unique consciousness that distinguishes them from Black men and white women and helps them sustain high levels of voter participation, engage in political organizing, and ultimately seek political office.

The networks of dissident citizenship give Black women opportunities and encouragement to seek office, name recognition among potential voters, and occasions for fundraising. Also in these spaces Black women develop skills that are transferable to the political arena, skills such as public speaking, fundraising, and a service résumé that community members respect. These women gain skills and express a heightened sense of confidence thanks to their community and volunteer experience. It is through such forms of participation that Black women develop social capital, and it is their network of potential voters and fundraisers that enable Black women to achieve political success.

Unfortunately, this type of work is often misunderstood as signifying *lack* of ambition because it is less individual and more communal. Because such work is rarely included in how we understand Black women's motivation to seek public office, the bulk of the literature consequently limits expressions of ambition to running in elections and moving up the political ladder (Lien and Swain 2013).

Data and Methods

This chapter introduces data gathered in interviews with 36 Black women from across the country who served or currently serve as elected officials, work within a political party, and/or are members of media. While Black women's numbers in political office are growing, much of what we know about their path to political office comes from studies that examine existing officeholders (see Carew 2012; Ward 2016; Brown 2014; Hardy-Fanta et al. 2016; Silva and Skulley 2019; Shah, Scott, and Gonzalez Juenke 2019). The interviews were conducted between 2017 and 2021. These women served (or still serve) as U.S. senators, state legislators, city councilpersons, and school board members in the South, Midwest, West Coast, and Northeast. These women represent not only districts of majority Black voters but also areas outside the South and places where Black voters were the minority. The interviewees responded to an email solicitation I sent to 75 Black women elected officials identified by the Center for American Women in Politics. As of 2020, the officials were currently serving or had served in state legislators or in statewide offices across the nation. In addition, through Facebook groups that target African American women, I posted a solicitation for Black women who served as local elected officials. All interviewees consented to being "on the record" and permitted the inclusion of their names in publications. I provided them with their transcript to correct, clarify, or strike any statement made during the interview. During the interviews, which ran from 45 minutes to an hour, I questioned the respondents about their motivation to run for office, the fundraising process, and their experience in office. I recorded, transcribed, then organized the results into themes.

The resulting data provided significant insight into how Black women learned to engage in politics. In order to explore the role of the radical imagination, I also gathered data from five focus groups (with 40 women in total) held from 2016 to 2019 in Florida, Illinois, Maryland, and Texas.[2] Four of these groups were composed of African American women undergraduate and graduate students who were highly engaged in their campus communities (they were members of campus organizations and several began their own organization to address a campus issue) and were interested in continuing to provide service via elected office and/or community activism.[3] The fifth focus group was composed of African American professional women who were well-informed and consistent voters. The young women who participated were not only from majority African American rural and urban communities but also from predominantly white suburban neighborhoods. The older women mostly resided in majority Black neighborhoods in the Washington, DC metropolitan area. In the focus groups, I led discussions on their views of current issues, politics and African American women as elected officials, and community and campus organizations in which they participated. Their comments reveal how Black women navigate marginalization, cultivate a sense of identity, and value engagement in organizations. Notably, for some, college was their first opportunity to engage in formal groups with Black women. These engagements often reflected their community experiences and the example of Black women in their home communities. I thought it was important to place both data sets in dialogue with each other to inform our understanding of how Black women acquire their understanding of community and political work and seeking office across generations.

The data presented in this chapter are not exhaustive; further interview and focus group responses appear in the following chapters. Yet the women's testimonies support my premise that for certain Black women there is a socialization process that that centers service, but it also offers means of political socialization that then creates a base of support for women to move outside of their immediate communities by seeking elected office. This has led Black women to seek political office not only (or even mainly) for the prestige of the position but also for impact—recall the chapter's opening epigraph. This desire to make an impact also helps determine which office Black women chose to run for. These women's testimonies also speak of their self-identity and expectations and the importance of networks in providing volunteers, mentors, and financial support for political campaigns.

Socialized at Home and in the Community for Agency and Action

At Delta Sigma Theta Sorority Inc.'s 2019 "Delta Days in the Nation's Capital,"[4] then treasurer of the St. Louis, Missouri, chapter Tishaura Jones commented regarding public service that "Black women run to do something; men run to be somebody."[5] Participating on a panel of

Delta members who served in elected positions, Jones spoke of the value of Black women seeking office, and she noted that what drives Black women to do such work is the greater purpose of seeing change in America and in their marginalized status. Specifically, the "something" that Jones said Black women run to do is the work of the radical imagination that emphasizes traditional and nontraditional forms of political engagement and the work toward justice, equality, and access. This type of vision and work toward it was consistently expressed by the interviewees and focus group members.

Focus group participants consistently confirmed that the socialization process that occurs during Black girlhood affirmed their identity while shaping the development of leadership skills and political interest. When asked how they would express their sense of identity, many of the participants noted that their dual-minority identity as female and Black makes them unique, and that this duality contributed to the high level of esteem they witnessed in Black women who served their communities. When asked if they viewed their identity as positive or negative, Sharon,[6] a 19-year-old sophomore from North Florida said, "Definitely yes, it's a positive, because I feel as a Black woman, we have a deep perspective that literally no one else has." Eunique, a 21-year-old college senior from Texas, expounded on which identity influences her the most, while contrasting Black women with other women: "I think my Blackness has more role, and my gender is kind of shoved in there, because I think Black women have always been a little bit more dominant than other cultures of women in my opinion. We have always been more upfront about how we feel about what is going on."

Several of the participants articulated how the complexity of racialized gendered identity shaped their awareness and motivated them to consider a political career. Jasmine, an 18-year-old college freshman from Missouri, said:

> I'm just changing my career plans and decided that I want to run for office. I... realized... my gender is just as important as my Blackness because I realized both [are] underrepresented groups within the political atmosphere but now I'm coming to understand more the context of my gender because I realize the type of male-dominated

society [into which] I'm planning on venturing, so I'm being more conscious of my gender now.

Several of the focus group participants expressed this unique socialization. One spoke in particular about the confidence and pride she saw her Black female classmates express:

Quiana, a senior from Florida, said that when she arrived at college "there was a sense of Black pride. Even at this PWI, (predominantly white institution) our Black women . . . have self-pride. And we carry that with passion, and we carry that with the pride that we have, like the essence you were saying. So, I can see how you're saying when you were talking to the older women and they probably had, you know, different reactions than us. Personally, I say I love being a Black woman. It's because someone was there to tell me that, hey, you're a Black woman. You need this now; you need to put out. You need to have a sense of self-pride, just because all the things that Black women have been through, it's not going to do anything but make you stronger.

One of her classmates followed up by discussing her confidence in her beauty as a Black woman:

Yeah, like how she said we're trendsetters and futuristic. I mean, I pay attention to hair. And so, like when . . . if you go way back, white women didn't like when Black women would wear their hair down. So, they would have them cover it up. So instead of us just walking around with ugly scarves all day, we started wearing pretty scarves. Then we started getting even more attention. So, what we're try—when they try to box us in, we['re] already going on to something else that's . . . going to make us shine.

The views of the focus group members confirm the role that socialization plays in how Black women learn to navigate their racialized gendered identities while beginning to engage in service and politics. The interviewees' experiences of their youth and their engagement with politics also confirms that socialization at home and within communities affects the likelihood of Black women emerging as political candidates.

The respondents spoke with great passion about the influence of their families and the persons they saw who engaged in politics. They discussed in detail working on campaigns of family members as children and teenagers. For some this included stuffing envelopes, knocking on doors, wearing campaign T-shirts, or tagging along to campaign events. In many cases it was a family member who influenced their political path and the work ethic they had in approaching campaigns. Former Georgia State Legislator Dee Dawkins-Haigler expressed that her political participation is in her blood, having watched her mother and grandmother participate in politics:

> I've always been in positions my entire life that dealt with some type of social justice, or political nature, even forming protests in high school, all the way up through college. And then I ran my mother's campaign for city council in South Carolina, West Columbia, South Carolina. She was the first African American, first female, and first woman.... First African American, first woman, first Democrat to hold a seat in Lexington County (South Carolina), which is like one of the strongholds of the Confederacy and white supremacy.
>
> The only pe[rson] that I saw really [politically] active in the community growing up was my mother, who was very active in the Democratic Party. Other than that, I didn't see Black women [being] very active, didn't even see a lot of girls my age interested in being in the political arena or even caring about social justice issues. Now, believe it or not, my grandmother was very influential in my life because she was one of the few Black women, or women, or Blacks, who was very active in the union movement. So, she was a union officer back when it wasn't even safe to be involved, engaged in the unions, and she would ... travel to Atlanta just to go to meetings dealing with the union, because she always felt like workers should have a voice, that Black people's lives had worth.

Meredith Lawson-Rowe, who serves as a city councilperson in Reynoldsburg, Ohio, also participated in politics as a child. She recounted:

[Since I was] a young girl, my mom has always been involved in social action. I've been in church, we've always been involved in community, community organizing, community building, giving back. I can remember as a young girl, maybe about eight or ten years old, my mother was a campaign manager for a local county commissioner, and he was our uncle. So, to me, that was, "Oh, Uncle Bob's campaign." And we wore shirts, and we passed out literature. And my mom has always been political, our church has always been political, so it's always been important to me to participate in serving those that don't have equal representation.

Teree Caldwell-Johnson who at the time of her interview served as vice chair of the Des Moines, Iowa School Board credits her parents with her commitment to service and understanding of politics. Her father was the first African American elected to the City Council in Salina, Kansas, and he would become the first African American mayor of the city. Both her parents were very active in civic organizations and social organizations. Caldwell's mother was a member of Alpha Kappa Alpha Sorority Inc. and Links Inc., which Caldwell joined as well. Caldwell informed me that their examples of commitment to community motivated her to be engaged and understand that running for office was a valuable tool for change.

The comments of Dawkins-Haigler, Lawson-Rowe, and Caldwell-Johnson suggest that they had grown up knowing it was important to engage in community and political work, but it was also important to serve with purpose. These statements confirm the value of exposure to political examples, as well as the value of accessible role models and Black women engaging in politics and service across generations. Their examples suggest that for the socialization of Black girls, up-close and personal examples of political participation, along with the opportunity to participate as children, significantly influences girls' future involvement as in politics as voters, activists, and candidates.

In a direct expression of the impact of the radical imagination, Arkansas State Representative Vivian Flowers centered her response to why she ran for office and continues to serve. Flowers passionately spoke of the self-worth and care she was raised with and on the desire to ensure that other girls experience the safety and worth she experienced as a child:

> I have wonderful parents who come from really beautiful families—not that we don't have our share of issues and drama and everything that every other family experience, but I just . . . I didn't grow up thinking I was less than, and I didn't grow up not getting what I needed. I grew up getting most of what I wanted, I didn't have to deal with my parents splitting up. I [have] . . . never been raped, I ain't never been molested, I ain't ever been beat up. The one time my brother got into a fight and I had his back, this boy hit me in front of my father, but I knew . . . I knew that no matter what, my dad was going to protect me, and it made me tough. I am safe and I'm free and I'm happy. And I just want that for everybody I represent. I just want that for them. And I want it to be where the government or white supremacists or mean, selfish, greedy people don't have any power or impact over another girl like me not being able to live her best life.

Flowers's vision of her leadership along with that of the other respondents shows us that the candidates understand the challenges their community members face. While these women also spoke of having ambitions and goals as politicians and professionals, these ambitions are anchored in the "something" of which Tishaura Jones spoke. This confirms that the ambition that elite Black women hold is inclusive of a purposeful service that influences their emergence as a candidate. The narratives presented are only a sample of what the women stated, but they reveal the influence of generational, elite political behavior that encourages Black women and girls to engage in politics. We also see that familial and community socialization and gendered and racialized experiences can open them to see the difficulties and obstacles involved in such service.

Socialized to Serve

Just as they came from communities that encouraged their achievement as a means to overcome the marginalization of racism and sexism, so too respondents consistently discussed the need to work at a very high level. This translated into knocking on more doors than did their opponents, being extremely well prepared for debates and media events, and finding ways to overcome limitations in fundraising. The memory of lessons learned as children, along with campaign strategies and a work ethic, reflects Black women's unique societal role as both a woman and Black. For many of them, seeking excellence was closely connected with ideas of what is necessary to thrive as Black women and to be in a position to win. Senator Carol Mosley Braun (D-IL, 1993–1999), the first Black woman to serve as a U.S. senator, recalled her mother's words to her: "I wanted to do the best job I could. That was my mother's line. Do the best job you can where you're planted. And that was my motivation—to do the best job I could where I was planted. And so, I just [put] one foot in front of the next. And then when it came time, I was in the U.S. Attorney's Office." Councilwoman Shanette Strickland's motivations were more specific: "If we only need 1,500 votes, you['d] better get to 2,500 votes [chuckle]. You got to work differently. You got to fundraise different. You have to have your message different to [the others who] knock on those doors."

Lydia Glaize, who currently serves as a Georgia State Representative was a first-time candidate in 2013 when she ran for city council in Fairburn, Georgia. Glaize stated that her interest in running came from her community work and the knowledge she gained by engaging in that work. She recalls precisely what pushed her to consider running. She was attending a meeting for a community organization, the Voter Empowerment Collaborative, and remembers:

> One of the local leaders was discussing what we called the Donut, which is the cities around [I-]285 [outside Atlanta]. And on the south side, those cities had become minority-majority cities. But the elected positions did not reflect the makeup and the demographics of the citizens of those cities. So, when we got in the meeting that night, one of the things that was said that stuck out in my mind [and] that really prompted me to consider running, was the word "voluntary apartheid."... What that meant was that people of color were the majority in these cities south of the airport, and yet the mayors and city councils were reflective of the [white] minority in the city. And

so, with that said, it's very similar to South Africa. There was apartheid somewhat, but [it was] voluntary because we didn't have many African Americans who had run for office. And the few that did, they lost every time, even in a [race] where [there were] at least six people running.

Glaize went on to say that upon making her decision, she found she had plenty of support to follow through, thanks to the connections she had forged through her community work in various organizations and in the local schools.

City Councilwoman Meredith Lawson-Rowe of Reynoldsburg, Ohio, was a reluctant candidate. It was her volunteer work on a campaign that led her to being asked and accepting the call to run. She had assisted a candidate for city attorney who later ran for city council. While helping with the candidate's city council run, she also helped another candidate run for city auditor. The former candidate later recruited her to run for office. Lawson-Rowe explained that she deliberately had to set aside all her preconceptions and lack of confidence:

> I told her [the city council member recruiting her] all the reasons why I couldn't do it: I didn't have the experience, I didn't have the education, I didn't have the political background, I didn't come from a political family, and all of these were the reasons why I could not do it. And she [told] me, "Well, that's not true, that's not true." She ... debunk[ed] all of [the] mess I had in my mind.

Angie Jenkins of Reynoldsburg, Ohio, who was also a reluctant first-time candidate and ran on the same slate as Lawson-Rowe, stated that her sense of community and volunteer work led her to politics. Her service gave her a keen understanding of the needs of her community and who was needed at the table to make pertinent local policy decisions:

> Well, for school board, at that time, my children were going to the Reynoldsburg school system, and I wanted to be a part of that process. Reynoldsburg went through many changes and the school board needed some people of color to serve, and they also needed

to have a voice in the community that looked like the children that were attending the schools in Reynoldsburg. Reynoldsburg was . . . chang[ing] as far as minority growth [went]. From there, I went on to volunteer for the Obama campaigns, and I volunteered for the Hillary [Clinton] campaign. I also volunteered for the local city councilwoman, Kristin Bryant, who is now on City Council. Once I started volunteering with her, then I started to volunteer for Councilwoman Strickland for the election that we won. I went to her meetings and decided that I was going to sign up to volunteer and help her run. And then Kristin Bryant, who's on City Council, came to me and said, "Why don't you run?" And she gave me some options of what I could run for.

These testimonials offer a view of the thought processes of women considering a run for political office. These women all were professionals, engaged in organizations that assist in fostering leadership, but they still had a confidence gap. The realization that they held the skills to become viable candidates defaulted to a realization that in addition to their concern about community issues, there also was value and a skill set that came from their community work. Interviewees continued to share their concerns about an initial run for office and how they overcame doubts.

Overcoming Doubts to Run

Several of the women interviewed stated their hesitancy to run for elected office due to what they perceived as their lack of experience. They were eventually persuaded by thinking of the impact they could make. The women were conscious that their opponents would be predominantly white and male candidates. They expressed concern, knowing that a white male would likely have access to far more resources than them, and were aware of the possibility for an election to become fraught with racial polarization.

One such woman who ran for office was Dr. Gethsemane Moss, who now serves as a school board trustee for the Benicia Unified School District in California and had previously served as an appointed commissioner for her community's Arts and Culture Commission. When asked about her confidence in running and about how she had made the decision to run for office, she stated, "No, I really [didn't] feel confident." Later, she explained, "There were three white men already running for two seats. I didn't want to fight that hard, and I didn't have a lot of time to think about it before the deadline to submit." Yet Moss decided to run in the majority white district after reflecting on the impact she could make, adding,

> I think another reason why I feel compelled to do it is because . . . in the wake of everything that's been happening with things around, around systemic racism and things like that, I realize[d] . . . in some of the communication that I've had with members of the board, that if I weren't there to offer a different perspective, they would just keep on doing things the same old way. So, I just felt like, oh my God, it became very clear to me that [the board members] are almost clueless in terms of what perspectives are needed for making sure that we're serving all students.

Angie Jenkins, who serves as president of the Reynoldsburg, Ohio, City Council, likewise not only expressed doubt in her ability to run but was also concerned about who her potential opponent would be and what the pattern of leadership in her community had been. When a friend asked her to run for council president, she said:

> I thought, "Well, president? I've never [even] served on city council. How can I be president?" I wasn't really familiar with that role and didn't think that I would win, just because I wasn't really familiar with what all that entailed. And [because] there were a lot of men that were serving in that role . . . I didn't think that I would be able to beat [them] because they'd been there for so long. And they're Caucasian men, so I didn't think that was going to be possible. Running as president also was a challenge because the person that been in that position, had been on city council, and then he ran for the presidency, and he had been in that position for a while as well. But I thought maybe the city would be looking for a change and because of the growth in population with minorities, I thought I had an opportunity there to serve and to win.

The trepidation that Moss and Jenkins expressed is consistent with the lived experiences of Black women in a society in which the identity and experiences of Black women are not valued. Yet both women decided to run in spite of the challenge, due to the perceived impact they felt their contributions could make on their communities. The sense that Moss and Jenkins had about how their identity could influence their potential success as candidate is also reinforced by the recruitment process that Jenkins and several of the women I spoke to experienced, they were encouraged to run by friends or personal acquaintances. This type of recruitment confirms that many of these women, while they held elite status within their sphere of influence as a result of their professions and community work, they were politically structural outsiders. It was not the party apparatus that informed these women they were viable candidates, in most cases other women and Black political elites encouraged them.

The Resources Dissident Citizenship Provides

In the decision-making process to run for office, central was the role of organizations. Every politician spoke of their volunteer work with organizations, recalling their efforts either as a board member, program coordinator, or as someone who stuffed book bags at an annual back-to-school event. Several respondents had formed organizations to meet a specific community need. All of these examples confirm the value of the socialization process that shapes Black women and the resources within their communities that foster the desire and value of political participation. Central to those resources are organizations that offer opportunities for Black women to gain valuable skills that increase their professional socialization and their ability to become a candidate. These include opportunities for public speaking, managing an effective meeting, fundraising, and interacting with other elite community members.

In addition to community service, another recurring theme was the role of working on political campaigns. This type of service also gave the respondents a broader sense of policy needs for their communities, understanding the inner workings of campaigns, and opportunities to cultivate relationships that would be useful during their own campaigns. New Hampshire State House Representative Charlotte DiLorenzo became engaged in politics through volunteering for the Obama 2008 presidential campaign and in 2011 ran for her town's new Democratic county office. She reports:

> What actually got me launched into politics or even being interested in politics was the Barack Obama campaign. I joined the campaign in around April of 2007 after hearing Barack speak in Hampton, New Hampshire. Back in 2011, we were getting ready for Obama's re-election for 2012. I spoke with some folks in the Rockingham County Democrats Office.... And my town did not have a town Democratic committee. We formed a town committee. And from there, I was the vice chair.

In separate interviews, Sarah Anthony and Tenisha Yancey, who both serve in the Michigan House of Representatives, also noted that their interest in running for political office was piqued by doing volunteer work on campaigns. Anthony noted that she had engaged in several campaigns to preserve affirmative action in the state and in a congressional campaign. While volunteering, she

> started to realize that many of the voices that I thought should be at these tables were not being adequately represented, particularly low-income folks and Black and brown folks, that their issues just were not being uplifted with fidelity. And through that process, I was able to gain a lot of inroads into communities that would ultimately help me when I start[ed] to put my name on a ballot.

Representative Yancey's experience prior to running was very similar. She told me,

> I've worked on judges' campaigns. I was exposed to the endorsement process and seeking endorsements and calling around and following up on endorsements for a few judges. On other campaigns, I did door-to-door knocking and just talking to people and getting their support. I also did phone banking and volunteering for a lot of local campaigns.

These experiences confirm that Black women participate in a variety of service opportunities and community engagement that often leads to political participation (Junn 1997; Tate 1991; Gay and Tate 1998; Alex-Assensoh and Stanford 1997; Scott et al. 2021). Take as another example County Commissioner Sherri Washington of Rockdale County, Georgia, who has an extensive service history. She is a member of the NAACP and the local chapter of Delta Sigma Theta Sorority Inc., and she is a founder of the local bar association for Black women. She ran repeatedly but unsuccessfully for a state legislative position, but realized during those failed runs that she nevertheless always won her county. She attributed that success to her strong community engagement, which led to her winning a local election and then re-election in 2020. Not only does volunteering connect one to a variety of networks, but it also provides an avenue for potential candidates to hone valuable skills as a candidate and public servant.

Among the interviewees, a consistent theme was the value of having had experience in community service prior to seeking office. Not only did it motivate women to run, but it also gave them an opportunity to gain the skills required to run for office. Shanette Strickland, who serves on the Reynoldsburg, Ohio, City Council, also attributed her success as a first-time candidate to her community and professional service providing her with connections:

> I'm involved with this business professional club, [and that] also [helped me] to network. I was in the community at my child's football games and connected with people in my community. I learned how to communicate in a different way. Everything that *I* think is an issue may not be an issue for [everyone else]. So, having those conversations, [I'd ask], "What do you want to see change here in Reynoldsburg? What are those things that you want to see, businesses, opportunities here in Reynoldsburg?" My IT background and connection to other IT people here in Reynoldsburg allowed me to [use my communication skills] . . . in my position today. Communication, from an IT perspective, negotiation from an IT perspective: these are all the skill sets that I use in my job today [for] advancing the infrastructure of my city.

Brenda Gilmore stated that her experience with volunteering helped her to develop transferable skills. Gilmore began volunteering during her childhood and through this developed strong organizational and fundraising skills. She chaired events for organizations such as the YMCA and worked in numerous women's organizations.

> I really had entry level jobs when I was volunteering when I was young girl, it may be making phone calls, or it could have been putting stamps on letters and send[ing] them out. I could be knocking on doors. I have great organizational skills. And I am good at fundraising, but I'd never thought about applying those skills to running for elected positions. I mean, I had been chair of different events at the YMCA and worked in a number of women's organizations where I would chair different [committees]. But I still didn't see that those skills were transferable to running for an elected office. But [in fact] I've used all those skills and the people and contacts as a great resource too.

Gilmore noted that although she did not always realize she was developing particular skill sets in volunteer positions, over time she became aware that the skills and networks she had developed through service would prove invaluable on the campaign trail and as an elected official.

For the respondents, seeking an elected office was an extension of their commitment to serving the community. Several of the respondents conveyed that they saw the role of Black women in politics as necessary. St. Louis Mayor Tishaura Jones observed, for example, that Black women enter politics because they notice something has gone awry and that being in office is more than a career choice: it is a way to effect necessary change and to right injustice. Multiple participants shared a similar perspective about seeking different positions, saying they had other motivations besides moving up the political career ladder. Judge Sheila Calloway, who serves as juvenile court judge in Nashville, Tennessee, stated when asked about her ambition to seek a higher judicial position:

> At this point in my career, I have not done all of the dreams and visions that I have for juvenile court, . . . so I definitely will run again

in two years, no question about it. After that, I don't know.... I would like to be in a position where I'm not just influencing and changing policies for this group of kids and this family, but [doing so] on a nationwide basis, I would like to do that. I would like to be one of the decision-makers or the policymakers that are helping to decide how juvenile court should run and the things that we should do, and moving us away from locking up kids and sending them to the adult system, and all of those things. I want to be a part of the national conversation about it.

In summary, respondents consistently confirmed that community and volunteer work is a strong predictor of candidate emergence. Their testimonies also help us understand that for Black women, seeking political office is not only about individual ambition but is also a form of political participation (Scott et. al 2021; Tate 1991; Simien 2005; Smooth 2006) through which to impact their communities. This desire to have impact is no coincidence but a result of a socialization process that prepares Black women to overcome challenges that racism and sexism present. These responses help us understand that Black women have a deeper motivation to serve and to use their elected position to enhance the experiences of community members. This aspect of the radical imagination for something greater for the community is front and center not only in the decision to lead but also in the desire to cultivate and participate in spaces that foster leadership and encourage political participation.

The Alternative Spaces of Black Women

The intersection of race and gender in which these Black women find themselves has led them to carve out spaces to cultivate and wield power to address their unique needs. Black women have unfortunately often found that opportunities for solidarity with white women were and are fraught with racism, and that white women often ignored the complexities of Black women's needs (Jones 2020; Giddings 1984). Black women also found it challenging to engage in social movements and organizations led by Black men, as these were typically spaces of patriarchal control and sexism (Giddings 1984; Robnett 1997; Simien and Clawson 2004). Black women have therefore sought out their own collective spaces with other Black women to advance their needs. The institutions they formed have been key in building political participation for Black women (Giddings 1984; Higginbotham 1994; Hunter 1998; Smooth 2018). These organizations became communities critical to the political and personal survival of Black women (Collins 2000; Jones 2020).

Most recently, Black women have used their collective voices to mobilize voters and particularly African American women to vote in the 2020 election. Black women have used organizations not only to get out the vote but also to influence the options available to voters via candidates and policies. Melanie Campbell is the convener of the Black Women's Roundtable, one of the largest networks of women focused on using civic engagement to improve the lives of Black women, their families, and their communities by improving access to healthcare, ending systemic racism, reforming the criminal justice system, lifting people out of poverty, and so forth. It is a unique blending of Black women with a variety of backgrounds: corporate board members and labor activists, college professors and student activists, nonprofit leaders and grassroots volunteers. Campbell was instrumental in organizing Black women to come together to campaign publicly for the Democratic Party 2020 vice president to be an African American woman.

As central figures in Black organizational life (Simpson 1998), Black women have long been trusted as informal community leaders in movements that have family overtones and religious roots, such as the Civil Rights Movement (Payne 1990; Robnett 1997), and in social movements in cities like Chicago (McCourt 1977; Drake and Cayton 1970). Black women are highly active in addressing the various issues that impact the Black community, such as environmental justice (Simpson 2014), the Civil Rights Movement (Robnett 1997), reproductive justice (Price 2020), and labor activism (Arneson 2006).

The relevance and impact of Black women's organizations role in advancing political objectives has a long legacy dating to the founding of the National Association of Colored Women (NACW) in 1896. The NACW was the first African American civil rights organization, and it fostered the beginning of the Black women's club movement. Simultaneously, Black women also formed structured organizations within churches and formed Greek letter organizations at Historically Black Colleges and Universities (HBCUs). These organizations and the ones to follow organized Black women and the Black community to address needs such as childcare, charity for the poor, financing social justice campaigns, and cultivating strategies to achieve equality, all while making the protection and elevation of Black women their main priority (Giddings 1984; Higginbotham 1992; Hunter 1998; Smooth 2018; Berry and Gross 2020; Jones 2020). The pivotal role of these organizations and the women affiliated with them became ingrained within the political and cultural life of the Black community.

One of the critical institutions within the Black community is the Black Greek letter organization (BGLO), mentioned in passing above. Founded between 1906 and 1963 to help Black students address racism,[7] sexism, and issues of justice and racial uplift, that these organizations exist to serve not only college campuses but also the larger Black community is evident by membership not ending upon college graduation, instead, members commit to a lifetime of service. The structure of African American sorority organizations is unique in comparison to other sororities. Would-be members have the opportunity to join at two different levels: as undergraduates while matriculating on a college campus or after completing their college education. Members engage in monthly business meetings to plan service projects and community outreach and fundraise to support their organization's mission.

For Black women, these Black sororities emerged "as spaces for young Black women on college campuses to assemble and advocate for the political, social, [and] human rights of Black people in the United States" (Daniels 2021, p. 13). These organizations engaged within the Colored Women's Club Movement tradition in that same era (Higginbotham 1994; Hunter 1998; Daniels 2021). This allowed college-aged young Black women to organize and mobilize with like-minded older women of the Black women's suffrage and social movements.

Membership in Black sororities has been shown to create high rates of political engagement (Simpson 1998; Dowe 2018; Daniels 2021). It has also been shown that sorority membership correlates highly with seeking public office (Dowe 2018; Daniels 2021; Austin 2022). Beverly Evans Smith, the 26th National President and CEO of Delta Sigma Theta Sorority Inc. stated:

> We have quite a few mayors who have run and won. We haven't yet broken that glass ceiling with Black women governors. I'm hoping that we do that sometime fairly soon. We certainly have congressional leaders; we have seven currently serving. So we have reached the point, even for Delta Sigma Theta from very early times, when we have been able to show that you can in fact be a Black woman who runs for office because we've had examples for them.

How Black women value their membership in these organizations is likewise reflected in a recollection of Vonda Searcy Moore, who attended the swearing-in ceremony of Atlanta Mayor Keisha Lance Bottoms in January 2018. Both Bottoms and Moore are members of Delta Sigma Theta Sorority Inc. In Moore's Facebook post she jubilantly recalled Mrs. Bottoms greeting the National President of the organization after someone from the crowd announced that the President of Delta Sigma Theta was on stage at the end of the receiving line. "Mrs. Bottoms makes an immediate 180-degree turn, drops everything (judges, press, statesmen etc.) and addresses our President. Atlanta got a mayor named Keisha and she is . . . a Delta." This anecdote may seem irrelevant to someone outsidethe Black community, but it speaks to the social value that Black female organizations provide their members, specifically, the network among Black female candidates.

Student focus group participants noted that organizations in which they participated informed their political knowledge and ambition by giving them a deeper sense of issues, alerting them to avenues for increased community engagement, and confirming that seeking office is realistic for them. Zara, a 21-year-old college junior from Chicago and a member of Zeta Phi Beta Sorority Inc. an African American sorority, noted that participation in her organization "teaches me . . . not [to] sit comfortably with what has been told to me." Her experience with the sorority has prompted her to increase her engagement in campus organizations that support low-income students.

> Socialization in general just makes me more aware. [E]very space I go into, it's like, "How can I make this better for low-income first-generation students? How can I make this better for Black women?" Because those are the two organizations I'm most a part of and those are my most salient identities. So, it just really teaches me to think critically about everywhere I'm going and how to make it more accessible and make it better.

A key aspect of membership in BGLOs is the level of support and assistance that members provide to other members. Karrie, a second-year doctoral student from Arkansas and a member of Delta Sigma Theta, appreciated the networking assistance these organizations provide, even when she didn't ask for it: "I intentionally used my connections with my sorority . . . I like the fact that these connections are made to be used. You don't meet people just to say you know them and then be through with it. No, you meet people, and they tell you what they could do for you." Karrie elaborated that sometimes members can become offended "if they know that they have resources that you can use or needed, and you did not ask."

Political ambition research shows that the absence of role models negatively affects women's political leadership and that role models are important for the flourishing of women's leadership. Karrie's words on role modeling within her organization confirms this, as did her appreciative comment, "Well, really, it's really given me the examples that I didn't have growing up, of Black women actually in office or Black women making decisions that mean something to the greater population [rather] than just my small town or all of that." In short, the value of organizations was not merely touched upon by the focus group participants, it was a continual thread in all the conversations.

All of the women interviewed belonged to either a BGLO, and/or a Black woman's civic organization such as Links Inc., or a community-based organization, and, as mentioned, some founded organizations to meet specific community needs. A common theme in the interviews was the value of the civic and social organizations to which the respondents belonged in not only helping to foster skills but also offering the women opportunities for networking and fundraising.

Lashrecse Aird, who served in the Virginia House of Delegates, spoke of the value of socialization through organizations.

> I think the socialization from my organization [Delta Sigma Theta] teaches me to . . . not sit comfortably with what has been told to me. . . . My organization, the Quest Scholars Network, we've been working on advocacy efforts for getting a space for . . . first generation low-income students on campus that's been years long of writing, legislating in the making.
>
> So I think just that socialization in general just makes me more aware of every space I go into, it's like, "How can I make this better for low-income first-generation students? How can I make this better for Black women?" Because those are the two organizations I'm most part of and those are my most salient identities. So it just really teaches me to think critically about everywhere I'm going and how to make it more accessible and make it better.

These organizations provide a network of women not only locally but throughout the country. While these organizations are restricted from campaigning for or endorsing political candidates, their members individually show themselves to invaluable in providing support to one another and to members of other Black Greek letter organizations. Interview and focus group participants who are members of Black sororities expressed the value of membership. There are members in every sector of the community who provide support, mentoring, and resources when needed. Tishaura Jones said:

> I am a member of Delta, and I often lean on my chapter sorors to help volunteer or show up when we have contentious committee hearings. And they do show up, they show up and they're dressed in red [chuckle] when they're trying to attack me at the board for whatever reason. I'm also . . . I would say, over these last eight to twelve years, I would say, I've spent a lot of time developing networks across the country. So I'm a member of the New DEAL Leaders, which is a group of state and local elected officials, all Democrats, who are committed to pro-growth progressive policies. And so there are state elected officials, mayors, city council, just building relationships

there. I'm also a member of Local Progress, which is run by the Center for Popular Democracy.

Sarah Anthony, a member of the Michigan House of Representatives, spoke of how her sorority, Alpha Kappa Alpha Sorority Inc., provided her with significant fundraising support:

> My most successful fundraiser was a women's fundraiser, in which I called every single member of my AKA chapter and just asked them, "Can you support me with $100?" . . . And I think that it showed, for me, the power of sisterhood, the fact that these women were able to not just lend their checkbook, but when I needed folks to handwrite envelopes to senior citizens, when I needed people to do my phone banking. Literally the entire chapter basically came [together] during the final stretch of the campaign and were in the union hall making phone calls for me for twelve-hour shifts for the entire weekend. That is an inherent network . . . without [which] I would not have won the race.

During her interview, Mayor Pro-Tem of Tallahassee, Florida, Dianne Williams-Cox spoke of the roles that her lifelong membership in organizations including Alpha Kappa Alpha had played. She noted the extensive leadership opportunities she had in the organization and how that led her to a network not only in Tallahassee but also throughout the South.

> Members of the sorority . . . were very supportive, not just in my local chapter that I'm in, but in our sister chapter, as well as chapters throughout our region. They all were contributors and supporters of my campaign. So having that type of network helped, and it also helped that I also held positions within the sorority as well, and so people got to know me up close and personal, not just somebody that's always running for office but somebody who was actually doing some work.

The sorority women interviewed noted that their organizations created opportunities and resources for Black women to run for office.

Their fellow sorority members locally and nationally became go-to persons for fundraising, and local members often provided support such as volunteering to knock on doors, stuff envelopes, and man the phone bank. They also noted that their work within these spaces provided them with a variety of leadership skills, from how to put together a meeting agenda to organizing large numbers of people to either fundraise or provide services. These testimonials attest to my argument of how the radical imagination brings forth the necessary resources for Black women to succeed as candidates.

In addition to organizations of Black women, the Black church has been critical to the cultivation of leadership and network opportunities for political candidates. Several respondents spoke of how their church and community involvement led not only to potential voters but also to tangible resources that assisted their campaigns. Juvenile Court Judge Sheila Calloway, for example, noted that her church family was not only extremely supportive, but that it also allowed her to rent at a reduced rate a campaign office in a building the church owned. Or consider City Councilperson Connie Alsobrook, who is a business owner in Covington, Georgia, and has an extensive history of community service. She spoke at length of how her work gave her name recognition and unsolicited campaign support from members of her community. That support included persons volunteering to pay for campaign mailers and campaign car magnets, and who made donations from out of state. Diane Williams-Cox also was extremely appreciative of the support she received from her church:

> I have a very supportive church family, very supportive family. We've been at our church for thirty-plus years. And they've watched me work in the church as well as working in community and work causes and make them aware of things that were going on in our community. So it was really a natural fit. Pastors at that church had been very involved in political action, such as a Tallahassee bus boycott, [which] was spearheaded out of the church that I attend. And so the current pastor kind of picked up that mantle and has continued in that vein and is very supportive of his members who seek public office. And so that helped.... At one time, I'm told we had seven thousand members on the roll. And so when your pastor supports

what you're doing, he kind of puts that out into the membership and people listen. And so that was helpful.

The role that organizations play in the cultivation and candidate recruitment of Black women cannot be overstated. Not only do these organizations provide pathways to valuable resources and network access, they also signal a commitment to the needs and interests of Black people. Most critical to this type of identity is the Black Church and HBCUs. The Black Church has a long legacy of not only meeting the spiritual needs of the Black people but also providing a space that often fostered resistance to racism and societal injustices while providing the Black community with social and economic support through businesses, such as funeral homes and day care, and meeting the need for job training and financial support for college attendance.

As stated earlier, the Black community saw education as a means to address the racism and injustices faced at the end of the nineteenth century. Through the leadership of Black and liberal white churches, white philanthropists and Blacks who gained a status of class HBCUs were formed became a central institution to provide education and professional employment for community members thus playing a critical role in advancing the educational and material lives of Black people. Virginia State Delegate Aird's experiences speak directly to the value that HBCUs and organizations offer Black women seeking office by providing an entrée to potential voters:

> I think those [organizations] were the difference because every time I needed to engage with a voter, I found the touchpoint. So I'm a Virginia State University grad, which is right here in this community. At this point, I had been living here for about six years when I ran. So I would say, "What church do you go to?" "Oh, my church membership is such and such. I'm in this sorority." "Who do you belong to?" All of those different touchpoints, I found some kind of "in" with people.
>
> Those relationships were the difference, in my opinion, between my successes and not, because if I could not find some sort of touchpoint, especially in a Black community predominantly, I don't even think I would have had the carpet rolled out at all. And I should

say that the four people who ran, one of them was born and raised [here], another was from this community but did not live within the boundaries. And then the other was totally from outside of the community and was also not well known. And so the strength ... [of] my race was definitely having some pre-existing relationships.

I contend that elite Black women have an elevated social status as a result of their community work and the expectations held by the community. Aird's comments speak to how organizational membership provided the resource to connect with potential voters and supporters. Not only did she find personal benefit from her membership in certain spaces, the community she campaigned in also saw value in the organizational spaces she engaged in, and, as a result, they were more open to listen to her and ultimately vote for her. The experiences of the Black women I interviewed illustrate the value of the often misunderstood and ignored communal nature of Black political engagement. While Black women are not monolithic in their views or experiences, what these women have shown in general is that their trajectory into politics was often not developed in isolation but through a community of family and peers and as members of valued institutions.

Discussion

I began this chapter by positing that Black women have developed a *radical imagination* through which they envisage a better society—a society in which they lead, from which they benefit, and which improves the lives of their community members. The framework I have developed moves beyond the extant literature's premise that the political ambition of Black women is less than that of white women or men. In the past, it has appeared so merely because political science approaches categorize political participation very narrowly, typically negating and downplaying mechanisms (beyond voting) in which Black women engage, such as community and civic engagement (Jordan-Zachery 2013; Alexander-Floyd 2017). Previous studies have also often ignored or devalued the rich social structures and indigenous resources within marginalized groups. Countering this, the data that my interviewees provided reveal the complex dynamics that contribute to black women's unique political socialization and resource development.

The testimonials presented confirm my theory of the role of the radical imagination: the unique position of Black women in society prompts their higher levels of participation—efforts to combat the invisibility of being a Black woman (Alex-Assensoh and Stanford 1997; Stokes-Brown and Dolan 2010). This begins early in a Black girl's life with a socialization process in which home and community have an impact on and care *for the community at large* rather than merely a few individuals. In addition, generational examples of service, the pursuit of excellence, and a sense of obligation to do something and not just to be something or to hold a title help women decide to run for office. This socialization has led Black women to engage in leadership and participate actively in their communities. Such engagement not only affects Black women's opinion of themselves, their identity, and their sense of agency, it also provides training mechanisms for Black women that with time empower them and influence their decision to delve into political careers, to cultivate valuable networks, and to have a greater sense of community needs once they are in office.

The experiences of the respondents are consistent with the strong standing of elite Black women in their communities. These experiences explain how Black women purposefully engage within their communities and develop a standing that puts them in a position to be recruited by community members and to have success as candidates. Once they have decided to run, their community standing facilitates the flow of resources to them through a network of organization members and community members who respect or have benefited from those candidates' prior community work. Respondents consistently confirmed that community and volunteer work is a strong predictor of candidate emergence (and ultimately success). Their testimonies also clarify that for Black women seeking political office, it is not only about individual ambition but it is also a form of political participation (Scott et. al 2021; Brown and Dowe 2020; Tate 1991; Simien 2007; Smooth 2006) that seeks to impact the communities in which these women reside. This desire to have impact is no coincidence: it is a result of a socialization process that is structured to prepare Black women to overcome challenges that racism and sexism present.

Tennessee State Senator Brenda Gilmore similarly testified that her local political work is what kept her in politics because of the impact she had through it, particularly on individuals:

> Well, I do enjoy being at the table, I have a big curiosity, a huge curiosity. So, I like knowing, being at the table when the decisions are made, I like helping people, and sometimes I get joy out of things that probably will never hit the newspaper, nobody else would know about it. It may be advocating for a child who's been suspended from school and wants to graduate and walk, and the principal has said they cannot walk with the other graduates. I get just as much joy out of that, working with the principal and the superintendent and the mom and the dad and the student, as I do maybe [from passing] a . . . really important piece of legislation. So, I think it's just the helping people part that I enjoy.

These responses help us understand that Black women have a deeper motivation to serve and to use their elected position to enhance the experiences of community members. This aspect of the radical imagination for something greater for the community is front and center not only in the decision to lead but also in the desire to cultivate and participate in spaces that foster leadership and encourage political participation.

The interviewees' reflections help us understand how and why Black women engage, and they alert us to the unique socialization and value of Black women. But their reflections also remind us of the invaluable resources in the Black community that open the door to influence in ways that compensate for Black women's limited access to other resources, such as finances and connections to political operatives. Not only that, their reflections also help us understand how Black women's deliberate engagement and development of a standing within their communities with time leads community members to recruit them to run for public office. Because they are already well-known in their community, these women then attract resources through the networks of people who respect or have benefited from the women's community work.

The questions I have attempted to answer about how Black women decide to seek office and what makes their runs successful elicited other useful information too. Many of the women represented in this chapter and in the data set reside in communities that were proactive about facilitating the development of networks of Black women. In some communities these networks developed as a result of family members participating in certain activities. In others, through civic and social organizations, women were able to develop networks and relationships in spaces reserved for Black women. Future research could usefully explore how Black women develop networks within multiracial communities, and how younger Black women without an extensive service and political background might yet cultivate networks and strategize for political success.

The limited existing literature suggests that Black women's unique socialization, politicization, and life experiences make their political activity exceptional. Some researchers posit that the double discrimination Black women face prompts their higher levels of participation in effort to combat the invisibility of being a Black woman (Alex-Assensoh and Stanford 1997; Stokes-Brown and Dolan 2010). This socialization process, which is shaped by generational examples of service, by nurturing a desire for excellence, and by a sense of obligation to do something and not just to be something or to hold a title, contributes to the decision to run for public office. This socialization has led Black women to engage in leadership and participate in community organizations "whose mission is institutional change" (Collins 2000, p. 23).

3
An Ambition That Resists Marginalization

> I am not wrong: Wrong is not my name.
> —June Jordan

In the previous chapter I explored how the radical imagination of Black women contributes to a socialization process that leads Black women to understand the value of political work and that it benefits both them and their communities. The socialization of Black women prompts them to carve out spaces of power via organizations and community service. These spaces and the actions women pursue through them are ones they use to respond to obstacles they face as private citizens and as politicians. I also showed in that chapter that resources they access through these spaces bolster their chances of both considering running for office and being elected to office because they provide a network of support, access to potential donors, and recruitment by community members. The use of these spaces cultivated by Black women are consistent with how marginalized groups more broadly cultivate resources.

Miller's and Dawson's research has shown that resources available to marginalized persons is found particularly within community networks and that this help shape political strategies, perspectives, and group consciousness (Miller et al. 1981 and Dawson 2003). Black women candidates' reliance on community resources has to do with marginalized persons often distrusting dominant institutions and relying instead on community leaders, newspapers, organizations, and social networks to understand and process their experiences (Brown 1994; Cohen 1999; Dawson 2003; Nunnally 2012; Harris- Lacewell

2004). This distrust is the result of being slighted for decades and being overlooked by the media, the culture, and politicians, as well as being marginalized and assigned stereotypical roles and capacities to hinder their political advancement and equal participation (Collins 2020).

The political implications and power of institutional marginalization and stereotyping cannot be underestimated—even though these images lack any basis in reality, such actions are effective in achieving their intended ends, specifically their agents retaining political power and undergirding the white-dominated social structure they serve. Ably demonstrating this is Carla Brailey's introduction to the world of politics; she was former vice chair of the Texas Democratic Party and a 2022 candidate for Texas lieutenant governor. During her first job in politics, she was having a conversation with a mentor about being a Black woman in the world of politics. Her mentor (a Black woman who was her elder) said, "Little girl, let me tell you something, you'll be OK as long as you don't take anything personal. 'Cause just remember, little Black girl, you're going to always be a little Black girl, and it'll never be about you, and if you'll remember that, then you'll be okay, you will survive it." Brailey recounts, "I survived and when snakes came I knew, if I was going to be here for the people, I had to let some stuff ride."

This conversation between Brailey and her mentor alludes to Black women's awareness of the structures and stereotypes that they navigate daily in life and in politics. Washington correspondent Tia Mitchell of *The Atlanta Journal-Constitution* noted how Black women's awareness impacts their relationship to political and media structures: "The adjectives we use to describe someone, sometimes those show unconsciously that we're trying to paint someone's approach or demeanor as more emotional or more riled up. And also I feel like sometimes with politicians, especially Black women, they're [Black women] very cognizant of being put in a box, not just by the media, but by the political structure all together, and that's a hard line." The actions of those who wield power can be and often are designed to restrict, discourage, and at times embarrass Black women, as long as the goal of the person(s) wielding power are met. These women's conversations is an example of how Black women share their "collective wisdom" to survive in a system in which racism functions not only through individual actions but also through systemic, structural inequalities that undermine

Black women via stereotypes, public rebuke, and shaming (Collins 2000). However, Brailey's goal to "be here for the people" is a reminder that the radical imagination of Black women enables them to maintain their resolve, awareness, and strategic way of navigating societal challenges so that they can achieve and serve in politics.

The Positionality of Black Womanhood in Society and Politics

Stereotyping Black women does not stop there. They are often characterized as lacking femininity and overbearing, and therefore not worthy of love; they are considered childlike and not intelligent, implying they need to be controlled by more intelligent whites. Rather than being regarded as caring mothers, Black women have been stereotyped either as lazy "welfare queens," who irresponsibly have children for whom they cannot care, or as domineering mothers who contribute to the ineptness and pathology of their sons (Moynihan 1965; Collins 2000; Harris-Perry 2011). "White womanhood," by contrast, has long been construed as pure and virtuous (Alexander-Floyd 2012; Collins 1990; Combahee River Collective 2015; hooks 1981; Jordan-Zachery 2007). These ideas remain evident in the gendered and racialized language and symbols used by candidates from both parties to attract and emphasize the value of white voters; for example, terms such as "soccer mom" or "suburban mom" speak to white women's worlds and ignore Black women who live outside the stereotyped world of Black families in inner cities or urban areas (Kurtzlebean 2018).

The effort to ignore or stereotype Black women is not only evident in campaign messaging, it is found also in public policy, in particular the recent conversation about teaching race—and more specifically critical race theory (CRT)—in public schools. The outrage over CRT and the attendant emphasis on the right of parents to contribute to or control curriculum in order to protect white children from feeling guilt about racism blatantly ignores Black mothers' decades of concern regarding what is taught in school and, even more fundamentally, their children's safety in public schools (Morris 2016; Streeter 2021).

These tropes masked as policy are used not only to attract white voters, but they also determine the type of candidate that political parties will recruit and the messaging that the candidate will employ. Such messaging is often to ensure the safety of white voters—at the expense of Black voters.

The efforts to campaign for and coordinate racially divisive policy are consistent with the distinctive worldviews of white and Black women and with who is likely to respond to such racialized appeals. White women have served as a buffer to protect white men and their power, and white women's votes in 2016 and 2020 show a pattern in which white womanhood becomes a politicized identity for voters (Junn 2017; Frasure-Yokley 2018). Exit poll data showed that 52 percent of white women voted for Trump, while Clinton received 43 percent of white women's support and 94 percent of Black women's votes (Roper Center 2016). Going into the 2016 general election, it was widely assumed by the media and political pundits that Donald Trump's gendered attacks on Hillary Clinton, along with video and audio of him discussing sexual assault and seducing married women, that white women would vote overwhelmingly for Clinton (Chozick and Parker 2016; Rucker 2016). However, this stark racial division in women's voting patterns came as no surprise to scholars who had since the 1950s studied the voting and opinion preferences of white women (Junn 2017; Maxwell and Shields 2019)—a pattern that showed white women typically vote with the Republican Party. White women are "second in sex to men, but first in race to minorities" (Junn 2017, p. 346) and have become a critical barrier against persons who have been placed in a category of being less than white (deBeauvoir 2001).

Black women have rarely been able to separate their intersecting racialized and gendered identity and positionality (Frasure-Yokley 2018; Collins 1990; Gay and Tate 1998; hooks 1981; Jordan-Zachery 2007; King 1988; Prestage 1977). The unique duality of Black women's identity is often seen as "other" in the space of politics. In my interview with the former mayor of San Antonio, Ivy Taylor, she spoke of how Black women in politics are often ignored and underestimated. She reflected that in many spaces Black women are not considered the optimal choice for leadership:

I think that people usually underestimate us [Black women] or don't think of us at all. The broader community doesn't look to us for leadership I think as often. I know in cities that have larger Black populations, there's more opportunity I think, for folks to be viewed as, "Oh, that's someone that we could push toward whatever position or we could back her." But my situation is a little bit unique here, and I even found that when I was a District 2 council member, I don't think that certain segments of the community viewed me as a heavyweight or someone who really brought substantial skills to the table because I was just the Black representative from District 2, which was considered less than in comparison to other districts. Even though I'm a Yale educated urban planner who had years of experience working in the city and on the planning commission and at nonprofits, I think people just never even took the time to find those things out. So now that I'm in this position [mayor], what I hope is that it gives people a different view of Black women in general.

Taylor's comments reflect how Black women are viewed not only as Black but also as "other" that can be ignored or dismissed. Her experience is not one of isolation as Black women have rarely been able to separate their intersecting racialized and gendered identity and positionality (Frasure-Yokley 2018; Collins 1990; Gay and Tate 1998; hooks 1981; Jordan-Zachery 2007; King 1988; Prestage 1977). The othering of Black women is to place them in a category of "another," an identity that is unique to them in which their gender and racial identities are ignored and their personhood is distinctive from any other group. This requires an intersectional approach to understanding the "identity" politics of Black women (Gay and Tate 1998; Crenshaw 1989, 1990; Collins 2000; Jordan-Zachery 2007; Simien 2007; Carew 2012; Brown 2014; Smooth 2006).

Stereotypes of Black women are, unfortunately, not only dynamic but also enduring in America. These stereotypes have the purpose of (1) putting Black women in their place, (2) oppressing Black women who attempt to achieve, and (3) shaming Black women in order to justify practices that oppress them. In politics, those stereotypes have been used to justify the limited access Black women have had to power through elected positions and in business, media, and other areas of leadership (King 1973; Collins 2000).

How are those stereotypes enacted? Often through "controlling images" constructed to place Black women in positions of servitude, labor theft, and exploitation, as well as to normalize social injustices such as racism, sexism, and poverty in everyday life (Collins 2000). White persons continue to perpetuate the three main stereotypes (of mammy, jezebel, and sapphire), and Black women continue to consider them as they choose how to present themselves to the world (Harris-Perry 2011).

Stereotypes and expectations about Black women in society also marginalize them within leadership structures both inside and outside their communities. Scholarship on the gendered leadership of the Civil Rights Movement has often noted this and has observed that men relegated any particularly strategic and talented women to the background while they themselves became the face of the movement (Lee 2000; Robnett 1997; Ransby 2003). During my interview with Sharon Pratt, the first Black woman mayor of Washington, DC, she shared her perspective on the role of Black women in their communities. "As far as African American communities go, we are often very matriarchal, but most of our institutions tend to be very patriarchal. You have a few major organizations where women have been in charge, but all of the civil rights groups going back to the movement have been led by men." Pratt's observations that Black women have had limited roles within organizations can also extend to questions of whether Black women should be elected at all, and if so, to what type of office.

This background of Black women in matriarchal roles extends to the perspective that Black women should be concerned only with certain (i.e., family-oriented) issues and thus serve only in a narrow selection of elected positions, such as on a school board or as a member of a city council. No wonder that Black women find their service as elected officials challenged and unwelcomed. Wilmington, Delaware's former treasurer, Velda Jones-Potter, noted that she served in a role not typically associated with women, let alone Black women, a position that controlled the arguably most significant city resource: money. She often felt that this contributed to the contentious relationship she had with the mayor. She told me,

> We as women and especially Black women aren't expected to handle or know how to handle money. A treasurer is a technical role with money. The treasurer is so different from where they want us or think we are supposed to be, like on the council. That is a major step, in that a council role is seen as more relationship and issue driven, while my role is technical and analytical. I'm not supposed to be here.

Jones-Potter is clear about the stereotypes that women and Black women face, but she is also clear about the power of her office. This type of self-recognition has been studied by scholars interested in the political activism of women of color (Brown 2014; Collins 1990; Pardo 1998; Phillips 2021). These women recognize the stereotypes yet also recognize their talents and strengths and that their personhood is shaped by others with whom they are connected (Collins 1990; Deveaux 1994).

In short, the behaviors and attitudes of those who attempt to control the lives, careers, and political trajectories of Black women are deeply rooted in American society and politics. They are examples of how responses to Black women are managed with the intention of influencing voters' perspectives and creating stumbling blocks to Black women's candidacies.

Black Women Marginalized as Candidates

Various researchers have shown that political candidates are perceived as viable if they have traits considered masculine, such as being assertive or tough. Those researchers also show that men are perceived as being more capable of handling certain issues, such as crime and national defense, while women are considered more compassionate and warm, more likely to prioritize family and women's issues, better equipped to deal with education issues, more liberal and Democratic, and more feminist than men (Sapiro 1981; Rosenwasser and Seal 1988; Alexander and Andersen 1993; Burrell 1994; Huddy and Terkildsen 1993; Kahn 1996; Sanbonmatsu 2002; Lawless 2004). These stereotypes about a candidate's personal traits being based almost exclusively on their gender strongly influence voters to choose either a male or female candidate (Sanbonmatsu 2002; Lawless 2004; Kahn 1996; Farris and Holman 2014).

Furthermore, African American women candidates face different stereotypes compared to their white counterparts. White women are deemed to be competent, nurturing, and caring (Koenig et al. 2011), while Black women are burdened with a variety of negative stereotypes, such as being considered controlling, angry, and tough (Littlefield, 2008; Orey and Zhang 2019). Because of these stereotypes, Black women are more vulnerable and susceptible to negative biases and, by extension, tend to be evaluated more negatively as political candidates and be less successful when running for political office.

The expectation that women will be more caring, compassionate, and sensitive aligns with the communal and supportive social roles ascribed to women. For Black women, such expectations are even more repressive because of their association with the stereotype of mammy. Even though she may be well loved and may wield considerable authority in her white "family," the mammy still knows her "place" as an obedient servant, and the assumption is that she has accepted her subordination (Collins 2000, p. 80). This image of mammy therefore symbolizes the dominant group's perception of the ideal Black female relationship to elite white male power. This dynamic of attempting to place a Black woman in a position of obedience and subordination was most evident during the 2020 presidential campaign that culminated in Senator Kamala Harris becoming the first Black woman vice president (Dowe 2020).

The Stereotyping of Kamala Harris

During the March 15, 2020, Democratic Party presidential debate, then candidate Joe Biden stated that he would pick a woman to be his vice president. So when Biden became the presumptive nominee, there were increased calls for the woman to be a Black woman. In order to raise public pressure and awareness of the fact that there were multiple Black women qualified to become vice president, Black women engaged in collective action emblematic of the long history of them resisting the hurtful tropes that continue to disqualify Black women from leadership opportunities (Dowe 2020). In April 2020, over 200 Black women signed an open letter written by a group of Black women activists, led by Melanie Campbell of the Black Women's Roundtable, calling for Biden to select a Black woman as his vice-presidential nominee. The letter was a collective voice that said to Biden, the Democratic Party, and the media that Black women are capable, talented, and will not be silent. Listing several Black women whose names were publicly discussed as possible running mates, the letter stated that these potential nominees

> were already leading in the roles they presently occupy and in the leadership positions they have previously held, from the local, state, and Federal levels, including domestic and foreign policy. They have the experience, qualifications and principled core values of a true leader that would make for the right partner to help catapult the Democrats to victory in November. Every one of these women has the skills, competence, and knowledge required of an effective governing partner who will help you lead America in this unprecedented moment in our history. (Sisters Lead Sisters Vote 2020)

This letter, along with a coordinated social media campaign and media appearances, is an instance of Black women's efforts to reshape the narrative around Black women and political leadership. This is consistent with research on how multiple stereotypes can compete with each other—and be overcome. The research of Kunda and Thagard (1996) showed that the stereotypical association of being Black and aggression can be overturned by simply describing a Black person as well-dressed or placing them in a business context. It might therefore be possible to replace negative with positive emphases about Black women. More recently, Brooks (2013) has studied how women in politics may not be evaluated by traditional standards of femininity at all because these women regularly violate those norms.

The mobilization efforts to advocate for a Black woman vice president gained traction in the course of the summer of 2020, with major media outlets posting op-eds and stories about the value of Black women as voters and insisting that the Democratic Party owed them their due, particularly given their grassroots efforts on behalf of the party (Graham 2020; Khalid 2020; Zhou 2020). While there was public lobbying on behalf of a potential Black woman candidate, there were also detractors as one particular woman's name rose to the top of the list: that of Senator Kamala Harris. Harris was the highest-ranked Black woman elected official, serving as the only Black woman in the Senate and the former attorney general for California. She ran a short-lived presidential campaign during the fall of 2019 that began with much excitement but fizzled due to lack of fundraising and low polling numbers. Facing an extra high bar within the Democratic Party, Harris found herself challenged as a woman of color. With the ghost of the 2016 election looming, party leaders and Democratic voters concentrated on which candidate could defeat Donald Trump, and a woman, let alone a woman of color, was not viewed as a winning candidate (Avalanche 2019).

As a member of the Senate Judiciary Committee, Harris gained national attention during the confirmation hearings of attorney general nominee Bill Barr and Supreme Court nominee Brett Kavanaugh. During both hearings, Harris pointedly questioned the nominees on a multitude of issues and their knowledge of legal statutes and precedents. The optic of a Black woman using her position of authority to question the credibility of white men led to praise from liberals. Meanwhile, the right railed against her and referred to her as "nasty," and conservatives considered her line of questioning "horrible" (Arnholz 2020). During her presidential run, Harris demonstrated herself to be a formidable opponent on the debate stage when she seized a moment and questioned the civil rights record of Joe Biden. However, following the debate, Harris was criticized as overly aggressive and disrespectful to Biden, challenging the ideal of what is the "respectful" place of a Black woman in politics.

During the official candidate-vetting process, it was leaked to the media by someone knowledgeable of private conversations that members of Biden's inner circle and those who were members of the official vice-presidential nominee search committee were concerned that Senator Harris was too "ambitious" and unlikely to be a team player. They feared she might rub people the wrong way. There was also angst over Harris's performance in the debate in which she challenged Biden. Chris Dodd, who chaired the search committee, stated privately that he had concerns about Harris and that she held no remorse for her debate performance (Korecki et al. 2020).

These comments were consistent with charges often levied against successful women and Black women in particular. They serve to remind Black women that they should aspire to only certain positions, and even then they should understand that their role is to be subordinate. In this political moment, Biden insiders launched a public smear campaign that activated the stereotype of aggression to attempt to force Harris (if selected) to perform a different stereotype of a passive mammy who was more amenable to their wishes. Interestingly the "leaked" comments did not question Harris' *ability* or merits to serve as vice president but rather presumed her inability to know her place and to be seen and not heard.

On August 12, 2020, Senator Harris was selected as the Democratic Party's vice-presidential nominee. At the moment, Black women across the country braced themselves for the onslaught of misogynoir language and actions toward Senator Harris. Black women on social media celebrated but also were prepared to defend Senator Harris and to keep her accomplishments in the forefront to resist the expected narrative that she was an affirmative action selection (Ebbert 2020; McShane 2020; Dowe 2020). This response was consistent with Cheryl Townsend Gilkes's findings that "Black women's assertiveness and their use of every expression of racism to launch multiple assaults against the entire fabric of inequality have been a consistent, multifaceted threat to the status quo. As punishment, Black women have been assaulted with a variety of negative images" (1983, p. 294). These negative images were evident in social media memes and sermons by white male pastors referring to Harris as a wench, jezebel, and other offensive terms that spoke of character images that harken back to slavery (Bidar and Patterson 2022; Marley 2020; Kuruvilla 2021). These attacks were not limited to social media: stump speeches by President Trump, the Biden-Harris ticket opponent, included them freely.

In my interview with Ayesha Rascoe of NPR, she commented about the way the public and media questioned Black women such as Harris.

> So when people think about what presidential looks like, this person looks presidential, this person feels presidential, I do believe that at

times, a Black woman is not thought of as what that looks and feels like. So when people are talking about or even when it's like, "Is this person ready?" I think there is more of a question, whether intentional or not, when it comes to Black women and their readiness and their preparedness. Are they going to be able to do this? Can they do this? I do think there's a question of competence that I feel like comes up in political commentary more, and maybe I notice it more because I'm a Black woman, than it does with white men who are allowed to be all sorts of different things and face criticism but not necessarily of their competence or their readiness. I think that that can be a part of the way the media, whether intentionally or not, can raise those questions more of a Black woman than they would, or a woman of color than they would of others.

Vice President Kamala Harris's journey gives us insight into the challenges that Black women face as elected officials and that Black women politicians are nuanced. Harris, an aspirational and ambitious person, and many Black women career politicians face retribution for not shying away from their personal aims. In the remainder of this chapter, Black women speak of more nuanced efforts to silence them and limit their access to political power and influence. It continues to rely on interviews conducted with elected officials and on focus group data, which present what Black women state about their perceptions of being Black women and efforts to marginalize and shame them as political candidates and politicians. Their comments do not indicate that Black women feel powerless but offer a glimpse into how they navigate politics in spite of stereotypes that hindered support from politicians, political parties, or potential voters. Lastly, they show that despite obstacles they encounter due to racism and sexism, Black women candidates are optimistic that they can win elected office.

The Ways of Marginalization

Stereotypes have long attempted to define and limit opportunities for Black women while shaping the perceptions of potential voters, the media, and political parties about Black women candidates. In spite of the limitations these efforts have placed on the political strength and advancement of Black women, the women themselves have demonstrated their resolve to continue to make strides in spite of expectations based on a marginalized view of them. This was evident in the comments from focus group participants. Focus group participants noted their awareness of the societal othering of Black women, yet they were also aware of how they and their community of Black women developed mechanisms not only to resist that societal othering but also to build themselves up. April, who is a 20-year-old junior from Miami, recognized the benefit of Black women seeking office and using that leadership role to respond to negative stereotypes. She noted,

> I can see value in it. I think it's important. Now, as far as . . . the challenges they'll face, Black women I think will always have that angry Black woman label. So, whatever they do in office, I think it should have purpose, effectiveness. . . . Whatever they do need to make a statement . . . so they can say. . . not all Black women act like how you think they act. Some of us, you know, [have] got class and we do what needs to be done.

April's comments acknowledge Black women having an acute understanding of how they are positioned within society, yet, there is purpose and value in engaging in politics and refuting stereotypes. This type of acknowledgment of the ways society attempts to limit and place Black women into a particular category was further addressed by other respondents. As a result of marginalization, group members are often evaluated by a stigmatized "mark," which affects how they engage society. Elise, a 20-year-old junior from Atlanta, said, "As Black women, we already have . . . so many stereotypes placed [on] us. Like if we come off too powerful, we're viewed as, you know, the b-word. And then if we are . . . more standoffish, when we're just minding our business, we come off more aggressive." Shaun, a 19-year-old sophomore from Jacksonville, Florida, followed up by expressing how society marginalizes the physical appearance of Black women through body shaming and rejection of natural hairstyles, but she noted how Black women resist.

> There is a lack of spaces for us to be ourselves. Like whether it's ... our natural hair, our curves, just who we are. Like we've constantly ... been exploited. And I just feel over it. For example, they have Melanin Mondays and Black Girl Magic—the hashtag on Twitter and all forms of social media. And I believe it's a way for us to uplift ourselves. Society doesn't really respect Black women or view us as human, [and] fine. [So] we're going to uplift ourselves, support each other, and we're going to take pride in not only our melanin, but our curves, our natural hair, and we're going to be OK with it.

These experiences expressed by young college-age women confirm the pervasiveness of stereotypes—but also Black women's commitment not to acquiesce but to overcome the perceived limitations that stereotypes express. These challenges faced by college-age Black women also plague older Black women who aspire to make an impact in the world of politics, as we see particularly in their interview comments about the politics of appearance.

The Politics of Appearance

Social science research consistently indicates that women and minorities face a disadvantage in attempting to present a professional image, not because of any inherent failings on their part but because of others' negative stereotypes, lower expectations, and workplace norms that advantage white male standards of behavior and appearance (Alvesson and Billing 1997; Rosette and Dumas 2007). This disadvantages white women and minority men and women. Gender is a double bind for women who want to display so-called professional characteristics—meaning typically male characteristics such as ambition, competitiveness, and competence. Thus, some women may choose not to accentuate their femininity or attractiveness (Heilman and Stopeck 1985) and opt to portray themselves as more, for example, competitive than they naturally are. This expectation of appearance and manner based on stereotypes affects not only their campaigns but also how they govern or hold office.

Take appearance: For Black women, skin tone, hair texture, and the combination of the two have distinct meanings. Since the Jim Crow era of the late nineteenth and early twentieth centuries, beauty culture and the politics of appearance for Black women were used as powerful tools to combat the prevailing and often contradictory stereotypes of them. Black women used the politics of adornment, such as straightened hair and accessories such as gloves, to signal their status and demonstrate their place in the newly changed American society (Lindsey 2017). Historically Black women have been evaluated by the extent to which their actions, style choices, and lifestyles adhere to those of whiteness, the self-designated arbiter of appropriateness (Higginbotham and Weber 1992; Hine 1997; Hobson 2003; Cooper 2017; Brown and Lemi 2021). That evaluation has a hierarchy, one that evaluates dark-skinned African American women as tougher, more aggressive, less intelligent, and less educated than lighter skinned African Americans (Maddox and Gray 2002). These hierarchies of attractiveness result in women whose skin tone and facial features more closely approximate whiteness being labeled as most appealing and darker skinned women as less appealing (Hunter 1998; Brown and Lemi 2021).

Several research respondents discussed the pressure to look perfect at legislative meetings and public appearances, and they noted how appearance could hinder or help access to opportunities. Dr. Carla Brailey, who, as mentioned, served as the vice chair of the Texas Democratic Party, noted that in politics there is a need for those in power to feel some type of familiarity and comfort with Black women, and a cue for familiarity is appearance. She said that her ability to assist Black women candidates and navigate state politics were facilitated by her physical appearance and education, which made her acceptable to political powerbrokers in her state.

> I'm familiar, I physically fit this script of the docile Black woman or who they hope to be docile. I've got this long hair, very light skin, hazel eyes, and PhD from Howard University. I fit the safe script. For them they see me and say this a safe Black woman, and as a result of me being perceived as safe I make other Black women I'm affiliated with safe.

Brailey's self-awareness of how her appearance is perceived as acceptable is grounded in the issue of colorism discrimination based on skin tone and physical features as they vary within and among racial groups (Hunter 2007; Weaver 2012). More positive meanings became attached to lighter skin tones, while darker skin tones and phenotypic features were attached to more negative attributes and beliefs (Hill 2000; Neal and Wilson 1989; Okazawa-Rey, Robinson, and Ward 1987).

The social construction of race in the United States was based on the "one-drop rule." Rather than differences in skin tone becoming an innocuous feature of racial identity, it became the basis for hierarchy in Blackness. The experiences of Dee Dawkins-Haigler, who is a darker skinned Black woman who served as a representative in the Georgia legislature, show how perceptions about hair and appearance affected her ability to legislate and network. Dawkins-Haigler noted that the style of her hair and whether or not she wore dresses determined if she would be invited to meetings by men—both Black and white. Dawkins-Haigler, who at times wore her hair in a short afro style, noted how fellow legislators responded to her appearance:

> I realized that my hair was blocking the door to access because people already had a conception, a misconception about who I was with that afro. So I said to myself that there really is something to this nonsense. That year I began to wear a lot more pant suits because I wanted to see something. I said, I'm going to switch it up on them next year. I came back the very next year with my hair weaved and straight, in addition I put on more skirts and dresses. The men invited me to every single meeting. I was like, "What in the world?" Even the white people felt more comfortable because I had a feminine European twist to my appearance. I thought this is some nonsense. But I'm telling you that stuff makes a difference. And I never thought that stuff was real until it happened to me, just your hair and your attire. I'm telling you.

The noted sexism here also speaks to the legacy of beauty standards imposed on Black women. Rockdale County (GA) Commissioner Sheri Washington, who is also a full-time practicing attorney, noted that she has been criticized for her appearance. She recounted a time when she attended a commission meeting directly from work and wasn't feeling well. She didn't have a chance to go home and touch up her hair or change. Washington was heavily criticized by the meeting's attendees, while her male counterparts, who often attended meetings and events underdressed or chose not to show up at all, received no criticism.

The scrutiny received, the expectation that Washington would present herself a certain way, and the suggestion that Dawkins-Haigler needed to wear her hair in a more "feminine" style, all these responses harken back to the legacy of respectability politics and of the Black community; in particular, Black women attempting to resist stereotypes that challenged their womanhood via their appearance and behavior. This cultural norm of what is appropriate and how leadership should present itself, rather than challenging the dominant values of the mainstream culture, appearance, and behavior, often acquiesces to double standards and heightened scrutiny of Black women (Higginbotham and Weber 1992; Brown 2014; Cooper 2017). This scrutiny is not only expressed by implied behavior of others, but it can also present itself in blatant public attacks.

Public Shaming and Rebuke

The presence of Black people and Black women in the United States has been situated as a problem that needs a solution. The alleged "problem" with Black women is that they, rather than the structural dynamics that are the inheritance of slavery, are the cause or contributor to poverty, segregation, crime, and so on. As Black women navigated spaces, whites perceived them as unfit to be within proximity to them. In 1965, this type of shame directed at Black women became articulated in public policy in the government-funded report *The Negro Family: The Case for National Action*, more commonly known as the Moynihan Report. The report asserted that Black family structures were deviant due to the dangerous and emasculating role Black women held within their homes. It described Black women as overbearing matriarchs whose mothering led to a pathology in the Black community that eventuated in crime, underachievement, and a perpetual culture of poverty. In great measure, this shame via public policies has contributed to the long-standing tropes of Black women as welfare queens and lazy low-paid workers who attempt to exploit the generosity of the federal government and abuse the tax dollars of honest white people.

Efforts to shame Black women in social and political spaces through rebuke and public criticism not only draws on stereotypes of Black women as lazy, dishonest, and sexualized,[1] they also have a psychological impact: embarrassing, eliciting self-doubt, and prompting persons to question whether they deserve to be in the space where the rebuke occurred (Harris-Perry 2011). Interview participants spoke painfully of being publicly chastised. These moments typically happened immediately after their political victory or early in their tenure and were intended to embarrass them and to imply that they were violating rules.

Following their election to city councils in Conyers, Georgia, Valyncia Smith's and Connie Alsobrook's decision to have a Black female judge swear them in to office was challenged. It was common practice for newly elected city councilpersons like them to select the official who would swear them in, and yet these two Black women were told their request violated that process, that they were being disruptive, and that a judge would be chosen for them. They protested but to no avail. Both Smith and Alsobrook were prepared not to participate in the swearing in if they were not afforded the same courtesy that had been extended to other councilpersons.

Ultimately, Smith and Alsobrook were sworn in by the judge of their choice. The incident clarified for them how they would need to engage with the business of the city and that this was not going to be their last challenge. Both women stated that they approached their tenure assuming they might need to be overprepared for meetings and events to avoid being "called out." Alsobrook knew that the sitting council members' staff perceived her as "young, new, a woman, and Black. They didn't think I knew anything." The response she encountered is unfortunately common among Black women navigating not only narrowly political spaces but also more broadly other professional spaces. It is emblematic of the adage that in order to achieve success Black people have to work harder to gain similar access as whites. Such interactions place an undue burden of time, resources, and stress on Black women

(Bell and Nkomo 2003; Harris-Perry 2011). This burden comes at a cost: less time is spent fundraising for future elections, communicating with constituents, networking with colleagues, spending with family, and resting and regrouping.

In Reynoldsburg, Ohio, Angie Jenkins, Shanette Strickland, and Meredith Lawson-Rowe—the three Black women elected to city council—spoke in separate interviews of an incident that occurred the day of their swearing in. The city operates under so-called sunshine laws to maintain transparency in government affairs. One of these laws states that three or more elected officials should not be gathered in one room discussing city business outside of an official meeting. Following the swearing-in ceremony, the new members were in a room with two other council members talking to the press. The city auditor stormed into the interview room and, directing his concern toward them while ignoring the other council persons, yelled, "You guys ain't supposed to be here!" in front of the media. Strickland, who was aware of the sunshine law the auditor was referencing, told the women to stay. The next day there was talk in city hall that the new members were uninformed and had violated the law. Strickland said she felt it was necessary to deal with the situation head on and consequently went to talk to the city auditor in person. When she knocked on the auditor's door, his assistant asked Strickland if she informed the city auditor that she was there to see him, Strickland responded. "No, I'm going to knock on his door and barge in, just like he did us." Strickland recalled her conversation with the auditor: "I told him, I said, 'I will not be intimidated nor bullied by you or anybody else here.'" "Oh, Ms. Strickland," he responded. "I'm not trying to do that." I said, "'The way you barged in on us, yes you did. We weren't doing anything wrong, and we invited you to stay.' I continued to tell him that he was elected like I was, and [that] I hope[d we could] work together as city officials."

Similarly, Charlotte DiLorenzo, who serves in the New Hampshire House of Representatives, found her transition to the elected position to be somewhat of a culture shock and was met with a rude welcome during the orientation process. During a break on orientation day, DiLorenzo was sitting in a lounge area drinking coffee and eating a donut before going to the main hall. She observed other representatives entering the main hall with their drinks and food, so she took hers too. DiLorenzo recalled, "And all of a sudden one of the doormen yelled at me and said you are not supposed to have drinks in there. DiLorenzo said in addition to persons taking in food and beverages, there was a table in the hall with cups and napkins that appeared to be for representatives. I said, "What do you mean? Other people have their drinks in there." I said, "Listen, don't you ever talk to me like that again. I am going to be around here for a long time, and I don't accept being treated like that." DiLorenzo said the response by the doorman was alarming, but more alarming was that her colleagues watched and did not intervene on her behalf.

These experiences reveal the complexities of how Black women navigate spaces that question their right to be present in them. Recent scholarship by Tenesha Means on Black women judges confirms that the experiences of disrespect and public rebuke are consistent across branches and happens while Black women are performing their official duties or in unofficial workspaces (Means 2022). These efforts to embarrass Black women in elected positions are reminiscent of stereotypes that Black people are inherently dishonest and deceptive and therefore ineligible to be in positions of authority.

The response of Black women has to be viewed in a nuanced manner. Because of the unique position that Black women face in society, often the response to stereotypes begets the formation of another stereotype the "strong Black woman." Many Black women in the public eye, including politicians, are faced with responding to disrespect and efforts to shame or rebuke either them directly or indirectly. Either way a response or no response will often fit a motif around who Black women are—angry or strong. It is often difficult for these women to respond to incidents with justified anger due to their marginalized status. Harris-Perry (2011) notes that for marginalized citizens who are denied access to the public sphere of discourse or are members of a group that is despised, they cannot be accurately recognized or seen. Therefore every response or action will be skewed. As a result Black women have often responded in ways that reinforce the trope of being strong. Black women politicians often seek to address challenges to their appearance or efforts to embarrass them by remaining undeterred. These limited views of Black women forces elected officials to establish appropriate boundaries and cultivate appropriate responses strategically while trying to remain in political spaces to be effective legislators in spite of challenges posed by individuals as well as political institutions.

Black Women, Political Marginalization, and the Democratic Party

Political parties have a significant impact on social hierarchies. These organizations reinforce how people think and engage politically by mobilizing and excluding groups. For example, the Democratic Party has a long history of ignoring the needs of the most consistent voting bloc—African Americans—and instead of trying to broaden the electoral base to include white voters and thus increase its chances of winning presidential elections (Frymer 2005; Sonenshein 1990; Gamble 2010). These efforts have contributed to the marginalization of African American voters in general and of African American women in particular *even though* with few exceptions white women have consistently voted for Republican presidential candidates since the collection of data on voting preference began in 1948 (Junn 2017; Tien 2017) The inability of the Democratic Party to address the viability of Black women as candidates mirrors the party's inability to address the political views and needs of its strongest voting bloc. Carol Mosley Braun, the first African American woman senator expressed the situation Black women find themselves in with the Democratic Party as this:

> Black women, the mules of the world as Zora Neale Hurston said. You start off being Black and you add to that being female, and what you got is a double whammy. So you wind up in a situation in which nobody really wants to see you coming, the men don't want to see you coming. The whites don't want to see you coming, particularly on the Democratic side. Put aside for a minute the Republican Party, because I can't speak to their dynamics, but on the Democratic side, Black people are the main Democrats, and without us the Democratic Party does not win elections, and so they actually positively have to depend on Black votes to get their white candidates elected, but they don't always want us.

The Democratic Party has long crowed about its electoral strength among women, support that has largely been thanks to Black women along with Latinas (Smooth 2006; Scruggs-Leftwich 2000). The scholarly study of the political gender gap often focuses on gender-based differences and emphasizes the choices of white women (Carroll 1999; Simien 2007; Smooth 2006). However, further analysis of the gender gap reveals that Black women are more supportive of the Democratic Party and a progressive agenda than their white counterparts, as evidenced by the gravitation of white women to the Republican Party going back to 1952 (Junn 2017).

The gap in party choice continued to be cemented in 2017 when Alabama elected the first Democrat to the Senate in 25 years. The highly contentious election, which gained national attention, drove an increase in voter turnout, with 98 percent of Black women voting for Democrat Doug Jones. However, it was the 2020 presidential election cycle in which Black women received increased attention not only for their voter turnout but also for their keen organizing skills through which they mobilized communities to register and to show up and vote. The success of Joe Biden's campaign during the southern primaries and general election victory in Georgia is largely attributed to Black women. Just as Black women are more likely to vote for Democrats (White and Laird 2020; Frymer 1999), so too they are more likely to run as Democrats, particularly in the South.

Being in and out of the Democratic Party Network

As the previous chapter showed, Black women are often recruited to run for office via community networks they have developed and not via political parties. While numerous women in this study found success in running without being directly recruited by someone from the political party, the impact of early support and recruitment by a political party cannot be dismissed. Carroll and Sanbonmatsu (2013) argue recruitment for female candidates is more influential in the outcome of political success than it is for male candidates. And yet party leadership's hesitancy to support women as candidates reflects the limited idea of what type of candidate is electable (Brown and Dowe

2020). Limited recruitment affects Black women's ability to secure campaign resources necessary to establish a viable campaign early, especially resources outside of their districts (Sanbonmatsu 2006). Yet resources provided via a party are critical for the success of Black female candidates, especially since we know that Black candidates raise less money and rely heavily on small donations and on donations outside of their districts (Thielemann 1992). With an increased number of Black women seeking office, it is imperative to understand if and when these women receive party support and the impact of that on their election and consequently their leadership.

The interview participants' reflections confirm the complex relationship they have with the Democratic Party. Some elected officials were able to capitalize on the relationship they developed prior to running with their local or state party organization. Those who had no formal relationships found limited opportunities to receive support and also felt challenged in soliciting and receiving support once elected. Several of the women who did not receive support as a candidate noted the benefit of party engagement and support. Nicole Whitaker, who serves as Ward Commissioner in the Township of Winchester, Pennsylvania, noted that party affiliation is critical in her community, where the Republican Party is the dominant party, and observed that anyone who is serious about serving should run as a Republican due to the one-party nature of the area. Whitaker reported that the local Republican Party was crucial to supporting her and other candidates with fundraisers and helping purchase items such as yard signs and campaign advertisements. She noted this was important not only to maintain party dominance in elections but also as a valuable support to first-time candidates who might have limited resources of their own for campaigns.

Party engagement traditionally is a way to gain access for consideration for leadership and candidate recruitment. For some of the women I spoke too, participation in party politics was beneficial but the benefits were limited once they declared themselves as candidates. Lashrecse Aird, member of the Virginia House of Delegates, listed the benefits she received as a result of her engagement with and leadership in the party network prior to running for office. Her service as chair of her of local Democratic Party led to leadership opportunities within the Virginia party and allowed her to develop a rapport with other Democrats in the state by engaging with their campaigns. While Aird benefited from relationships with the state party, she observed that Black women outside of the party network had very little hope for success. Many of the women who attempt to run are challenged by not knowing, for example, the process of filing to run for office, by having limited name recognition, and by insufficient fundraising, she said. This lack of mentoring and support speaks volumes to potential voters and donors:

> You have to have a team of people you've asked that believes you should be doing this work and that are going to serve as extensions of you to grow your network of people who believe enough in you to give some money. All politics is local, no matter what level you're running for or you are trying to engage in.

Aird went on to say that her state party structure doesn't have a recruitment arm for new candidates but is more structured to protect current members and is closed to persons who are viewed as outsiders.

North Carolina House of Representative member Vernetta Alston echoed the value of party relationships. Her interactions with the state Democratic Party have increased and become more regular over the years as she moved from a city council position to the state legislature. "There is a House Caucus in the North Carolina Democratic Party that is very active. We [Democratic members] hear from them, at least by email, almost every day, to keep tabs on where everybody is. And so that support generally across the board has been substantial." Alston noted that the local Democratic Party in Durham was building an African American caucus, which she hoped would increase leadership of African Americans and increase their representation as elected officials.

While some women were pleased with their experience with political parties, there were others who either had mixed experiences or total disappointment. Conyers, Georgia, City Councilperson Connie Alsobrook, like several others, had engaged with the local Democratic Party prior to running for office, and she credited her candidate recruitment by the local party as stemming from her participation. She first became involved with the local party in a grocery store when its secretary introduced herself and invited Alsobrook to a meeting. This invitation led Alsobrook to learn more about her community and provided her with opportunities to assist local candidates with their campaigns. For Alsobrook, this party work was what cultivated her interest in running for office. Alsobrook's experience is unique because too few Black women gain an opportunity to experience working in the upper echelon of their local party, which can exclude them from valuable information that is needed when deciding to run for office. However, when she actually decided to run, the party did not help her, and Alsobrook publicly stated her discontent with the lack of support:

> The Democratic Party did not assist me in me running for office. And yes, I did call them out on that. I did let them know in a meeting that they were not helping Valyncia [Smith] and myself. There were persons who didn't realize that I was involved in the party early on and helped solidify a democratic presence it in the city.

During the election and shortly after, she challenged the party's inability to assist candidates. The party responded that it did not involve itself in elections, but she felt that was an excuse and that the party could have done more to signal to its members that she was a viable candidate and that therefore they should support her with donations and simple acts such as sharing social media posts.

Dianne Williams-Cox, city commissioner of Tallahassee, Florida, who has an extensive history of engagement and leadership with the local and state level of the Democratic Party in Florida, also observed limited party support for Black women:

> The local party does all that it can to help some candidates. Now, we're supposed to not choose as a party, we're not supposed to choose a candidate, especially if you['ve] got multiple Democrats in the race. But then there are those who, individually, they'll get a collective and then they do what they do kind of behind the scenes. We have had chairs who are very fair chairs and did the right thing, but we've had some that was . . . not that they weren't fair.

Williams-Cox continued to discuss her concern about what she sees as bad optics; that is, a pattern in which Black women in leadership faced opposition from white men who were less experienced or credentialed. This pattern she noted repeated the notion that the work of Black women was necessary, but that, nevertheless, the face of leadership and the party should be white and male.

The comments of the aforementioned women were a sample of multiple conversations in which respondents noted challenges with party support, even if they received some support at various stages of their political career. While these women primarily noted challenges while running, several women also noted challenges once in office.

One of the most significant impacts of party support and early engagement with a candidate is fundraising. During her interview, Michigan State Representative Sarah Anthony described both the double standard that Black women face when seeking donations and the impact of not having the full support of a political party:

> There is a fundamental difference in how fundraising goes for Black women. I am not one that doesn't do the work; I will stay on the phone for hours and beg folks. But there is something that happens between when I make the ask for $1000 and but come away with less, as to say, "She'll be okay with $250." For folks like me who are actually doing the work, it can be very deflating. The other thing that is a structural problem with the Democratic caucus, in Michigan, is that the majority of Black women who are serving are coming from highly concentrated Democratic urban communities.
>
> When you look at who the Democratic Party is trying to support and throw financial resources toward, they're trying to get the national interest groups to pour money into, it's not our communities, it's not our seats. They will look at us as, Well, we'll have a Democrat there anyway. So, whether it is Sarah, who's the Black woman or whatever Democrat comes, we're going to have that vote regardless. But what that does, is it diminishes our chances [of] not just having a seat at this table. What does it look like to advance even further and higher in the Democratic Party? I don't know, but last year I put my name in the running to be speaker of the House.

Anthony went on to state that during her campaign to lead in the legislature she was told that she lacked fundraising skills. She also noted that interest groups weighed in saying, "Hmm. We don't know, we don't know. And it was all the dog whistle, coded language of, Well, what's your leadership style, or You come off as a little bossy, or You come off as a little assertive . . . aggressive." All of the things that women, but particularly Black women, see and hear every day.

Anthony disappointedly informed me that she received such criticism not only from her white colleagues but also from Black colleagues who felt she didn't raise enough money. What stung particularly was that such critique does nothing to address the structural challenges Black women face. She felt the true measure of leadership was how she worked with people from both parties, and that her negotiation skills were particularly laudable but overlooked. But as long as fundraising will be a benchmark not only to receive support before but also after entering the legislature, Black women will always face challenges. She noted, "It's the fact that because of how this . . . political world is structured, Black women will continuously have a difficult time fundraising because of where we come from, because of who the donor pools are, and because of systemic racism."

Anthony's experience points to the influence of stereotypes regarding the effectiveness of Black women as leaders and fundraisers. Scholars have shown that these doubts by political parties are particularly problematic for Black women seeking election in districts that require crossover appeal with white voters. This hesitancy poses difficulty in launching a successful campaign due to challenges in securing the necessary resources to do so (Sanbonmatsu 2006). It is argued that the two-party system "created democracy" (Schattschneider 1942) and that consequently party competition is an avenue by which to advance inclusion and promote the needs of the disadvantaged (Dahl 1967). However, Frymer (2005) notes that African American scholars see the two-party system as limited and exclusionary in nature (Walton 1972), as is evident in the positionality of Black women candidates in the Democratic Party. The Democratic Party has often perceived the support of Black voters both as a means to victory and as a destabilizing force that pushes away white voters.

The previous chapter highlighted that Black woman have high levels of community engagement that can assist them in seeking office. While the women with whom I spoke had cultivated a significant network that provided financial and tangible resources, they all noted the limited support they received prior to winning their races. Tenisha Yancey, who serves in the Michigan House of Representatives, informed me that her community work and network were referenced as the reason why the Michigan Democratic Party did not directly recruit her or provide her with support: the party felt she didn't need it. Yancey observed that attitude, however, did not seem to apply to her white counterparts who also had community ties when they ran for office. Moreover, when she transitioned to her legislative position she heard of other Democrats who received support as candidates, including her opponent. "I know for sure that there were several members in the Democratic caucus who were helping one of my opponents who was a white female. They were using their resources and helping her to get elected, and then I get elected, and it's like, 'Yeah, I'm here now, so how are we going to mend this relationship?' Some of them don't realize that I know how much they helped my opponent, but I knew."

Due to the knowledge that certain Democrats, in particular white politicians, were able to access resources that she couldn't, Yancey was hesitant to discuss her reelection campaign with her Democratic colleagues and became concerned about heightened interest in her reelection efforts by some of her colleagues:

> There was one who used to call me every single day asking me, "Well, are you using the van? Are you using the van?" The minivan is a system that you can use from your cell phone to track how many doors you're knocking and the neighborhoods you have been in. And I don't know who else could have access to mine, but I didn't use the van and I'm glad that I didn't because some of these people were way too interested to know whether or not I was using the van, especially when I found out later they were actually actively helping my opponent.

Such experiences of Black women and party politics reflected the varied structures of local and state parties. What was consistent among the women who held a leadership position in their state party as either caucus members or as leaders was that the Democratic Party was often lacking in the number of Black women who engaged in party politics as leaders, which affected the role the party played in providing support for current and potential Black women politicians. These observations speak to the deeper challenges that Black women face within political parties and in finding support for their political aspirations more generally. Like other institutions, political parties reflect the biases and culture of the community and society in which they exist. These stereotypes position Black women as outsiders. The testimonials confirm that party structures institutionalize placing Black women outside of party support that is important for candidate emergence and electoral success. Parties cannot be expected to be more open to seeing Black women as viable candidates if their structure limits the voices of Black women as leaders and those who would champion a different model in candidate recruitment.

Limited Leadership and Opportunities Within Democratic Party

Black women who have served in leadership positions in Democratic Party circles acknowledged a significant challenge in the party's support of Black women. Arkansas House member Vivian Flowers, who has served as chair of the Legislative Black Caucus, noted that it was important for the few Black women in positions of leadership to be proactive in getting Black women not only to vote but to also run for office. Flowers, who is involved with in the Democratic Party in the region and actively engaged in a network of Black legislatures across the country, said that from her perspective:

> At th[is] time there aren't any real resources to support women who are looking to run for state and local office. There are groups like Emerge with the Party but that isn't Black woman specific. I want to use my space to be a resource for information, be a resource for women to become educated voters, be a resource for women who are interested in running for office, and as such, to strengthen and

enhance the role of women in our families and in politics right now, especially Democratic politics, focus some of our work and some of our priority and mission on not just voting but winning office.

As an "insider," Flowers's statement gives credence to the experiences of the Black women in this study. The Democratic Party has outsourced its outreach to external groups that are committed to increasing the participation of women and women of color in politics. That Flowers sees her role as an advocate to assist Black women is emblematic of the radical imagination's resistance to institutional marginalization. That Black women cultivate a vision and path not only for themselves but also for others is a core aspect of the radical imagination. While Black women are often committed to assisting others, they are also still committed to holding institutions accountable for their role in the continued perpetuation of ideas about where Black women belong and that their work should be in service of the institutions in which they reside.

The Democratic Party's ability to win elections has largely been tied to the political strength of Black women. The turnout of Black women voters and their ability to mobilize other voters has become critical for Democratic Party success in most elections, especially at the national level. Yet this overwhelming dependence on Black women has not translated into the party deeming Black women critical to shaping the direction, messaging, and policies of the Democratic Party or to being among its leaders. Dr. Menna Demessie, who served as vice president of Policy Analysis and Research at the Congressional Black Caucus Foundation, noted the challenges that Black women have faced in rising to key leadership positions in the Democratic Party. She noted seeing a handful of Black women who were major fundraisers and organizers for the Democratic National Committee, but she did not see other Black women rise to positions of influence within the party. She noted the irony of this dynamic, for "if they were not doing what they were doing, the party wouldn't be [successful]." Dr. Demessie observed that the Democratic National Committee selecting leaders who are rarely Black women while relying on the labor of Black women to keep the party winning elections should elicit shame and change. But it doesn't.

Karyn Bradford Coleman, who serves as chief of staff for the Democratic Party of Arkansas, made a similar observation:

> Executive directors—there are four Black women in the entire country who do the same job that I do because this is typically a white male's job and some white females. When you have institutions and spaces that are geared to protecting whiteness, we don't do a good job of making sure that inclusiveness is a part of our agenda. And so what happens is, there are one or two figures such as a Senator Kamala Harris or Stacey Abrams, and because those figures become transcendent, people feel as if they have done their job. And they don't understand that if the town that I'm from in Des Arc, Arkansas, with less than two thousand people, if the city council is made up of all white males, but the town demographic is thirty-eight percent African American, you've [actually] not done your job.

The profound comment of Coleman offers a structural analysis of the limitations of the Democratic Party in not only advancing the ambition of Black women but also developing a structure that is inclusive. This dynamic is a painful reminder that political parties should be viewed as institutions that shape how people engage and think politically. Exclusion influences and mobilizes groups, but it also unfortunately reinforces ideas in society about the excluded groups—in this case Black women. As Demessie and Bradford confirm, despite receiving substantial electoral support from Black women, the party reflects a society that views Black women as laborers whose work should benefit them. No wonder Black women have long acknowledged feeling exploited while recognizing that of the two parties the Democratic Party's policies align best with their policy needs. Vivian Flowers's analogy ably sums up the relationship:

> I would liken it to our relationship with men—beautiful and supportive but it's going to always be exploitive because of the history and the existing structure of it. The party is not run by women, the consultants and the whole economic infrastructure of it, there's no sharing with Black women, people don't make sure we get contracts,

that we get mentored. The ones who get in there, got in there however they got in there, and they do the best they can with what they have, but it's just not a lot of avenues because we're not only competing with each other, we're more so competing with other white women. Because you've got the woman moniker, and then you've got Black women, and that's always been such a one-sided relationship where we pretend, I think, that it's mutually beneficial. But it's really almost abusive, more so than even the party or men. You know what I mean?

I think the history and the infrastructure and the money of the party are really, really important. Just like women are expected to get married to be validated as women, to be validated as worthy of being treated as a lady, to be validated as, "You must be really beautiful because a man wanted you, and now you can have children," as if you can't have children without being married. That's why I would liken it to the relationship we have with men.

Flowers speaks to the positionality of Black women not merely in political parties but also in society as whole. Black women live at various intersections of injustice as a result of their identity and history. They have consequently had to be forward thinking when navigating how to survive for themselves and their families. The injustices Black women face come in the form not only of opinions but also of practices of institutions to which Black women have access and from which they seek justice. The analogy of an intimate relationship between a man and a woman clarifies just how exploitive the nature of Black women's political work is, particularly in the face of a marginalizing structure that presumes Black women have no other options for their liberation. However, Black women do recognize the exploitative nature of the relationship and take ownership of their labor and ambition. Black women candidates and elected officials uniformly expressed a belief that their political party can and should do more to recruit diverse candidates. The narratives shared by the women in the study forcefully underscore that their party gives them no real support or even welcome despite them being reliable voters and often strong candidates.

Discussion

Following the election of Donald Trump, the changing political and social climate ushered in an increased tolerance of public bad behavior where instances of public hostility toward Black female elected officials, organizations, entertainers, and members of the media increased; yet it is something that their white and male counterparts ignored. The conscious and public dismissal of Black women and the harsh representations of them that are endorsed via media channels and public officials are consistent with the political marginalization that Black women have encountered for years.

Throughout the chapter I presented data that chronicled the daily challenges that Black women face in society and political parties. Their experiences confirm why our traditional understanding of ambition is a better explanation for white women who do not face outsider status as a result of an intersectional identity of race and gender. In the previous chapter I explored the socialization process of Black women. That process is often structured to prepare Black women for the institutional barriers and marginalization they will face. The efforts to marginalize Black women through words and actions is an attempt to limit Black women's to respond and prevent future efforts to minimize their presence and influence.

As evidenced in the testimonials, the women were not necessarily shocked by the efforts to shame or ignore them but often attempted to respond in ways that they deemed appropriate, which would allow them to continue to be an effective politician.

The women interviewed uniformly expressed a belief that the political party had a role in either advancing or minimizing their ability to be successful candidates. While some felt supported by the party and others did not, there was a consensus that their political party could and should do more to recruit and support Black women as candidates. These nuanced experiences are extremely telling, especially for those who had engaged with their party prior to running. It is typical that party engagement should lead to increased access to information and opportunities for recruitment and campaign support. But for these women, those types of engagements did not always offer a beneficial return on their investment. This is a telling feature of American politics and parties as institutions primarily because Black women are reliable voters and are often strong candidates. This precarious position supports my argument that Black women are developing political ambition on a margin that exists not only by norms and behaviors, but it also remains as a result of institutionalized behaviors by political parties.

4

Black Women's Leadership

Connecting Socialization, and Careers

> I'm no longer accepting the things I cannot change... I'm changing the things I cannot accept.
>
> —Angela Davis

During a May 2019 House Financial Services Committee debate to repeal the 2013 Bureau for Consumer Financial Protections auto-lending guidance in an effort to prevent discrimination, Republican Congressman Mike Kelly of Pennsylvania unceremoniously interrupted Congresswoman Maxine Waters and attempted to scold her. He said she was not the appropriate person to comment on the auto industry and discrimination, and he stated that the nation was "coming together as a people in spite of what you say." Kelly also incorporated the "make America great again" rhetoric of then President Donald Trump by saying that conversations about discrimination were *hindering* making the nation great. Although Kelly flouted protocol by interrupting Waters and speaking directly to her instead of to Tom McClintock, the Republican chair, McClintock neither corrected Kelly nor stopped him from finishing his direct rebuke of Waters. Yet when Waters attempted to respond, McClintock attempted to prevent *her* from speaking and reminded *her* of protocol.

Congresswoman Waters responded concisely that she was aware of procedure, and that it was McClintock who was not following the rules. Then, turning to speak directly to Kelly, she continued: "I want you to know that I am more offended as an African American woman than you will ever be." She went on: "And this business about making American great again: it is *your* president that's dividing this country.

And don't talk to me about the fact that we don't understand . . . No, I will not yield. Don't tell me we don't understand. That's the attitude given toward women time and time again." When McClintock again attempted to interrupt Waters, she retorted: "You did not interrupt [Kelly] when he was making those outrageous remarks about him knowing more about discrimination than I know about discrimination. I resent that and I resent the talk about making America great again" (Rogo 2020).

The moment went viral, and Waters' statement "No, I will not yield" became a catch phrase and meme to symbolize the dissatisfaction Black women often feel in the workplace when they experience disrespect by having their ability and intellect questioned. This moment was a clear example of Black women being told to stay in their places, that their lived experiences are not valid, and that their presence should be ignored. Kelly, for his part, exhibited an attitude that women should have a limited role in politics because they can only offer limited expertise. Studies have shown that people believe male politicians are better suited than female politicians to deal with issues of crime, defense, and foreign policy, and that they are more intelligent, more decisive and forceful, and better suited to promote public policy (Brooks 2013; Lawless 2004). In this case, the debate was about the auto industry, which has long been identified with images of masculinity and with white male blue-collar workers, although over 20 percent of the industry currently consists of female workers (Coffin and Lawrence 2020). Though Black workers now comprise only 17 percent of the total auto industry workforce, at the height of the auto industry 30 percent of the workers were Black (Dawson 1994).

Kelly was likewise dismissive of Waters's expertise on issues of economic development. Yet she has served as ranking member or chairwoman of every Financial Services subcommittee since 1995. Indeed, the political career of Maxine Waters exemplifies the strategic manner in which Black women represent their constituents. Waters currently represents the 43rd Congressional District of California, which consists of Inglewood, Torrance, and parts of Los Angeles, including the airport. Waters's extensive service on the Financial Services Committee may seem odd to some who might assume that that a Black woman representing a majority non-white district (50 percent Latino,

19 percent Black, 12 percent Asian) would serve on a committee such as Education and Labor or Homeland Security, which addresses immigration. However, this committee addresses issues such as consumer protections and small-business development, international finance, and public and private housing. This broad array of issues significantly affects the economic health of Waters's district, given that predatory financial-lending processes, limited access to resources for small-businesses development, and lack of affordable housing are all issues of great concern to her minority constituents.

Congresswoman Walter's placement on this committee and her leadership are worth noting. Walter's career and committee assignments express a nuanced understanding of the needs of her community. This is similar to the efforts of the women interviewed who decide to lead politically; they have made deliberate choices about collaboration and sought legislation that directly benefited their constituents. Likewise, several of them hold the self-possession Maxine Waters exhibited in response to her colleagues' dismissal of her is like the leadership shown by other Black women in politics.

Throughout the text I have explored how Black women's political ambition is cultivated. This chapter will shift to how Black women transfer the skills and awareness of community concerns to professional spaces and how both their awareness and professional experiences influence their political careers. The spaces in which ambition is cultivated also are spaces that offer leadership development and skills to meet the needs of their constituents. For many Black women who were acculturated with an emphasis on service and community while recognizing their unique social position, professional life becomes another prism for their identity to be challenged, skills questioned, and opportunities for growth limited (Bell and Nkomo 2003; Barnes 2016). In those same spaces Black women professionals incorporate the skills and community ethos gained from their civic and social organizational engagements and participation in religious institutions. Similar to the ways that the marginalized status of the Black community and Black women contributed to a distinctive socialization process and network of organizations, Black women have faced marginalization in the careers and professional networks that are considered pathways to a political career. Therefore it is necessary to explore how Black women who found themselves often shut out of those "traditional" careers transferred their leadership skills along with an awareness about policies and inequities that impacted the communities they would eventually serve as elected officials.

Developing Black Women as Leaders

Our understanding of how political women lead relies on two research strands: one about what women do once elected, and the other about how they learn to govern. Recent literature on what women of color do once elected informs us that they are deliberate in their choices about how to legislate (Smooth 2001; Garcia Bedolla, Tate, and Wong 2005; Bratton, Haynie, and Reingold 2007; Fraga et al. 2007; Bejarano 2013; Minta and Brown 2014; Brown 2014; Brown and Gershon 2016; Hardy-Fanta, Pinderhughes, and Sierra 2016) and that they use their political power in legislative bodies to address the needs of Black women and their communities (Smooth 2001; Gay 2001; Cohen 2003; Tate 2003; Fraga et al. 2007; Reingold and Smith 2012; Rouse, Swers, and Parrott 2013; Brown and Gershon 2016). This they often do by being deliberate about establishing useful relationships and about collaborating in their work, by cosponsoring legislation, and by deliberately championing issues that affect their constituents (Brown 2014).

As previously stated, political ambition theory posited that certain careers were pathways to politics for both men and women (Carroll and Sanbonmatsu 2013; Lawless and Fox 2005). Because women had limited access to careers in business and the legal profession, it was argued that opportunities to interact within political networks were limited, and consequently women would have limited ambition and opportunities for political engagement. While Black women found themselves shut out of these careers, there was nonetheless an increase in the number of Black women seeking office (Prestage 1991; Gamble 2010).

Literature based on studies of African American women officials since the 1970s confirm that these women often come to their positions better prepared than their colleagues in terms of the prestige of their former occupation and their educational background (Prestage 1977;

Darcy and Hadley 1988; Moncrief, Thompson, and Schuhmann 1991; Williams 2001). This finding is consistent with the role that socialization plays within the ambition on the margins framework in which indigenous spaces offer these women skill development, leadership opportunities, and encouragement to purse academic and professional degrees. We have a limited understanding of how Black women attain the skills to pursue political careers. Much of what has been studied comes from testimonies in biographies and autobiographies of Black women elected officials and those who have served in political parties (Chisholm 1973; Brazile 2004; Brazile et al. 2018; Abrams 2018). Likewise, a growing number of biographies and studies of how Black women hold informal and formal leadership positions in civil rights organizations and social movements show how women gained the necessary skills (Robnett 1997; Ransby 2003; Lee 2000; Blaine 2018; Jones-Branch 2021). We know that political leadership training that targets such women also cultivates such leadership strategies. In this chapter, I extend our understanding of not only the careers Black women held prior to obtaining office but also the transferable skill sets they bring to governing, which is grounded in community, and contributes to impactful leadership for their constituents.

On-the-Job Training

Historically, Black professionals have been disproportionately concentrated in the government sector. In the early 1980s, 67 percent of all Black professionals and managers were concentrated in the government compared to 17 percent of professionals of other racial and ethnic identities. Among upper level administrators, 42 percent of Blacks worked in government (Pickney 1984). Though the number has declined, today, with more career options available to them, those with careers in government still total around 20 percent. When asked about their careers prior to serving as an elected official, many of the women mentioned having worked in local governments, state agencies, or nonprofits that worked closely with local government agencies. The testimonies of these women confirmed that their leadership skills and political ambition were shaped by the training and expertise they developed in those spaces, and that likewise those positions had increased their understanding of the role of public policy in addressing the inequities that their communities and future constituents face.

Angie Jenkins, Reynoldsburg, Ohio, City Council member, is an alum of Xavier University, an HBCU in Louisiana, and she engaged in community service, in particular service for the schools and athletic programs that her children were involved in. Jenkins had worked in state government for 15 years, first in the Ohio Department of Health, then in the Ohio Information Technology Office, and finally in the Ohio Attorney General's Office. Throughout her career as a classified employee, she experienced changes following every election cycle; depending on which party was in the majority, her boss and the policy focus could change. During her career, most of her coworkers were in unclassified positions, which meant they could be moved from office to office or be fired depending on the desire of the governor and those in key political positions. During her career she grew to understand the fluidity of personnel and the effect that political appointees had on financial and policy implementation. Jenkins noted that with each change in the governor's office, there were transitions in higher level positions, with people coming and (not always by choice) going; as a result, she learned to adapt.

During such periods of transition, Jenkins not only honed her skill set to work effectively in a fluid office environment, she also gained unique insight into the politics and funding of critical issues such as healthcare. These new insights were coupled with an awareness she held about challenges women of color faced while seeking healthcare. Jenkins recalled that one administration sought to eliminate agencies and offices that informed women about abortions. During that administration, she recalls that one doctor left the Department of Health because he disagreed with the policy. Working amid such revolving-door circumstances and changes in policy, she gained an appreciation for the complexity of the issue and its potential to affect women beyond those who sought information on abortion services. The proposed changes affected women of color particularly because the policy shifted funding away from the already underfunded public health offices dedicated to addressing the overall health of women while providing access to safe and healthy maternity and childbirth experiences. Jenkins observed that her state lacked funding for what she referred to as "health equity" and that this limited funding had a significant impact on the resources available to local communities. She noted: "Working in state government, there's just a lot of roadblocks that are in place at the state level and then again, at the local level. And politics is just sometimes difficult to work around when people have other agendas and it's not for the sake of the community."

Jenkins's found that the value of her experiences and understanding the needs of persons who had limited access to healthcare were evident in the first crisis that she and her fellow council members faced during her first few months in office—the COVID-19 pandemic. She brought to the table a great understanding of existing health disparities and how an increase or decrease in funding could make a particularly significant difference during the pandemic—for good or ill. She noted that though access to healthcare and vaccines for the elderly was prioritized during the pandemic, others (like minorities and persons with pre-existing medical conditions) enjoyed no such priority, resulting in disproportionate rates of disease and death among such groups. Jenkins' understanding of and experience working with limited funding and health inequities during her earlier career, along with her sensitivity about marginalized communities being impacted directly by healthcare policies, became an asset during the pandemic. For example, Jenkins recognized and spoke to the council about the need for mask mandates before major cities, such as Columbus, initiated one. She was ignored, but perhaps her suggestion primed the council, for when a different council member advocated for masks a week later, the council accepted that suggestion wholeheartedly.

Alaska State Senator Elvi Gray-Jackson knows what it is like to be forgotten, not only as a Black woman but also as a municipal worker. Her experiences influenced her approach to her career and the people who needed to be heard and represented. Gray-Jackson articulated that she gained invaluable understanding of government financial management during her career. She began as an executive secretary to the transit director of Anchorage, later became senior budget analyst, and ended her career as director of the Budget and Legislative Services Office. In 2005, Senator Gray-Jackson worked for Municipal Light and Power as director of the Alaska Energy Railbelt Authority, a joint action agency with three electric utility members. In describing her career, Senator Gray-Jackson noted, "Through formal education and on-the-job training, I worked my way up from administrative assistant to budget analyst. Then I got promoted to senior budget analyst. Then ultimately, I got promoted to the director of the Assembly Budget Office." Like Angie Jenkins, Gray-Jackson witnessed the ebbs and flows of changes in political leadership. In 2005, such changes affected her. For though the assembly is supposed to be nonpartisan, the leadership moved to the right and, being a "proud Democrat," Gray-Jackson stated that there was a political effort to "get rid of her office. This played in the media for three weeks." It was such experiences and observations of political maneuvering that motivated Gray-Jackson to seek elected office.

Black women not only have worked at high rates in government sector, but they are also a core group of employees and leaders in nonprofits. Jheanelle Wilkins, who currently serves as a Maryland state delegate, was interested in social injustices and political processes as a young person. While in college she joined political organizations such as the Young Democrats and civic organizations such as Alpha Kappa Alpha Sorority Inc., the oldest Black sorority. Wilkins commented that her engagement in her sorority allowed her to learn how to develop effective service programs and engage in a professional meeting setting. She is currently employed by the Leadership Conference on Civil and Human Rights as the director of state and local affairs. The Leadership Conference is the oldest and largest organization formed to develop a coalition around civil rights issues. Wilkins commented that she gained an appreciation for service while watching her mother visit people on their church's sick and shut-in list. Those visits translated into a desire to help those in need. As an immigrant, her family was proud to vote, and she had a strong interest in policy impacts on vulnerable groups while in high school and college. While in high school Wilkins interned at the Leadership Conference. As an intern Wilkins stated her time at the organization "really opened my eyes, that internship, to how people can push and advocate from the outside, how people can organize and demand a change, and that internship just really ignited a passion for just better understanding policy, how to organize on issues." Upon graduation from college,

Wilkins was employed by the Leadership Conference. She noted that in her in position she developed a deeper understanding of issues that were discussed in the media through a national scope, such as ensuring people were accurately counted in the census or immigration policies that often significantly impacted her state and community. Wilkins also commented that this understanding of issues and the needs of her state and community, along with her desire to assist her community, contributed to agreeing to run for office when an open seat in her district became available.

Former Wilmington, Delaware, Treasurer Velda Jones-Potter's path to elected office was likewise shaped by her career, but in a different way. She transitioned to politics from an opportunity that arose in her corporate career as an engineer. When asked about that transition to elected politics, she noted that her political career trajectory had not been a straight line:

> I'm an engineer, and I have a master's degree in finance, and I spent the first seventeen years of my career in the private sector in a major corporation, the DuPont Company. My exposure to public service in the realm of politics, elected office, was first really through my husband; he was very active in local civic associations and in politics. And frankly, from that exposure, I had no interest [chuckle] at all. I was very satisfied with making my contribution and doing my service through volunteer work, board service, philanthropy. I had no interest in the dynamics that I saw in politics. But while I was at the DuPont Company, the mayor—the first African American mayor of the city of Wilmington—contacted me and asked me if I would come to the city to assist in a major problem that the city had under his leadership.

Jones-Potter became part of a loaned executive agreement plan—not a specific program but an accommodation designed to assist Jones-Potter's service to the city; DuPont augmented her salary, and she accrued service with the company in a public-private partnership. Jones-Potter saw this as an opportunity to contribute to her city. During her two-year term in the partnership, she found success and relied on her leadership skills and financial expertise.

> We helped the city turn a surplus within the eighteen months that I was director of finance, and the response was just so positive to the kind of leadership that I brought. Much of it's sort of personal style of leadership, but also the business practices that I was able to bring from my experience in the corporate environment. And I loved having the impact on lives of people through my professional skills, but really having a more direct impact on people. So what I'd say about that whole experience was it was really life changing for me. And I knew at the time that I just didn't have the same passion for bottom-line corporate results, financial results, in that arena that I did for helping people, and improving the lives of people.

Jones-Potter expounded that she had a long-standing commitment to service as evidenced in her active engagement in organizations, such as the National Coalition of 100 Black Women and Delta Sigma Theta Sorority Inc., in which she said she gained an appreciation for collaborating with persons who had differences of opinion but were committed to a mutual goal. She found her transition to working within a political space fulfilling because it allowed her to deepen her level of service to her community and city while using her unique skill set to assist with critical issues that affected her community. Jones-Potter returned to DuPont and later left to work at a venture capital company that owned a financial services company. Along came an opportunity from newly elected Governor Jack Markell, who was then state treasurer. With two more years left on his four-year term, he asked Jones-Potter to serve out the rest of his term so that he could assume the governorship. She would become the first Black woman to hold a statewide seat in Delaware.

Teree Caldwell-Johnson, who currently serves as vice chair of the Des Moines, Iowa, school board, is similar to many of the women in this study. She is an alumna of Spelman College (an HBCU) and a member of Alpha Kappa Alpha Sorority Inc. and several other influential organizations comprised of professional Black women, including Jack and Jill of America Inc., which is focused on strengthening African American children through leadership development and service. Her career included working around the country in city and county managers' offices, including a seven-year stint as a county's manager in her hometown. She also served as the executive director of the Solid Waste Authority, which had responsibility for 17 different municipalities in the region, and several of the Waste Authority's members were elected officials.

Caldwell-Johnson's extensive career in city and county management gave her an acute insight into various community issues, the complexity of crisis management, and fiscal management, while working closely with elected officials. Caldwell-Johnson did not see herself as an elected official until she felt she needed to address significant challenges within the neighborhood she served. Caldwell-Johnson explained that she currently served as the president and CEO of a housing and human services nonprofit, which manages approximately 350 low-income Section 8 housing units located across the street from an elementary school. "Seeing some of the challenges that were happening within the neighborhood where I serve, [I] decided at that point that I needed to step in and utilize my voice and my position to hopefully make a difference with some of the decisions that I thought were going to have a net negative impact, not only on the people that live in the neighborhood where I'm currently employed, but also on the students in terms of their educational pursuits."

The issue that propelled Caldwell-Jackson to run directly affected the communities that her agency served. The superintendent at that time decided to close several different elementary schools under the guise of low enrollment—including the school across the street from the houses she managed. She stated:

> It was hard for me to envision closing a school in a neighborhood where we had fifty percent of our residents, probably six hundred who were children ages zero to eighteen. And a large portion of them elementary-aged students. And so I started doing a little bit more research and found out that students from my neighborhood were being bused to seventeen different elementary schools in the community. So if you're busing kids away from the neighborhood school, of course you're going to have low enrollment in the neighborhood school. And it was at that point that I decided that I needed to fight, not only for our neighborhood, but I needed to fight for our students.

> And so I decided to enter the race. That wasn't the sole issue upon which I ran, but it was certainly a motivator for wanting to run.

Not only did her professional experiences shape her understanding of how she could impact issues as an elected official, they also impacted how she is currently navigating issues as an elected official. During the interview in the summer of 2021, Caldwell-Johnson expressed concern about the increasingly partisan nature of the state legislature, partisanship that was affecting both the dynamics of the nonpartisan school board on which she served and its approaches to local education policy. Although she is concerned, she confirmed that her years working in city and county managers' offices prepared her to navigate uncharted territory on behalf of the school board.

These testimonies confirm that the literature that argues a narrow career path supports women's political ambition is not applicable to the fostering of political ambition in Black women. First, the career spaces that many Black women find themselves in are often outside of business and legal professions. As the women in this study confirmed, for much of the Black middle class, professional opportunities often come through career paths in governmental and nonprofit sectors. Second, when Black women enter career spaces, many are not novices when it comes to recognizing opportunities to affect change across various issues for persons who, in the words of Elvi Gray-Jackson, are "left behind."

The women in this study brought to their careers an understanding of the inequities that Black women and other underserved populations face. They all had spent considerable time in organizations and educational institutions that are committed to advancing Black communities while providing socialization in professionalization and leadership. Career placement is not just about being in positions to foster networks that develop pathways to electoral victory; for these women, their career choice becomes a place to marry skill sets that develop in indigenous Black communities with opportunities to gain a more nuanced perspective about policies that impact their communities. In addition, when reporting about their career paths in government agencies, several respondents said they entered government as political employees.

Politics as a Career

While some women enter politics through careers that are impacted by political decisions, others begin their careers in spaces that make those political decisions as legislative and policy aides. One example is Arkansas State Representative Vivian Flowers, who, upon graduating from college, took a job at the Bureau of Legislative Research, which she held for five years. The position gave her an understanding of public policy, government processes, lobbying, the maze of committees, and the legislative workflow. This led to Flowers serving as committee secretary of the bureau and working with legislative analyst Willa Black Sanders of Little Rock, who was one of only a few African Americans at the bureau. In discussing her career trajectory, Flowers stated that the position and relationship with Sanders led to her serving as executive director of the Legislative Black Caucus. This in turn opened more doors and exposed Flowers to the national scope of legislative leadership and the network of African Americans in legislatures across the country.

It is important to note that Flowers served before our current era of social media, when business was conducted through personal relationships and email was used for work only. This required her to build relationships that would later facilitate not only her ability to campaign but also to legislate. She recalls: "By the time I served, you fast-forward all these years, I knew the landscape. The political, the partisan landscape had changed, but the policy infrastructure and the institutional infrastructure were still the same. And many of the lobbyists were the same. And so, by the time I ran I got a lot of support from lobbyists." As stated earlier in the book, networks that Black women cultivate often connect them to political elites and mentorship. For Flowers this happened in her workspace. Her experiences confirm the value of relationships for Black women to move from outsider status to insider status.

Joni Alexander, who currently serves as a city council member in Pine Bluff, Arkansas, was raised in Pine Bluff but after college in Virginia she did not return home immediately. She became a schoolteacher in South Korea for two years, and then returned home to serve as the chief of staff in the mayor's office. It was then that Alexander learned that 47 percent of the youth in her community lived below the poverty rate. In her role she attempted to implement a youth program because she knew that cities with demographics and challenges similar to those found in Pine Bluff had dedicated departments to address the needs of youth. To gain support for the department, Alexander started "to present all of this information [research on other cities]; I met with each council member individually because I wanted their feedback, I didn't care if they would support, I needed feedback. They were all in support of it, except for one. And that was great because we had a lot of dissension back then."

The mayor for whom Alexander worked was not re-elected, but Alexander took her knowledge about youth programs and poverty and went to work at a youth organization with the goal of building the program she had been unable to build while working for the city. It was a challenging task since she didn't have the same social capital as when she was connected to the mayor's office and had access to city resources. While working at this new position, she was recruited to run for City Council. In her platform she focused on three issues, issues she learned about while working in city government, issues she had also attempted to address as an elected official. She recalled:

> So I knew city government in and out, and one thing I feel like people don't give credit to are the actual people who work in city government. I wanted to be a voice and support for them. I wanted to look at some of our antiquated legislation and change those things and also introduce new legislation to help with things going on in the city. I wanted to be transparent, and I wanted to provide a platform of communication between the citizens and the elected officials.

Alexander's experience helps us understand the value of working within political spaces for Black women who seek office. These spaces not only allowed Alexander to gain insight into the political process and challenges in her community, but these spaces also allowed for her to have an access point to engage more fully with community members that would eventually allow her to become a viable candidate.

Former Texas Democratic Party Vice Chair Carla Brailey likewise entered the world of politics through direct employment. Upon earning a PhD in sociology, she decided not to enter the professorate and was approached to apply for a job in the administration of then incoming Washington, DC Mayor Anthony Fenty. In that capacity, she served in many roles that included providing direct oversight of nine community relations and constituent services offices. She also oversaw 140 boards, including the city's influential Sports Commission and the Public Service Commission (formerly known as the Public Utilities Commission). While serving, she gained valuable insight, she noted, especially into the often ignored role of boards and commissions, while dealing with appointments and the jockeying that goes on for board and commission positions with the highest profiles and the largest budgets. Brailey learned a valuable lesson that helped her understand party and state politics, namely, "politics is not politics without an exchange." Brailey noted that these experiences during her employment in city government fueled her interest to run for office. Though she did not win the city council seat, she would successfully move up the ladder in state politics and ultimately became the Texas Democratic Party vice chair, and in 2022 she was a candidate for Texas lieutenant governor.

Black women have found other avenues to gain access to politics and opportunities for training and culturation that allows a successful transition to elected office. The lived experience of these women broadens our understanding of the pathways to political careers. These experiences not only provide opportunities, they also develop skill sets for strategic and politically astute behavior once elected. How? Of all demographics, Black women continue to be the most represented in the labor market while continuing to be involved in political work. Wendy Smooth posited that the participation of Black women is a "paradox" given that so many Black women have limited access to resources typically deemed necessary to political participation in general and running for office in particular. How does this happen? One answer lies in Black women's location in the workforce. Governmental agencies, nonprofits, and other spaces offer Black women opportunities not only to become acculturated into the ins and outs of politics but also to become policy experts and experts in the impact of policy decisions on the communities in which they reside.

Strategic and Purposeful Leadership

Political representation is highly significant in determining which issues, policies, and communities' needs are prioritized (Pitkin 1967; Fenno 1978; Mansbridge 1999, 2003; Dovi 2007). Once engaged in representation as political leaders, there are gendered differences in leadership styles (Rosenthal 1998), in the types of constituency service that men and women undertake (Thomas 1991), and in their communication patterns during legislative hearings (Kathlene 1994). Women are more likely to sponsor bills on education, childcare, and health, often referred to as "women's issues" (Burrell 1994; Sanbonmatsu 2002; Swers 2002). Black women in particular legislate somewhat differently than both other women and Black men due to their gendered and racial identities and experiences (Bratton, Haynie, and Reingold 2007; Fraga et al. 2007; Reingold and Smith 2012; Smooth 2001). Black women act cohesively in state legislatures (Brown 2014) and have distinct policy interests that have a direct effect on the Black community, such as education, healthcare, and criminal and social justice issues that are often considered progressive (Barrett 1995; Orey et. al. 2007; Brown 2014).

Networking and collaborative attitudes are critical to the success of Black women in legislatures (Smooth 2001; Brown 2014). One theme that interview participants consistently mentioned was the need to be collaborative and strategic in legislating. Many of the women found themselves in situations in which their political party held a minority in their legislative body. In addition, they found that Black members in general and Black women in particular were often isolated and ignored. Women consequently deliberately developed allies, even if they were only temporary allies for the purposes of passing a piece of legislation.

Tennessee State Senator Raumesh Akbari serves in a legislature in which the opposing party holds a super majority so advancing legislation on behalf of her constituents can be challenging. To gain support in this legislature Akbari has to work not only to cross partisan boundaries but also to overcome cultural norms and racism.

> It's difficult because you have to build a connection with someone and get them to think completely outside of who they are and how they've been raised and who they've been around, because the demographics of Tennessee. You don't have a lot of Black and Brown people that are populating these areas outside of our urban cores, our cities, and the immediate surrounding area. So for me, it's about trying to find common ground. I know this issue is going to impact Black and Bown folks, but I also know it's going to impact white folks too. And so how can we reach that middle ground, whether we're talking about education or criminal justice reform, even healthcare, even though I can't seem to get [all of] them on the same page, . . . [I can at least try to get] some of them.

Akbari's efforts are noble and, as she acknowledged, can be extremely difficult, as was the case in 2019 following the murder of George Floyd. Some persons across the aisle at first seemed to be open particularly to having policy conversations, but ultimately they tended to default to political rhetoric, moving them into a stance that is directly oppositional to all the policy that Akbari was attempting to get passed.

In a separate interview with Akbari's colleague, Tennessee State Senator Brenda Gilmore, she approached the political disadvantage similarly:

> I think, one, it has to do with relationships. I think that that's probably the most important strategy—the relationships you build with individual legislators. And so I think this past year in the Senate is probably one of the most successful legislative years that I've had. I passed eight bills, I lost two. One, I really didn't care about, I was carrying it for my House sponsor, so I ain't losing sleep on that at all. The other one that I lost, I really did care. I really wanted it to pass. It would've made a significant difference in the lives of people who have been recently incarcerated and released in terms of getting back and making their lives whole again. And the reason I think I was so successful this year is because I intentionally made it my business to slow down and to spend time with individual legislators who I used to have champion some of the particular bills that I have. Since we, my caucus, we're in the minority. There's a super majority caucus in

both the House and the Senate. I am a Democrat, and there are only six of us in the Senate . . . out of thirty-three members. So even if we didn't show up, they would be able to carry on business without my caucus. So there's no way that I could pass legislation without the support of reaching across the aisle.

Gilmore went on to say that, in addition to relationships, she found success in turning to and involving particular stakeholders who can reach out to committee members. The legislative task requires a lot of homework, she said, homework that entails determining the stakeholders and who will be opposed to the bill, why, and what their talking points will be. In addition Gilmore commented on the value of having help even if it is from only one person:

> [The legislative process is] just so much, and you are so overwhelmed with all the different pulls that you have on you that you need somebody to help you touch all those bases and run interference.

Like earlier generations of Black political women, such as Septima Clark, Gilmore understands the value of empowering the community with knowledge about the system. By providing information about the value of contacting legislators, attending meetings, writing letters and emails, and making phone calls, Gilmore stays connected to the community and to the issues that concern them. This type of community engagement is important and can make a difference in the legislative process. Gilmore referenced a piece of environmental legislation that had to do with students in middle school and high school, and she noted that one of her constituents visited every legislator on the committee to explain why the bill was important and to ask whether they would vote for the legislation. The constituent came back to Gilmore and reported who had committed and who had said no. Gilmore found this information invaluable as she sought allies for the legislation.

While there were some women who were able to develop strategies to pass legislation, some faced obstacles and developed strategies to overcome not only a learning curve in a new position but also persons who ignored their presence. Angie Jenkins, who arrived in politics after retiring, noted the challenge of learning how best to function as council president. Some of her challenge was her approach to leading in a collaborative way. During her career, even though she often found herself in a politicized environment, she achieved success seeking consensus with others and brought this attitude to her elected position. In discussing her viewpoint of her role on the city council Jenkins noted:

> I feel like we're supposed to work as a team. And I'm not doing anything for résumé purposes, and I'm not saying anyone else is. But for me, I'm just trying to do it for what I think is . . . best for the city. And I'm doing it and asking for other opinions before putting it on an agenda. . . . And I'm asking other people on city council because I thought we were working together as a team and not solo. But from those two examples, I've learned that instead of asking, "What do you think? How do you feel about this?," I'm just going to put it on the agenda, and we'll talk about it in city council. So that's just a few examples of what I've had as a struggle for me, personally, and trying to work through barriers that I felt were barriers for me.

Jenkins went on to elaborate that she learned that her collaborative approach is not always reciprocated, which prompted her to consider a different strategy. In her role as council president, Jenkins is responsible for bringing forth legislation for the council to discuss. Jenkins felt it was imperative to develop a new strategy given the pressing issues the council needed to address during the COVID-19 pandemic. She recounted:

> What I've learned is that instead of asking, or asking for an opinion, or asking what they think about legislation, I just need to go to the attorney and to the clerk and say, "Can you not reinvent the wheel, but can you find this legislation where other cities have done it [i.e., a mask mandate] and put it on the agenda?" Because my role is the agenda for city council, so I don't need to ask anyone's permission. But I was trying to be a team player and trying to get feedback before putting something on the agenda.

As Jenkins grew in the office and consulted her counterparts in neighboring municipalities, she not only learned to be a team player but also realized her role allowed her the right not to ask permission for everything, especially pressing issues, such as a mask mandate at the beginning of the COVID-19 pandemic and how to fairly provide affordable housing.

While most of the women stated that they navigated legislative and political spaces using diplomacy and seeking allies, there were several who found themselves in contentious relationships with other members of their legislative team, as former Treasurer Velda Jones-Potter found in her difficult and at times confrontational relationship with the mayor. Jones-Potter entered politics as a seasoned professional who had also served at the state level. Her understanding of politics and finances coupled with her transparency often put her office at odds with the mayor. Jones-Potter thought that the center of the tumultuous relationship was that the mayor felt the treasurer should report directly to him, whereas she understood the role as managing city finances in line with the law and the best interests of citizens. Consequently Jones-Potter felt she was alone in how she responded to the mayor.

> When he uses heavy-handed tactics with other people, they just roll over and do what he says. That's on them. But as for this office, I'm elected by the people of this city, I'm accountable to them, and frankly I have an obligation to bring forth the best ideas and you're entitled to do the same. And where counsel ultimately makes a decision, let's just allow them to do that.

Jones-Potter's strategy of following the dictates of her elected position and allowing legal counsel to advise ultimately paid off; The conflict about the role of the treasurer and managing city expenses was decided by a judge who agreed with Jones-Potter and her interpretation of her fiduciary authority.

Carroll Fife, a member of the Oakland, California, City Council gained national attention for her advocacy work on behalf of the homeless population in her community and state. With that national attention came $250,000 in campaign funds. It typically takes $100,000 to run for a council seat in Oakland, so Fife's haul was unprecedented. Once she joined the city council, Fife went to work to address policing and homelessness. She was successful in "re-imagining public safety" task-force recommendations about police responsibilities along with reallocating $18 million from the police department to other programs centered on crime prevention. When asked about how this type of major legislation faired with her colleagues, she said:

> My colleagues know that I'm the only person with a real base. No one has raised as much money as I have. No one has had the volunteer base that I have. I still have six hundred volunteers since I won. I have not stopped organizing. I just had a volunteer call last night after my live stream with ten of my core volunteers who door knock and phone bank every week. That hasn't stopped. We, I raised my council budget 'cause we have a budget allocation that we can raise to do our work.
>
> I want to work with my council colleagues, but I'm doing that on behalf of the people who asked me to run and who put me there, and that is what I'm fully committed to, and that's just not necessarily how people operate. They also know I can raise money. They know that, all of the council members know that, the mayor knows that, our state legislature knows that, and so that gives me a little bit of support and leverage when necessary, but it's something that I just have to stay aware of and keep organizing because the power is with the people.

Black women in legislative bodies have learned to be collaborative to have their agendas fulfilled. In hyper-partisan spaces as well as in environments that tend to be dismissive of such women, women use their well-honed skill sets and political savvy to win victories large and small. In so doing, they also seek to make the legislative body more deliberative and efficient—but they will go it alone if no one accepts the challenge to work together.

Making a Better Space to Legislate and Serve

Research has found that women tend to challenge institutional structures, norms, and expectations in their legislative work, particularly in Congress (Amer 2005; Dittmar, Sanbonmatsu, and Carroll

2018). Similar to Dittmar et al.'s (2018) research on women in the U.S. Congress, I find that Black women challenge the norms and institutional structures in how they conduct their legislative work. Many of the women I interviewed recognized that their duties in their respective legislative body was not only to produce legislation but also to improve structures to enable a more efficient legislative process and meet the needs of their constituents.

Her corporate workplace experience gave former Wilmington, Delaware, Treasurer Velda Jones-Potter an opportunity to implement processes to make the state and local government run more efficiently.

> I find there to be such great opportunity in government to bring practices that in the private sector are just commonplace, and yet in government aren't at all part of the processes. So the kinds of inefficiencies and the lack of use of metrics, and goal setting, and accountability for deliverables and results; those things that are second nature to me, and that I understand how they help value be created, and yet I don't see them in practice.

For Jones-Potter, enhancing the mechanisms by which government functions was a means to ensure that policy decisions would be more effective for citizens and would ensure that they received greater benefits with minimal waste of taxpayer resources.

Likewise Angie Jenkins, who serves as president of the Reynoldsburg, Ohio, City Council, noted that inefficient processes hindered both council members and citizens who desired to understand the decision-making process of the council and where their tax dollars were going. When Jenkins took up her role, she participated in the orientation process for new councilpersons. This included mock meetings that were structured to orient the incoming councilpersons to the flow of the meetings and to the local legislative process. Jenkins felt that the sessions were "hideous"; not only were they extremely long, they also did not allow for deep understanding of the processes that determined what was being spent and why. When asked why the city business was conducted in the manner that it was, she didn't receive any concrete answers. This was simply the way things were done. After two years in the position, Jenkins felt as if she was still learning the process and decided to be proactive. She began working with the clerk to assist with the meeting flow. This led to an adjustment of the agenda, which allowed more time to discuss pertinent information while minimizing conversations that could instead be moved to the council website and social media pages. Jenkins found that these tweaks began to help the meetings flow more smoothly and purposefully.

Valyncia Smith, a city councilperson in Conyers, Georgia, ran for office promising transparency to her constituents. As a self-described millennial, she was aware that many people did not read printed newspapers or watch local news, where much of the information about council business was found, instead many of her constituents found content online. Smith began to place the council agenda on her own social media platforms. She reported, "I ran on transparency and the need to increase correspondence and partnership about economic development and youth programs. I want the people to know what they should know." Not waiting for the city to increase information on its website, Smith took matters into her own hands. "Information is now archived on both of my social media pages, the agenda, the budget, or any kind of resources that are available to the community." The city has now followed suit, increasing the amount of information about council business it posts on its website.

In 2017, Jheanelle Wilkins was appointed to fill an open seat in the Maryland House of Delegates left vacant by a delegate who was elected to the state senate. She noted there was a learning curve, largely due to fact that when she entered the House of Delegates, it had been in session for two weeks. "The legislating is happening and I'm just dropped in there. And I think that what really helped was just utilizing some of the networking, organizing skills that I already had, one of those being building relationships." Wilkins went on to note that skills she acquired from her career and activism gave her the confidence to meet with legislators she admired to seek advice on how to be an effective legislator. Those inquiries early on in her legislative career not only allowed her to build relationships, but it also led to opportunities for increased leadership in committees and in critical conversations concerning legislation.

Other respondents also noted that they had questions or concerns about how business was conducted in their legislative bodies and that information was not readily available to them on how to be effective in their new roles. It's natural for any first-time elected official to have a learning curve, but for Black women in these spaces for the first time there can be other factors at work that make it hard to become familiar with what's expected and how things work. Said Valyncia Smith:

> Information was not only limited for the public but also to new councilpersons especially those who were not traditionally in leadership—Black women. There is no guideline—and I'm sure for good reason—on what an elected official does in this capacity. If it wasn't for the incumbent who retired giving me accessibility to him, to talk to him or call him if I'm confused about something or I don't understand something, or I have a question, I can only imagine the amount of numbers and phone calls I would have to make to other municipalities to figure it out. I'm sure people who have preceded me did not have these issues because they didn't look like me.

Smith's perspective speaks to the increased challenges Black women face once elected. However, these women continue to find ways to make the legislative space efficient and effective. Certainly Black women rely on their experiences as professionals to engage in the political sphere, but this does not minimize how they use their leadership to advance the needs of their communities. Community is indeed one of the primary factors that motivates political ambition, but it also commonly becomes a significant component of the policies that Black women champion.

Service to Community

As African Americans increased their share of elected positions nationally, research was initially concerned with whether these legislators were best suited to advocate for constituents of their shared racial background. With time, this literature expanded to encompass other minority groups, most notably Latinos (Swain 1995; Tate 2003; Casellas 2011; Minta 2011; Rouse 2013; Wilson 2013). The research has largely confirmed the expectation that descriptive representation by race has significant consequences. Moreover, that research has shown that politicians from underrepresented groups affect public attitudes and participation, both directly and indirectly (Bobo and Gilliam 1990; Gay 2001, 2002: Bowen and Clark 2014).

The intersecting power structures of Black women's race, gender, and age influence how Black Women experience and enact leadership and how others perceive them. In their leadership roles, these women seek to enact significant policies for those they represent. Indeed, studies increasingly show that officials who are women of color have a quite particular policy impact (Barrett 2001; Garcia Bedolla, Tate, and Wong 2005; Orey et al. 2007; Bratton, Haynie, and Reigngold 2007; Philpot and Walton 2007; Brown 2014). In particular, the presence of Black women as elected officials in itself increases and accelerates the representation of underrepresented groups, thereby enhancing the legitimacy of American democracy and fulfilling the aim of the radical imagination.

Though several of my interviewees represent districts in which African Americans are in the minority, they have succeeded in addressing far more than the needs of their African American constituents and constituents who have been marginalized due to their ethnicity or income/wealth status. Take, for example, Elvi Gray-Jackson, who currently serves as a state senator in Alaska, was in the Anchorage Assembly for nine years, and prior to that was a staffer in the Anchorage Assembly. The state of Alaska has a Black population of only 3 percent. But while serving as a staffer in the Anchorage Assembly, Gray-White felt it was critical that Anchorage, Alaska, not only acknowledge Martin Luther King Day but that it also be a paid holiday. During her career, she always took the day off unpaid. She recounts:

> For seventeen years every Martin Luther King Day, I'd take a leave day. And for about five years, the television station used to interview me every year to talk about why I felt it was important to take a leave day. And then they'd interview another employee who didn't think it was an important. . . . They did this for about five years, and one year, I was on an elevator with one of my assembly members and he said, "Oh, I saw you on the news last night talking about why you

take Martin Luther King's Day off. I was so impressed." And I said to myself, "Were you?" Aloud, I asked him, "Were you impressed enough to support making it a municipal holiday?" And he said, "Okay, yeah."

Gray-Jackson gathered six assembly members to sponsor the bill. Gray-Jackson did the research for the Memorandum of Intent, including finding out which cities in the state had a public holiday in honor of King. She reported that "in 1999, Martin Luther King Day became a holiday in the municipality of Anchorage because of my efforts, and I'm so proud of that." Although she was not an elected official when the holiday was enacted, she took the same passion about the King holiday to the Anchorage Assembly when she was elected to it. Her assembly district consisted of 34,000 people, including some Pacific Islanders and Asians, but it was primarily white. Within the school district, over a hundred different languages are spoken. While in the assembly, she worked until her colleagues formally recognized all cultural days and holidays of all the communities in Alaska, not only the white ones.

That Black women politicians like Gray-Jackson worked on behalf of minorities was a common pattern. Several of my respondents noted how strategic action was needed to provide substantive legislation for Black constituents. The women of the Reynoldsburg City Council—Meredith Lawson-Rowe, Angie Jenkins, and Shanette Jenkins—worked to pass the CROWN Act (Create a Respectful and Open World for Natural Hair), which prohibits discrimination based on hair style or texture and an antidiscrimination ordinance for the LGBTQ community. All three women noted that legislation that specifically addressed Black women was more likely to come from them—the implication being that if they didn't do it, no one else would. They were able to address all manner of concerns, from the discrimination that Black women faced on account of their hair to an antidiscrimination bill brought by one of their white female colleagues.

Teree Caldwell-Jackson of the Des Moines, Iowa, School Board noted that the diversity of the school board also reflected the diversity of the community. At the time, the board consisted of a majority of women who were African American, Latino, Asian, and white. The makeup of the board and community has influenced the issues the board has taken up and the policy interests of Caldwell-Jackson. She noted that the board was very proactive in developing actions that showed that the district fully supported DREAMers' and Latino students' access to public school education no matter the immigration status of their parents. Currently, the board is exploring what might improve the academic performance of African American boys and boys of color, as they are the lowest performing academic group. In discussing her approach to the issue, Caldwell- Jackson said, "If we can focus our attention on bringing up their proficiency and their scores, then everybody should rise. We felt we needed to utilize an equity lens. It is important to meet the needs of our lowest performing subgroups so that we can indeed meet the needs of all of our students."

For Raumesh Akbari in Tennessee, it has been more of a challenge to pass legislation that will specifically benefit her constituency given the super majority of Republicans in the legislature. Akbari told me that she has sponsored a significant amount of legislation that could directly affect Black Tennesseans, but that in almost every case that legislation had failed due to the legislative imbalance. However, she *was* able to pass legislation that improved access to healthcare for persons with sickle cell anemia, a blood disorder that disproportionately affects Black people. The bill called for TennCare, the state's Medicaid program, to review all forms of treatments and medications for sickle cell and to learn how TennCare could both fund treatments and fund public education campaigns about sickle cell disease. Akbari noted it was a major victory to be able to address the health disparities that Black people and poor Tennesseans face in relation to chronic diseases.

Dr. Gethsemane Moss serves as a trustee (board member) of the Benicia school district in California. Though there is little diversity, the district has made a concerted effort to meet the needs of African American parents. At the time of the interview, Moss told me she was working to formalize the Benicia African American Moms Group. The group informally came together in 2015 to have meetings with the superintendent and the different school site administrators to address issues and concerns that they had for their children, as well as to be more proactive to work with the administrators. The formal group, she said, will "be a full African-American parent network, so that way, it's there all the time, and then we know that issues will always be addressed." She also encouraged the school district to attend the California Association of African American Administrators and School Superintendent conference, which is a large, statewide conference.

Discussion

This chapter confirms another area of ambition theory that is not applicable to Black women, namely, the role careers play in candidate emergence. The scope of careers that Black women find themselves concentrated in are not within the narrow confines of business and legal professions. The fields that many of the women are situated in traditionally did not offer networks or resources that would facilitate a political career. But for Black women, they often bring with them skill sets and networks that allow them to navigate their career in a way that they are able to gain new skills and understanding about policy implementation while also utilizing an equity lens to recognize policy inequities. The testimonials in this chapter also support my argument that the networks Black women engage in benefit them with opportunities to expand their network with political elites and potential mentors.

The unique history and experiences of Black women inside and outside their communities have shaped their socialization and leadership development profoundly. This unique cultivation of being Black and a woman led the great Congresswoman Barbara Jordan to say:

> I believe that [B]lack women have a very special gift of leadership, because we have been called upon to lead in very trying times. And history has recorded the fact that [B]lack women rose to the forefront in times of struggle during periods of conflict about civil rights. But we don't have to go that far forward to recall that there was also leadership even in the days of slavery in this country. (Gill, 1997, p. 3).

Congresswoman Jordan observes that the leadership cultivation of Black women is unique and has been shaped by history and by the needs of the communities in which these women reside. As my theory ambition on the margin posits, the communities where these women live provide socialization and networks that help shape the worldview and political agency of Black women. The women I interviewed confirm Jordan's view and shared how Black women leading within both professional and political spaces affirms their commitment to communities and their ability to strategize to address issues that plague those communities. The skills that Black women bring forth led them to collaborate, be strategic, and make their legislative bodies more efficient.

5
What Do Black Women Need from Black Women Elected Officials?

> Our politics initially sprang from the shared belief that Black women are inherently valuable, that our liberation is a necessity not as an adjunct to somebody else's but because of our need as human persons for autonomy.
> —Combahee River Collective

Black women's continued high level of electoral participation has significantly affected election outcomes in recent elections. In 2017, after Republican Roy More was accused of multiple instances of sexual misconduct toward underaged girls, for the first time in 25 years Alabama elected a Democrat named Doug Jones to the Senate. This victory was largely attributed to Black women voters (Naylor 2017). Exit polls revealed that 96 percent of Black voters supported Jones, with 98 percent of Black women and 93 percent of Black men voting for him (Burlij 2017). Following the victory, the hashtags #ThankyouBlackwomen and #Blackwomen trended on social media, hailing Black women as the true winners of the election. Likewise, during the 2020–2021 election cycle, the state of Georgia was critical to the success of Democratic candidates. And Black women political organizers were deemed vital to Joe Biden's ability to win the state during the general election that sent him and Kamala Harris to the White House (Herndon 2020).

In a special election in January 2021, Georgia elected its first African American and Jewish senators, in so doing giving Democrats control of the U.S. Senate. Again hashtags followed lauding both Black women's participation in the electoral process despite the COVID-19 pandemic and their commitment to minimizing the effects of voter disenfranchisement efforts. While it is important to acknowledge the political engagement of Black women, the pronouncement that Black women "saved Democracy" only more deeply entrenches stereotypes that Black women do and should labor on behalf of others, as well as the idea that Black women are "an inexhaustible national resource, reliably saving our democracy in spite of the oppression we have, and continue to face, at its hands" (Brewton-Johnson 2021).

In Chapter 3, I explored the role of stereotypes and efforts to marginalize Black Women as political leaders. These same stereotypes shape public perceptions of Black people and Black women in particular (e.g., Stephan and Rosenfield 1982; Weitz and Gordon 1993; Niemann et al. 1998; Collins 2000; Harris-Perry 2011). The stereotypes also affect how Black women access and engage with public policies (Gilens 1996; Schram et al. 2009). Obviously if these long-standing tropes affect Black women voters, then they also affect Black women elected officials' efforts to legislate. Throughout this text I propose a framework to explore the candidate emergence of Black women. This chapter moves us a step further in the process of understanding why we see Black women as candidates and elected officials amplifying issues such as education, healthcare, and social justice.

To hear the voices of Black women as voters deepens our understanding of the community connections that support and elevate Black women to elected office. Ashley Daniels (2021) refers to this process as the "Black Women's Political Ethos" in which the ways Black women's unique feminism, political behavior, and the presence of Black political spaces contribute to how Black women make decisions about Black women candidates. Engaging with the ideas of Black women voters can shift perceptions of Black women as a hashtag while providing insight into the policy focus of many Black women elected officials.

Descriptive and Substantive Representation of Black Women by Black Women

The foundational text *The Concept of Representation* by Hannah Pitkin (1967) outlines three forms of representation: substantive, descriptive, and symbolic. Pitkin defines *substantive representation* as "acting in the interests of the represented in a manner responsive to them" (209). She defines *descriptive representation* as occurring when a legislator shares some descriptive characteristic with their constituents, while *symbolic representation* refers to what a legislator means to a particular group. Of these, Pitkin argues that substantive representation offers the greatest opportunity for quality representation because it requires the representative to take action, while the other forms of representation can exist in a static state in which citizens may see little to no policy solutions that affect change.

The presence of Black elected officials provides all three categories of Pitkin's typology for Black constituents. The research on African American congresspersons posits that they are more likely to introduce symbolic legislation that recognizes other African Americans (Tate 2003; Sinclair-Chapman 2002). In addition to being at the forefront of this type of symbolic work, African Americans are also more likely to introduce bills that explicitly or implicitly concern the interests of Black people, and they are more likely to address issues of racial equality than white Democrats, regardless of the percentages of African Americans in their districts (Baker and Cook 2005; Grose 2005; Orey 2000; Clark 2019).

Black women in the electorate not only influence election results but also contribute to an increasing descriptive and substantive representation of African Americans. Once in office, Black women champion the interests of Blacks and underrepresented populations, supporting progressive agendas more than their white female counterparts (Smooth 2006). We know that Black women legislators view themselves as having a unique role in legislative politics and that they often manifest this uniqueness in their campaign messaging (Hancock 2014; Brown and Gershon 2016; Smooth 2001).

This sense of a unique role often leads Black women to offer high levels of descriptive representation at a much greater rate than their male counterparts (Brown 2014; Frasure-Yokley 2018). Such descriptive and substantive representation contributes to the likelihood that Black women will support Black women candidates at high rates (Philpot and Walton 2007).

Data

In April 2017 I held a focus group with 15 college-aged women in Florida (Focus Group A), and in March of 2016 I met with 10 women who reside in the Washington, DC, Maryland, and Virginia area known as the DMV (Focus Group B). The participants in Focus Group A ranged in age from 18 to 20 years old. These women were classmates and had interacted with one another in class and outside it in social settings. The student's hometowns were in various municipalities including Chicago, Atlanta, Tallahassee, Miami, Dallas, Houston, Charleston, New York, and San Francisco. Their homes were located in differing types of neighborhoods including ere in predominantly white suburban neighborhoods, majority African American rural and urban communities, and in neighborhoods populated by several large immigrant communities. The participants in Focus Group B ranged from 38 to 55 years old. These professionals were book club members who had been meeting monthly for over five years. They discussed not only the assigned books, but, as a close circle of friends, they also discussed family, careers, and day-to-day life. These women mostly resided in suburban neighborhoods across the DMV area, though some lived in Washington, DC itself.

The conversations these two groups had with me offer insight across generational and geographical locations. All the women were registered voters, and Group A included several members who had voted in their first presidential election in 2016 while others were looking forward to voting in future elections. The idea of Black women in political leadership was not foreign to either group, as participants lived in areas where Black women in politics was common, either in their own communities or in the surrounding areas. They expressed a desire to see Black women lead effectively, and to them that meant engagement with the community and addressing issues of concern for Black women.

The participants were highly informed about various issues and challenges within their communities and campuses. They were keenly aware of issues that were often discussed among politicians and the public, such as abortion, guns, and LGBTQ rights, and how these issues were typically discussed among Black women. In discussing their perceptions of elected officials, they offered nuanced understandings and concerns not only about issues that officials faced but also about how Black women were empowered to enact change while also dealing with everyday discrimination. The college students were engaged with their campus communities, and they therefore mentioned not only experiences at home but also in their campus communities.

Black Women's Views

The focus groups began by me asking the women to describe how Black women are perceived in society. In both groups the women spoke of the challenges Black women faced. They described Black women as strong, beautiful, and bold, but due to stereotypes Black women were presented in the media and viewed very differently. In Focus Group A, Alexandria, a 20-year-old from Brooklyn, noted, "If Black women come off too powerful, we're viewed as, you know, the b-word. And then they say we are standoffish when we are just minding our business, but when we speak up we are aggressive." The group continued by discussing how white society often doesn't consider Black women to be physically beautiful and yet white women mimic or at least desire certain aspects of Black women's physique, such as full lips, as evidenced in the physical transformation of celebrities. These women did not see Black women or themselves as less than or victims.

As the women talked about the image and behavior of Black women, I was able to shift the conversation to how Black women think about social issues and politics. I asked the group how they viewed their own political perspectives and whether they would classify themselves as either conservative or liberal. I followed up by asking if their viewpoint was similar or dissimilar to Black women with whom they typically interacted. The women self-identified as liberal and said that at times they felt they were more liberal than other Black women, especially on social issues such as abortion and LGBTQ rights. The women in this group spoke about gaining an awareness of issues and feeling empowered to speak on them. These women held strong opinions about the nuanced thoughts and attitudes Black women hold and the fact that Black women can hold conservative opinions on some issues and liberal ones on others.

Chloe, a 20-year-old student from Houston, opened this segment of the conversation by stating that the role of the church influenced the attitudes of a lot of Black women, which dictated which issues they were more conservative about.

> Black women, because of our history of being in church, we can be conservative about how you are to behave and act in public, but a lot of Black women are more liberal when it comes to like different things like gun control. But when it comes to abortion, of course, they were more like conservative.

Jade, a 19-year-old from the Atlanta metro area, agreed and offered how liberal she saw herself. "In regard to abortion, gay marriage, things like I would say I'm different to what people assume Black women are. Because, most Black women are considered conservative on those issues and I personally am not conservative in those issues. I consider myself more liberal.... So, therefore, I don't think I meet the stereotype of Black woman's political views."

The conversation continued, and the women often invoked issues as examples of where Black women are conservative: abortion, guns, and gay rights. For Lydia, a 19-year-old from Chicago, she noted the gun culture of the South and attitudes that Black women and families she knew held.

> In terms of gun control, I find that a lot of Black women do not own guns. Since I've been in Florida, I would say that the South, like they are very big on guns and self-defense. So I see now that a lot of . . . a lot more Black families overall own guns. In terms of abortion, Black

women are anti-abortion, at least the ones that I know about. They're very religious, and they believe in Christ and they consider that to be a form of murder. So abortion is a no-no.

The group continued to comment on the social conservative aspect of Black women opinions, but they also clearly stated that they themselves were liberal on these issues. Dana, a 19-year-old from Charleston, joined the conversation by saying:

> I think a lot of times people assume that Black women are conservative in some ways, and ... because of the history of African American people, or Black people in general, just being known as very spiritual and also very heterosexual. I guess my views don't kind of fit into the societal norm of what a Black woman should sound or be like. I would say my viewpoints are very liberal-leaning radical in comparison to some Black women.

Kendra, a 20-year-old from Houston, said that she was sometimes conservative and sometimes liberal, depending on the issue.

> I can qualify myself as liberal when we're talking about housing or when it comes to welfare and basically aid from our federal government, but then you start talking same sex and things like that. I think a lot of my religion comes into play, so I tend to take more of a conservative stance on things. So I think for me, it does become a challenge to just say that I agree with each side because I just go by issue.

The group then began to more deeply analyze why Black women felt the way they did about some issues. The majority saw a generational divide. Kelly, an 18-year-old from Tallahassee, saw the nuanced opinions this way:

> I think it depends on what issue you're actually talking about. So if you're talking about an issue such as gay marriage, I feel like my views would be different than an older African American woman. So I think that we may have different views on that specific topic and maybe interracial relationships or something like that. So I think it

just depends on the actual topic we're discussing. I think some of us think different than some Black women who are older than us.

Following Kelly's comments the participants began to nod their heads in agreement and said they were clearly liberal on hot-button social issues but it was Black women over 35 that held more complex opinions.

Participants in Focus Group B confirmed the views of the college students in Focus Group A. When asked to discuss their ideology and the opinions of Black women, several of the women acknowledged that they held a conservative perspective on certain issues and that this was guided by their personal faith. Sharon, aged 48 from a Maryland suburb, opened the conversation by saying that her opinions were not guided so much by her racial or gender identity as by her faith. "My opinions in those regards should be based on my religious beliefs. So that's how I would vote on or not vote on it or converse about it as it relates to religion." Nicole, aged 40 and from the District of Columbia, commented that her opinions were also religiously motivated, and she used abortion as an example to substantiate this.

> My opinions are also religious based. So there was just a protest about abortion here a few days ago, and I think women should have their own say about it, but I feel it should only be done if the woman was raped or in danger of dying.

Lisa, a 47-year-old resident of Maryland, offered a different perspective.

> Yeah, I think the whole Roe versus Wade thing is still a big issue, and most of the men politicians speaking out, how many times have you had a baby? How many times have you been pregnant? The men speaking out, honestly. . . . I mean there are certain circumstances. . . . If a woman is raped, she don't want to have a baby. A lot of people [are] saying, "Hey, we shouldn't pay for these." For some of these people in these communities, they can't afford that. And you bring in a child into the world, that you can't afford to raise, what kind of quality of life [are] they going to have? And it's a lot of men politicians speaking out against it, saying [we] don't have money for Planned Parenthood, mostly conservatives. So that's the big issue.

Following Lisa's comments, the group shifted to actual policy and more liberal views that they held. Renee, a 42-year-old from a northern Virginia suburb, spoke about access to healthcare:

> I think people should have access to healthcare. I've been there and understand what it means to not be able to see a doctor because you don't have it [insurance]. And I would say most people in the African American community don't go to the doctor anyway. But now that I do have full healthcare, I go there every time.

The sentiment in the group was similar about access to healthcare. As the group continued to discuss the challenges regarding healthcare, they also spoke of personal experiences with receiving healthcare with and without insurance, as well as how a problematic healthcare structure affects Black women. The women spoke of health challenges that Black women face disproportionately, such as fibroids, and how limited access to affordable healthcare harms Black women daily.

The group of professionals who worked in various sectors, such as federal agencies and the private sector, and mothers who still had school-age children then began to discuss other policy issues, such as equal pay for equal work and public schools. The women saw themselves as more liberal on those issues. They told stories about themselves or other Black women being passed over for promotions and about there being an unspoken but widely known inequity in the salary scale in the office. They also expressed frustration with the quality of public schools within their communities.

The comments from both groups reveal both that the opinions of Black women are nuanced and that they are likely generational for certain issues. The women in Focus Group B are professionals who have had multitude of experiences and were not embarrassed to share their viewpoints and the personal reasons why they arrived at them. They also connected their personal opinions to broader public policy and the needs of others. The younger women were very clear about how they understood issues as well and the divides among Black women. Both groups offered insight into how Black women think and discuss policy issues among themselves and what shapes these ideas. Both groups presented a spectrum of ideas from conservative to liberal.

A Black woman running for office would not only need to speak to these issues, but she also would need to be skilled at addressing them in a way that accounts for the diverse ideas of Black women.

Views on Black Women Politicians

The conversation about the role of Black women as elected officials led to robust and intense conversation. Some women in Focus Group A felt quality representation was needed regardless of race, but that if the representative was a Black woman people would expect her to be particularly responsive to the needs of Black women. Twenty-year-old Makalya from Charlotte, North Carolina, noted that her off-campus job was in a low-income community and that she expected a Black woman would understand the needs of the kids with whom she works. Makayla said that though a Black woman elected official would likely try to "uplift" that community, Makayla would want the person to be fair to everyone she represented and not show favoritism to Black people. Nineteen-year-old Angela from Macon, Georgia, agreed with Makalya:

> In terms of politics and Black women in office, I agree with what previous students said: it all depends on what your goals are, what you plan to put in place. Because we've experienced women that don't have Black people at heart. Sometimes they are solely looking out for themselves. So I believe that it's up to us to hold them accountable, especially if during their campaign they promised or said they would pay attention to issues in the Black community or ethnic minority communities.

Kelly followed up by saying, "As far as knowing what she [the Black woman politician] is capable of doing, I expect her to completely fulfill all of her obligations, especially if she's using being a Black woman as a way to reach other Black people." Here, Kelly is noting not only how Black women's identity and experiences within the Black community influence how they campaign but also how likely Black women are to support Black women candidates (Philpot and Walton 2007; Daniels 2021).

The participants then gave personal examples of the limitations of Black women in leadership. Twenty-one-year-old Jasmine from San Francisco referenced the student government election on campus.

> I would obviously have high expectations for a Black woman]...I [would obviously] expect her to do what she said she was going to do. Our school actually had a Black vice president before. I have to take into consideration our school's politics, and taking that in consideration I know for a fact there's only so much she can do. Just her being a Black woman in our campus government... really means nothing, because our university has a very unique[ly] structured student government, which is surrounded by white sororities and fraternities.

Twenty-one-year-old Joi from St. Louis likewise commented about Black women and campus politics:

> We just had elections for student government, and I'm clear that I'm not going to vote for you just because you are Black, but I'm going to vote for you because you show me that you, one, have the experience, [and] two, show me that you can be a leader. I didn't vote in this election because I just didn't feel like the persons had enough experience or had enough leadership experience to carry the whole student body and do their job correctly. I guess I am holding the Black woman to a different standard... to our white classmates, she [might] be a token candidate, but for us we need her to be able to represent us.

The group continued to discuss how they wanted a Black woman to lead and what value there is in having Black women in leadership positions. Kendi, a 20-year-old from Dallas, said:

> I feel like as Black women, we have a deep perspective that literally no one else has. And to have that in a place of power, that can be really remarkable, granted that they identify as our community. And want to focus on certain things that we as Black women need.

The Focus Group B participants had an equally robust conversation about Black women in office. The DMV area that these women represent has a long history of Black women in leadership. At the time of the interview, both Washington, DC and Baltimore had Black female mayors. Although not considered a part of the DMV, Baltimore is close enough that many high-profile issues there gain coverage in the Washington, D.C. news outlets. At the time of the interview, Baltimore prosecutor Marilyn Mosby had recently brought charges against six police officers in the death of Freddie Gray. Not only did the case gain national attention, but it was also viewed as a local issue by the women in Focus Group B. They also expressed their expectations for substantive representation and acknowledged the limitations that can be placed on Black women. These limitations included a Black woman elected official not being able to make many public mistakes because if she did, she could possibly be characterized as inept by the media. This was a striking observation since several of the participants noted they often held Black women elected officials to a higher standard. Cynthia, a 48-year-old from a Maryland suburb, noted that Black women have been leading even when they weren't seen and that their presence and prompting made Black male leaders get things done.

This led to the group speak candidly about their experience with Black women leaders and the heightened expectations that they placed on them. Leslie, a 40-year-old who was a lifelong resident of Washington, DC, frankly stated:

> Yes, I vote for Black women, and we have always had Black women in politics in D.C. and now we have our second Black women mayor. But for the women there's an expectation that we don't necessarily expect that a white male or white female to understand what we go through in the Black community. They should, but we don't expect them to. But we do expect someone that looks like us to understand and be able to and address those issues.

Sharon added, "I expect her to understand. She should know our plight, our plight that we've gone through and done. And [she] should understand what our kids need, what our community needs in general and family. . . . You know, the men are the heads of the family but [we [women] run the show." Both Leslie and Sharon's comments speak to an idea that Black women are generally socialized very similarly and should behave with a racialized gendered consciousness. This is consistent with the scholarship that supports the idea that Black women have a unique consciousness that influences political behavior (Simien 2012; Simien and Clawson 2004; Daniels 2021).

At this point in the conversation the women began giving personal observations of local politics and how the D.C. mayor, Muriel Bowser, was perceived. Because of their proximity to Washington, all the women, even those who did not reside in DC, had an opinion. Nicole said:

> I guess I hold Black females that are in political positions to a higher standard. I'm like, "you should be doing more, you should be doing this." I don't know why. Maybe it's because I'm a Black woman, but I'm like, what are you doing? You could be doing more. I've been upset with Muriel Bowser a few times because sometimes she has been slow to respond to issues and she doesn't seem to anticipate the fall out when she does something.

Leslie followed up with a nuanced critique:

> Muriel Bowser does a good job with some things, like she opened up all these nicer homes this year because this is what she had . . . plan[ned] to do. OK, isn't this going to be nice? And she opened up across all the wards. I like that, but I'm just thinking: You['re] a Black woman and you['re] an elected official, [so] you['ve] got to be in the places where you['re] need[ed]. You can't just go where it look[s] good.

Erica, 45 years old, shared a similar sentiment to Focus Group A participants about showing up in communities. She said,

> We need Black women politicians, but we need them to be seen and in our communities. I don't always want to see my mayor or councilperson at a ribbon cutting, go to a school, community center, the places you went when you ran for office. I feel that way about all politicians, but I guess for Black women I think I feel it more. If you showed up when you ran, show up after [too].

I asked the group why they felt they held this double standard. Cynthia stated, "For Black women there is a feeling that they will be there for each other, and it shouldn't end because that Black woman [now] holds office. You need to be where you're needed. You should do what is needed."

Both groups felt that the community welcomed Black women as leaders, but they themselves did not offer them their blind support or their votes without a return. Their expectation was that Black women politicians should not only deliver on campaign promises, but it should also be within the communities that support them, tending to matters as they arise. The women also noted how the gendered racial identity of Black women candidates provides the candidate access to indigenous spaces such as churches and civic, cultural, and community events. By entering these spaces or reiterating their membership in these spaces, the candidate is signaling to Black voters an understanding of their needs. Therefore these voters (Focus Group B) expect their elected officials, particularly Black women, to understand and make a deliberate effort to enact policies that benefit the communities where Black women reside.

Issues on Which Black Women Should Focus

The final discussion in both groups focused on policies that respondents would like Black women politicians to address. In Focus Group A, Chloe spoke about local issues and that Black women politicians sometimes seemed to have a narrow focus:

> I feel like women in those positions, especially on the local level, only focus on education, and it's mostly about the schools and students that are already achieving at high levels and doing college prep. Where I live [Houston] there are a lot colleges, community colleges, and big universities. I feel like [the politicians] should equalize how much effort they put into . . . elementary school and public schools and emphasize success . . . whether or not someone plans to go to college.

Rather than have a particular policy in mind, Joi was more concerned about the approach a Black woman should take toward any policy:

> I just want them to take what they've experienced as a Black woman into whatever they choose to focus on. I just expect you to take what you've learned, not only by being Black but also [by] being a woman, take that into doing what you're going to do for the community. Take those experiences and say, "If I do it like this, it affects different things this way and maybe it will be better."

Adding to the gender analysis of the conversation, Alexandra raised the issue that in the Black community conversations and efforts focus primarily on Black men while Black women and girls are often ignored. She said, "I think as Black women we tend to focus on the plight of Black men. For a Black woman politician, I would want to see someone who would focus on everything for the race as a whole but also someone who would want to focus on the struggles Black women have every day." The comments by participants in Focus Group B confirms my premise that Black women's effectiveness is not just about the symbolic presence she may hold; her ability to offer substantive representation is largely tied to her having and maintaining a gendered racial socialization that centers the needs of the community.

Similar to their earlier responses, Focus Group B relied on their observations of what was happening in their communities and in local politics. Rene's primary concern was the quality of local schools:

> I really want a politician—especially locally, since that matters so much—to address why I live in a really nice neighborhood but my neighborhood schools are trash. All of the kids go to private schools, but in the white neighborhoods that are pretty much the same, people have similar jobs, the houses are the same size, . . . their kids have decent schools they can walk to. My coworkers always talk about what their kids do at school and all the extra stuff they get to do in school like chess club, taking a foreign language that isn't Spanish. It's not fair. I want a Black woman to say something about this because she has probably lived this.

Sharon addressed the value of someone who would take a different approach to issues:

> Right now everything is just bad. Crime has never gone down. Sometimes the violent stuff doesn't happen as much, but pretty much every day on the news the first fifteen minutes is about robbing and stealing. Police are crazy, so people are afraid to call if they need help. I don't think a Black woman can be a superhero. I'm more realistic than that. But I want her to bring a different idea to how to solve the problems Black people have been dealing with for too long.

These comments reveal that these Black women assume that most Black women should have a particular commitment to the needs of their (Black) community. This assumption harkens back to the socialization model I explored in Chapter 3.

Discussion

The data presented in this chapter reveal that for Black women voters the symbolism of a Black woman elected official is not sufficient for Black women constituents to feel they have received substantive representation. These women offered a concise expectation that a Black woman can provide quality substantive representation if she is committed to the needs and ideas of progress of the Black community. This sentiment brings back the ideas of Chapter 2 in which I offered the socialization model of Black elite political women that includes a consciousness and sense of community responsibility. This socialization model does not only apply to elite Black women. The focus group participants clearly expressed a strong sense of racial and gender consciousness. As stated earlier, elite Black women who navigate networks and leadership circles garner a particular social capital. This social capital brings about access to political and social gatekeepers while placing on elite Black women an expectation that they will engage in activities that will benefit the Black community. Clearly the women in both Group A and B have expectations of Black women who serve as elected officials.

Another factor that should be addressed is how these women understand their own lives and those within the Black community. Throughout the group meetings, the women spoke of challenges they and other Black women faced in accessing healthcare, a quality education, and equal pay, as well as a concern about crime. Despite the gains that the middle-class women in Focus Group B have made along with the potential middle-class life of the college students, there was still a strong awareness of challenges. The increased number of Black women earning advanced degrees have increased the overall number of Black advanced degree recipients. Black women are earning 71 percent of master's and 65 percent of doctoral and medical degrees earned by Black students in total (American Association of University Women 2022). Despite such gains, African American women across sectors, including professionals and managers, still earn less than white men and remain segregated in particular segments of the workforce that have few opportunities for advancement (Childers, Hegewisch, and Mefferd 2021). In short, despite their economic and educational advancements, the everyday life of Black women is still marred by discrimination and limitations. This recent survey data along with the concerns the focus group participants shared reflect research that has shown that African Americans can and do infer self-interests from group interest more generally (Dawson 1994; White and Laird 2020). Therefore, as long as group members are aware of disparities that affect group members, they will evaluate police, parties, and candidates with a strong sense of racial consciousness.

The participants also confirmed that although Black women are more likely to engage in politics that have a more liberal policy perspective on many issues, that perspective is not universal; the older women in the study were more likely to express more conservative ideas about social issues. I attribute this generational divide largely to socialization differences. Younger Black women have been exposed to a more diverse society at a younger age. Not only did many of them grow up in racially and ethnically diverse communities, but as a result of technology, they also had far greater access than previous generations to a range of ideas and issues prior to entering college where traditionally many young people first become exposed to persons outside of their communities. It is interesting to note that the younger women were conscious of the differences in opinions across generations, while members in Focus group B did not address a difference, voicing only how they felt. This is likely due to, for many of them, the fact that persons in leadership were closer to their age and that outside of family members their day-to-day interactions did not include younger Black women. The generational divide within the group has a significant impact on which Black woman candidate will be successful. These women presented nuanced ideas that require the same care and perspicacity from politicians speaking on these issues.

Overall, this chapter informs us the expectations Black women have of Black women elected officials. These expectations confirm the position of leadership and expectation of action that is placed upon Black women elected officials. While the groups did not present a monolithic approach to issue perspectives, what is clear is that Black women have a firm belief in the value of Black women leadership within their communities. As stated in the epitaph, there is a shared belief that Black women are inherently valuable.

6
Conclusion

> Freedom, by definition, is people realizing that they are their own leaders.
>
> —Diane Nash

Throughout the book I introduced each chapter with an epigraph by a Black women: Fannie Lou Hamer, Ella Baker, Rosa Parks, Dorothy I. Height, June Jordan, Angela Davis, the Combahee River Collective, and Diane Nash. For me and many others, these women embody the highest qualities of leadership and institution building. They were visionary risk takers whose activism confronted oppression, empowered Black women in particular and Black people in general, and lifted others that society had left behind. By their actions, these women sought to build a world that would bring everyone, not only Black people, a greater measure of freedom. Their words of wisdom give us insight into the radical imagination of Black women that is so central to the framework of my argument in this book.

In each chapter, you, the reader, have engaged with the voices of Black women from across the country. Through their words, these women who have served or are serving in public office gave us a candid portrait of the process of preparation for such offices, decision-making, and legislating. Their stories gave us insight into their doubts, hope, resolve, reflections, and determination. Central to their testimonies is a belief that their political journey is purposeful and beneficial to others. These women were introduced in different ways to the idea that political work and seeking public office is worthy work. For some, it was through their parents and grandparents. For others it was through a desire to bring about justice and joy, a desire that was often transmitted to them through the care and socialization they experienced in their homes and communities. For others, a combination of volunteer work and lessons learned in a college classroom sparked their sense of political purpose. Regardless of how their journey began, these women all reported that the value of their role as an elected official is bigger than themselves and that their leadership advanced their communities and society at large. That gave them tremendous satisfaction.

To understand how these women and other elite Black women decide to run for office, I offered my theory of *ambition on the margins*. With that framework, I argued that Black women make conscious decisions about when to enter politics and which office to seek—often with the encouragement and help of their friends and communities. They look for opportunities where they can make the most impact for their communities while navigating a marginalizing political structure that offers them limited resources or support in seeking political office. The main premise of the book has been that Black women have political ambition, but that this ambition cannot be defined in the traditional terms of the political science literature.

The political science literature, often confined by somewhat narrow boundaries, not only focuses on white men as the prototype of a political actor, but it has also developed paradigms of political behavior that either ignore or belittle the communities in which Black women are raised, live, and conduct political work. For those reasons, I have instead relied on the work of Black women political scientists whose scholarship understands and elevates the complexity of Black women's political engagement and the factors that contribute to their candidate emergence, scholars such as Alexander-Floyd, Brown, Jordan-Zachery, King, Locke, Prestage, Simien, Scott, and Smooth.

By eliciting and emphasizing the personal narratives of Black women, I have not only explored how Black women emerge as candidates, I have also, I hope, nudged my discipline to understand and to see the communities and institutions that nurture such women whose political engagement extends beyond voting. For these women have shown a profound commitment to American democratic ideals through their organizing, voting, and leadership; their commitment is no less and perhaps greater than that of the white candidates my discipline typically examines. These ideals and commitment were not only evident in the voices of Black women from the South or Black women who represented majority Black districts or municipalities. Many of these women serve(d) areas outside the South, such as Alaska, Iowa, California, Ohio, Pennsylvania, and New Hampshire, where they could not rely on a majority Black voting block to sweep them into office; they needed support from a multiracial voting block that included white voters and second- and third-generation immigrant communities.

Thanks to the voices of these women, readers better understand the status of Black women within their communities, the impact of their work, and how they experience and navigate a political world that still questions their viability as candidates and their acumen and wealth of knowledge as political actors.

An Ambition That Exists on the Margins

Throughout the text, I emphasized that the political participation of Black women is robust and that it can include running for office, not only voting or supporting. Black women historically have viewed political participation as a means to achieve full equality, and it is also for that reason that they have engaged in politics through activism, voting, mobilization, and seeking office.

Chapter 1 announced the book's theoretical framework of ambition on the margins. It became the roadmap for my argument that the political ambition of Black women is shaped by their collective socialization and the indigenous networks within the Black community. Those networks yield both opportunities for leadership development and access to the political network of the Black community. Together, those give candidates and leaders access to potential voters, volunteers, and donors. This ambition develops in spite of and because of the marginalization that Black women face in their day-to-day lives.

Chapter 2 explored the first step of candidate emergence: the socialization process of Black women by providing an overview of the inner world of Black communities that centered on indigenous institutions. Black women held their own understanding that their womanhood was distinctive and deserved the respect that was granted to white womanhood. This community is fostered and developed through the racialized and gendered socialization process and the network of community organizations and volunteer work that elevates the standing of Black women in their communities. Within those networks, Black women gain skills and support from similar women. But they also have opportunities to gain access to political gatekeepers within the Black community. Several of the interviewees stated they were recruited or encouraged to run by influential community members. Yet some women reported that despite these networks and this support, they still doubted their ability to run for office. Why? Some respondents knew very well that voters do not always welcome Black women political candidates or regard them as having the experience and skills necessary to run for office. In such instances, it was typically the community networks of other professionals, organization co-members, and community members who successfully encouraged these women to seek office and gave them the necessary support.

Chapter 3 moved further into the theoretical framework of ambition on the margins by exploring various facets of Black women's marginalization. It began with a brief case study of Vice President Kamala Harris and efforts to diminish her ability and ambition to become vice president. The questioning of Harris's "ambition" sheds light on the role that political elites and society expect of Black women—and how they often try to thwart their ambitions. By perpetuating age-old stereotypes, they show that they expect Black women to stay in their place, to be grateful for what they have, and, basically, to be subservient. In so doing, they willfully denigrate Black women's political acumen and aspirations. Focus group and interview data presented in this chapter showed that Black women are keenly aware of these pervasive stereotypes within political structures, and how they suffered from them personally. Yet these stereotypes not only temper their ability to acquire leadership positions within their party, to fundraise, and to develop fruitful collaborative relationships within legislative bodies, they also motivate them to draw on their own grit and the help of others to lead.

Chapter 4 explored how Black women learn to lead. One strand of political ambition literature has argued that career placement within the private sector offers opportunities for skill development and recruitment, therefore increasing women's political ambition. This strand of literature makes many assumptions. For example, it ignores the fact that many Black women's professional career mobility arises in careers outside of the legal and business professions. Due to limited opportunities in those fields, Black professionals often obtained career mobility and middle-class status from government and nonprofit sector careers. Thanks to their network of civic and community organizations, Black women were nonetheless professionally socialized. For by engaging in these organizations, they engaged in regular business meetings, fundraising, and learned other skills that they subsequently brought to the political realm. The women I interviewed told me how it was through their professional, social, and community organizations that they learned about how public policy development and decision-making processes often disproportionately affected the communities in which they resided. That insider knowledge spurred them to action.

Chapter 5 explored Black women's perceptions of public opinion topics and the substantive leadership that Black women candidates can provide. The two focus groups were clear that they wanted Black women's political leadership to be grounded distinctively within the particular needs of the Black community. Their feedback amplifies the literature about Black women having a stronger sense of racial group consciousness than they have of gender consciousness (Conover 1988; Gurin 1985; Simien and Clawson 2004). This contributes to the likelihood that Black women will vote for Black (women) candidates (Philpot and Walton 2007). However, the interviewees' feedback also suggested that their awareness of the discrimination and marginalization that they and perhaps particular political candidates face increased their expectations of Black women leaders.

In conclusion, though scholars like Smooth suggest that the positionality of Black women in society and in politics remains a "paradox," I have attempted to temper that paradox. I have done so by modulating the pervasive image of a political Black woman as a laborer who arrives on a ballot without a community, history, or ambition, and who should be quiet, ignored, or work on behalf of others. I say and have shown that Black women are strategic and deliberate actors, and I hope I have reshaped some readers' perceptions about Black women as political actors, have challenged some understandings of how and why Black women seek office, and have disputed and reimagined the often limited understanding of what Black women want from elected officials and public policy. By reporting firsthand experiences of Black women, especially Black women who have run for public office, I have advanced our understanding of candidate emergence, demonstrated how political socialization and community influence and engender ambition, and shown the extent to which those communities provide resources for Black women to run and to win public political office.

APPENDIX A

List of Interviewees

Aird, Lashrecse. Former Virginia State House Delegate
Akbari, Raumesh. Tennessee State Senate
Alexander, Joni. Pine Bluff, Arkansas, City Council Member
Alsobrook, Connie. Conyers, Georgia, City Council Member
Alston, Vernetta. North Carolina State House Representative
Anthony, Sarah. Michigan State House Representative
Bradford Coleman, Karyn. Former Chief of Staff Arkansas Democratic Party
Brailey, Carla. Former Vice Chair of the Texas Democratic Party
Caldwell-Johnson, Teree. Des Moines, Iowa, Public Schools School Board
Calloway, Sheila. Juvenile Court Judge, Davidson County, Nashville, Tennessee
Dawkins-Haigler, Dee. Former Georgia State House of Representative
Demessie, Menna, PhD. Former Vice President of Policy Analysis and Research, Leadership Institute at the Congressional Black Caucus Foundation, Washington, DC
DiLorenzo, Charlotte. New Hampshire State House Representative
Fife, Carroll. Oakland, California, City Councilmember
Flowers, Vivian. Arkansas State Representative
Gilmore, Brenda. Former Tennessee State Senator
Glaize, Lydia. Former Fairburn, Georgia, City Councilperson
Gray-Jackson, Elvi. Alaska State Senator
Jenkins, Angie. President of Reynoldsburg, Ohio, City Council
Jones, Tishaura. Mayor, St. Louis, Missouri
Jones-Potter, Velda. Former City Treasurer, Wilmington, Delaware
Lawson-Rowe, Meredith. Reynoldsburg, Ohio, City Councilperson
Mitchell, Tia. Washington Correspondent, *Atlanta Journal-Constitution*
Mosely Braun, Carol. Former United States Senator, Illinois
Moss, Dr. Gethsemane. Trustee, Benicia Unified School District School Board, California
Pratt, Sharon. Former Mayor, Washington, DC
Rascoe, Ayesha. Journalist and Host, National Public Radio (NPR), Washington, DC
Smith, Beverly E. 26th National President, Delta Sigma Theta Sorority, Incorporated
Strickland, Shanette. Reynoldsburg, Ohio, City Councilperson
Scott, Elsie, Member, Black Women's Roundtable
Smith, Valyncia. Conyers, Georgia, City Councilperson

Taylor, Ivy. Former Mayor, San Antonio, Texas
Washington, Sherri. Rockdale County Commission, Georgia
Whitaker, Nicole. Vice President, Upper Chichester Township Commission, Pennsylvania
Wilkins, Jheanelle. Maryland State Delegate
Williams-Cox, Dianne. Tallahassee, Florida, City Commission
Yancey, Tenisha. Michigan State Representative

APPENDIX B

Interview Questions

Politicians

1. What is your current profession?
2. Are you a member of civic and social organizations?
3. What motivated you to seek political office?
4. How many political offices have you held?
5. Were you asked to run for office? If so, by whom?
6. What role if any did organizations such as Black Greek Letter organizations, civic organizations, or religious institutions play in supporting your campaign/getting out the vote?
7. Did you gain skills in your work in organizations that assisted with your political campaign?
8. How did your career/profession impact your understanding of your role as a legislator?
9. What challenges do you face in providing leadership and voice for Black women on issues such as gun control, abortion, healthcare, etc.?
10. On what issues does your voice/opinion stray from the public opinion of Black women?
11. What are your perceptions of the barriers/challenges African American women face in having issues they faced addressed by yourself and other politicians?
12. How did/do you build collaborations with your colleagues?
13. What is your relationship with your political party leadership in your community and legislative body?
14. What issue(s) are important to you that you would like to address while in office?

Party Members

1. What is your party affiliation and role?
2. How do you engage with Black women running for office?
3. What are your observations on how your party recruits Black women to run for office?

4. Does your party have a pipeline process for Black women to acquire leadership roles within the party structure?

Media

1. What media outlet are you affiliated with?
2. Have you worked at other media outlets?
3. Have you observed stereotypes used in reporting on Black women?
4. Are there stereotypes that are frequently used in the coverage of Black women elected officials?
5. Are there strategies that Black women elected officials utilize to minimize impact of stereotypical coverage?

APPENDIX C

Focus Group Questions

1. Do you consider your opinions about issues such as gun control, abortion, healthcare, etc. liberal or conservative?
2. Is your perspective different from Black women you interact with?
3. What comes to your mind when you hear the phrase "Black Lives Matter?"
4. What are your perceptions of the barriers/challenges African American women face in having issues they faced addressed by politicians?
5. Do you have a different expectation of Black female elected officials than male officials or other women?
6. What important issue(s) would you like elected officials to address?
7. Are you involved in campus/civic organizations?
8. Do these organizations impact your campus life? If so, how?
9. Are you interested in running for elected office in the future?

Notes

Chapter 1

1. Karine Jean-Pierre served as Joe Biden's senior campaign advisor; Erin Wilson served as Biden's national political director, and Symone Sanders served as a senior advisor.
2. Then Senator Harris on the presidential campaign trail in Iowa in 2019. See Dittmar, Kelly and Glynda Car, "Kamala Harris' Kiability Was Not Electability," *Ms. Magazine*, https://msmagazine.com/2019/12/19/kamala-harris-liability-was-not-electability/.
3. See "Unfinished Business, Women Running in 2018," Center for American Women in Politics, https://womenrun.rutgers.edu/.
4. In Chapter 2, I address the value of organizations and institutions indigenous to the Black community that help cultivate the political socialization of Black women.
5. On October 22, 2018, former President Jimmy Carter used his official letterhead to send then-Republican nominee Brian Kemp a letter asking him to resign as Georgia's secretary of state.
6. See "Democracy Diminished: State and Local Threats to Voting to Post-Shelby County, *Alabama V. Holder* as of August 14, 2018," NAACP Legal Defense Fund, September 9, 2019.
7. In 2016, Black women were three of the 14 non-incumbent women elected to the U.S. House or Senate. Senator Kamala Harris (D-CA) became the second Black woman ever to serve in the U.S. Senate, Representative Lisa Blunt Rochester (D-DE) was the first woman elected to Congress from Delaware, and Representative Val Demings (D-FL) joined Florida's congressional delegation. Both Rochester and Demings won open seats in non-majority-minority districts.
8. Framingham voted in the spring of 2017 to become a city instead of maintaining a town government.
9. African American women candidates emerged in 1918 in New York after the state legislature approved women's suffrage. See Terborg-Penn 1998.

10. Professional organizations such as the National Association of Black Social Workers and the National Black Nurses Association formed in the late 1960s and early 1970s to not only meet the professional needs of members but also to promote professional practices that allowed for Black communities to receive better services.
11. See Reston 2019; Givhan 2019.
12. See https://www.nytimes.com/2019/08/10/us/taylor-dumpson.html.
13. See Codeswitch Podcast, NPR Trump's Anti-Social Media for a discussion of President Trump's hostile rhetoric toward African Americans. https://www.listennotes.com/podcasts/code-switch/president-trumps-anti-social-D1CZtUBhiqM/
14. See Rebecca Morin, "Black Female Leaders Criticize Pelosi, Schumer for 'failure to protect' Waters," *Politico*, July 7, 2018.
15. See both 2017 and 2018 Power of the Sister Vote Polls *Essence Magazine* and the Black Women's Roundtable.
16. Black women voted at the second-highest rate of any race/gender subgroup in 2016, despite dropping in turnout from 2012.
17. Representative Ayanna Pressley defeated the party incumbent in 2018; Representative Jahana Hayes did not receive her party's endorsement in 2018; Representative Lucy McBath did not receive support from the influential group EMILY's List; and in 2020 Cori Bush defeated the party incumbent.

Chapter 2

1. EMILY's List is the largest national resource for women and was created in 1985 by Ellen Malcom to fund campaigns for Democratic pro-choice women. The name is an acronym: "Early Money Is Like Yeast," it makes the dough rise. This acronym/saying is emblematic of the conventional wisdom that receiving campaign donations early is needed for successful political campaigns.
2. In line with standard practices in focus group research, the author stopped collecting data once she stopped hearing new information. See Morgan 1996. These geographic states were selected due to available funding opportunities at the time.
3. Interview questions and demographic summaries appear in appendices.
4. A legislative conference of Delta members that features speakers, including key policymakers, members of Congress, congressional staff members,

and policy experts. Sorority members meet with congresspersons from their respective states.
5. Jones was elected mayor in April 2021, becoming St. Louis' first African American woman mayor.
6. Pseudonyms are used to identify participants. The corresponding demographic information is accurate, and occupations, titles, etc. reflect respondents standing at the time of the interview unless otherwise noted.
7. Out of the nine organization that are BGLO, only two were founded at predominantly white universities: Alpha Phi Alpha Fraternity Inc. and Kappa Alpha Psi Fraternity Inc. The other seven were founded at an HBCU, Howard University.

Chapter 3

1. Recent incidents at American University, the White House Press Room, and commentary on Congresswoman Maxine Water's and ESPN personality Jamelle Hill's appearances demonstrate how Black women are commonly stigmatized to reinforce stereotypes and discredit the value of their voices and actions. See Sarah Larimer, "After bananas and nooses on campus, here's how a student body president copes," *Washington Post*, June 26, 2017; Olivia Beavers, "Reporter April Ryan on Spicer confrontation: I shook my head 'in disbelief,'" *The Hill*, March 29, 2017; Concha, "Joe O'Reilly mocks Dem Maxine Waters for wearing 'James Brown wig,'" March 28, 2017; Richard Deitsch, "ESPN suspends Jemele Hill two weeks for violating social media policy," *Sports Illustrated*, October 9, 2017.

Bibliography

Aberbach, Joel D., Robert D. Putnam, and Bert A. Rockman. *Bureaucrats and politicians in Western democracies.* Harvard University Press, 1981.

Abrams, Stacey. *Minority leader: How to lead from the outside and make real change.* Henry Holt, 2018.

Aldrich, John H. "Rational choice and turnout." *American Journal of Political Science* 37, no. 1 (1993): 246–278.

Alex-Assensoh, Yvette, and Karin Stanford. "Gender, participation, and the Black urban underclass." In *Women Transforming Politics: An Alternative Reader*, edited by Cohen, Cathy, Kathy Jones, and Joan C. Tronto, 398–411. New York University Press, 1997.

Alexander, Deborah, and Kristi Andersen. "Gender as a factor in the attribution of leadership traits." *Political Research Quarterly* 46, no. 3 (1993): 527–545.

Alexander-Floyd, Nikol G. "Disappearing acts: Reclaiming intersectionality in the social sciences in a post-Black feminist era." *Feminist Formations* 24, no. 1 (2012): 1–25.

Alexander-Floyd, Nikol. "Why political scientists don't study Black women, but historians and sociologists do: On intersectionality and the remapping of the study of Black political women." In *Black Women in Politics*, 3–17. Routledge, 2017.

Alvesson, Mats, and Yvonne Due Billing. *Understanding Gender and Organizations.* Sage, 1997.

Amer, Mildred L. "Black members of the United States Congress: 1870–2005." Library of Congress, Congressional Research Service, Washington, DC, 2005.

American Association for University Women. "Fast facts: Women of color in higher ed, 2022." https://www.aauw.org/resources/article/fast-facts-woc-higher-ed/.

Anderson, Carol. "Brian Kemp's lead in Georgia needs an asterisk." *The Atlantic*, November 12, 2018. https://www.theatlantic.com/ideas/archive/2018/11/georgia-governor-kemp-abrams/575095/.

Arnesen, Eric, ed. *Encyclopedia of US labor and working-class history.* Routledge, 2006.

Arnholz, Jack. "When Kamala Harris took on Brett Kavanaugh and Bill Barr." ABC News, August 12, 2020. https://abcnews.go.com/Politics/kamala-harris-brett-kavanaugh/story?id=72331829.

Austin, Sharon D. Wright. "The elections and governance of Black female mayors." In *Political Black girl magic: The elections and governance of Black female mayors*, edited by Sharon D. Wright Austin, ix. Temple University Press, 2022.

Avalanche. "Beliefs about gender in America drive perceived electability." 2019. https://www.avalancheinsights.com/beliefs-about-gender-in-america-drive-perceived-electability.

Avery, James M. "The sources and consequences of political mistrust among African Americans." *American Politics Research* 34, no. 5 (2006): 653–682.

Baker, Andy, and Corey Cook. "Representing Black interests and promoting Black culture: The importance of African American descriptive representation in the US House." *Du Bois Review: Social Science Research on Race* 2, no. 2 (2005): 227–246.

Barbara Lee Family Foundation. "Keys to the governor's office." 2001. https://www.barbaraleefoundation.org/research/keys-to-the-governors-office/.

Barker, Lucius Jefferson, Mack H. Jones, and Katherine Tate. *African Americans and the American political system*. Pearson College Division, 1999.

Barnes, Riché J. Daniel. *Raising the race: Black career women redefine marriage, motherhood, and community*. Rutgers University Press, 2015.

Barrett, Edith J. "The policy priorities of African American women in state legislatures." *Legislative Studies Quarterly* 20, no. 2 (1995): 223–247.

Barrett, Edith J. "Black women in state legislatures." In *The Impact of Women in Public Office*, edited by Susan J. Carroll, 185–204. Indiana University Press, 2001.

Baxter, Sandra, and Marjorie Lansing. *Women and politics: The invisible majority*. University of Michigan Press, 1980.

Baxter, Sandra, and Marjorie Lansing. *Women and politics: The visible majority*. University of Michigan Press, 1983.

Beal, Frances M. "Double jeopardy: To be Black and female." In *The Black woman: An anthology*, edited by Toni Cade Bambara, 98–120. New American Library, Inc., 1970.

Beauboeuf-Lafontant, Tamara. *Behind the mask of the strong Black woman: Voice and the embodiment of a costly performance*. Temple University Press, 2009.

de Beauvoir, Simone, de. *The second sex*. Translated by Constance Borde and Sheila Malovany Chevallier. Vintage. 2001.

Bejarano, Christina E. *The Latina advantage: Gender, race, and political success*. University of Texas Press, 2013.

Bejarano, Christina, Nadia E. Brown, Sarah Allen Gershon, and Celeste Montoya. "Shared identities: Intersectionality, linked fate, and perceptions of political candidates." *Political Research Quarterly* 74, no. 4 (2020): 1065912920951640.

Bell, Ella L. J., and Stella M. Nkomo. *Our separate ways: Black and white women and the struggle for professional identity*. Harvard Business Press, 2003.

Bernhard, Rachel, Mirya Holman, Shauna Shames, and Dawn Langan Teele. "Beyond ambition." *Politics, Groups, and Identities* 7, no. 4 (2019): 815–816.

Berry, Daina Ramey, and Kali Nicole Gross. *A Black women's history of the United States*. Vol. 5. Beacon Press, 2020.

Berry, Jeffrey M., Kent E. Portney, and Ken Thomson. "The rebirth of urban democracy." Brookings Institution, Washington DC, 1993.

Bidar, Musadiq, and Dan Patterson. "Twitter slow to remove tweets targeting Vice President Harris, report finds." *CBS News*, June 9, 2022. https://www.cbsnews.com/news/twitter-slow-to-remove-racist-sexist-tweets-targeting-vice-president-kamala-harris-report-finds/.

Black, Gordon S. "A theory of political ambition: Career choices and the role of structural incentives." *American Political Science Review* 66, no. 1 (1972): 144–159.

Blain, Keisha N. *Set the world on fire: Black nationalist women and the global struggle for freedom*. University of Pennsylvania Press, 2018.

Bobo, Lawrence, and Franklin D. Gilliam. "Race, sociopolitical participation, and Black empowerment." *American Political Science Review* 84, no. 2 (1990): 377–393.

Bowen, Daniel C., and Christopher J. Clark. "Revisiting descriptive representation in Congress: Assessing the effect of race on the constituent–legislator relationship." *Political Research Quarterly* 67, no. 3 (2014): 695–707.

Brady, Henry E., Sidney Verba, and Kay Lehman Schlozman. "Beyond SES: A resource model of political participation." *American Political Science Review* 89, no. 2 (1995): 271–294.

Bratton, Kathleen A., Kerry L. Haynie, and Beth Reingold. "Agenda setting and African American women in state legislatures." *Journal of Women, Politics & Policy* 28, nos. 3–4 (2007): 71–96.

Brazile, Donna. *Cooking with grease: Stirring the pots in American politics*. Simon and Schuster, 2004.

Brazile, Donna, Yolanda Caraway, Leah Daughtry, Minyon Moore, and Veronica Chambers. *For colored girls who have considered politics*. St. Martin's Press, 2018.

Brewton-Johnson, Morgan. "Once again, Black women are heroes. It's time to pay up." WBUR, February 8, 2021. https://www.wbur.org/cognoscenti/2021/02/08/black-women-stacey-abrams-kamala-harris-morgan-brewton-johnson.

Brooks, Deborah Jordan. *He runs, she runs*. Princeton University Press, 2013.

Brown, Elsa Barkley. "Negotiating and transforming the public sphere: African American political life in the transition from slavery to freedom." *Public Culture*, no. 7 (1994): 107–146.

Brown, Nadia E. *Sisters in the statehouse: Black women and legislative decision making*. Oxford University Press, 2014.

Brown, Nadia, and Pearl K. Ford Dowe. "Late to the party: Black women's inconsistent support from political parties." In *Good reasons to run: Women and political candidacy*, edited by Shauna L. Shames, Rachel I. Bernhard, Mirya R. Holman, and Dawn Langan Teele, 153–166. Temple University Press, 2020.

Brown, Nadia E., and Sarah Allen Gershon. *Distinct identities: Minority women in US politics*. Routledge, 2016.

Brown, Nadia E., and Danielle C. Lemi. "'Life for me ain't been no crystal stair': Black women candidates and the democratic party." *Boston University Law Review* 100 (2020): 1613.

Brown, Nadia E., and Danielle Casarez Lemi. *Sister style: The politics of appearance for Black women political elites*. Oxford University Press, 2021.

Bryner, Sarah, and Grace Haley. "Race, gender, and money in politics: Campaign finance and federal candidates in the 2018 midterms." Peter G. Peterson Foundation, March 15, 2019. https://www.pgpf.org/us-2050/research-projects/Race-Gender-and-Money-in-Politics-Campaign-Finance-and-Federal-Candidates-in-the-2018-Midterms.

Burlij, Terence. "The 7 most revealing findings in the Alabama exit polls." CNN, December 13, 2017. https://www.cnn.com/2017/12/13/politics/revealing-alabama-exit-polls/index.html.

Burns, Nancy, Kay Lehman Schlozman, and Sidney Verba. *The private roots of public action*. Harvard University Press, 2001.

Burrell Barbara, C. *A woman's place is in the House: Campaigning for Congress in the feminist era*. University of Michigan Press, 1994.

Calhoun-Brown, Allison. "African American churches and political mobilization: The psychological impact of organizational resources." *The Journal of Politics* 58, no. 4 (1996): 935–953.

Caputo, Angela, Geoff Hing, and Johnny Kauffman. "How a massive voter purge in Georgia affected the 2018 election." APM Reports, June 22, 2020. https://www.apmreports.org/story/2019/10/29/georgia-voting-registration-records-removed.

Carew, Jessica Denyse Johnson. "'Lifting as we climb?': The role of stereotypes in the evaluation of political candidates at the intersection of race and gender." PhD diss., Duke University, 2012.

Carroll, Susan J. *Women as candidates in American politics*. Indiana University Press, 1994.

Carroll, Susan J. "The disempowerment of the gender gap: Soccer moms and the 1996 elections." *PS: Political Science & Politics* 32, no. 1 (1999): 7–12.

Carroll, Susan J., and Kira Sanbonmatsu. *More women can run: Gender and pathways to the state legislatures*. Oxford University Press, 2013.

Casellas, Jason. "Latinas in legislatures: The conditions and strategies of political incorporation." *Aztlán: A Journal of Chicano Studies* 36, no. 1 (2011): 171–189.

Cathey, Libbey. "Trump mocks Harris' name, says having her as president would be 'insult' to country." ABC News, September 9, 2020.

Childers, Chandra, Ariane Hegewisch, and Eve Meffered. "Shortchanged and underpaid: Black women and the pay gap." Institute for Women's Policy Research, July 27, 2021. https://iwpr.org/iwpr-publications/fact-sheet/short changed-and-underpaid-black-women-and-the-pay-gap/.

Chisholm, Shirley. *The good fight.* Harper & Row, 1973.

Chozick, Amy, and Ashley Parker. "Donald Trump's gender-based attacks on Hillary Clinton have calculated risk." *New York Times*, 2016.

Clark, Christopher J. *Gaining voice: The causes and consequences of Black representation in the American states.* Oxford University Press, 2019.

Coffin, David, and Amanda Lawrence. "Demographic diversity in U.S. automotive manufacturing." Executive Briefing on Trade. U.S. International Trade Commission, September 2020.

Cohen, Cathy J. "What is this movement doing to my politics?" *Social Text* 61 (1999): 111–118.

Cohen, Cathy J., and Susan J. Carroll. "A portrait of continuing marginality: The study of women of color in American politics." *Women and American Politics: New Questions, New Directions* (2003): 190–213.

Cole, Elizabeth R., and Abigail J. Stewart. "Meanings of political participation among Black and white women: Political identity and social responsibility." *Journal of Personality and Social Psychology* 71, no. 1 (1996): 130.

Collins, Patricia Hill. "Black feminist thought in the matrix of domination." *Black Feminist Thought: Knowledge, Consciousness, and the Politics of Empowerment* 138 (1990): 221–238.

Collins, Patricia Hill. *Black feminist thought: Knowledge, consciousness, and the politics of empowerment.* Routledge, 2000.

Collins, Patricia Hill, and Sirma Bilge. *Intersectionality.* John Wiley & Sons, 2020.

Conover, Pamela Johnston. "The role of social groups in political thinking." *British Journal of Political Science* 18, no. 1 (1988): 51–76.

Conrad, Cecilia. "Black women: The unfinished agenda." *The American Prospect* 19, no. 10 (2008): A12–A15.

Cooper, Brittney C. *Beyond respectability: The intellectual thought of race women.* University of Illinois Press, 2017.

Crenshaw, Kimberle. "Demarginalizing the intersection of race and sex: A Black feminist critique of antidiscrimination doctrine, feminist theory and antiracist politics." *University of Chicago Legal Forum* (1989): 139–167.

Crenshaw, Kimberle. "Mapping the margins: Intersectionality, identity politics, and violence against women of color." *Stanford Law Review* 43 (1990): 1241.

Crenshaw, Kimberle. "Demarginalizing the intersection of race and sex: A Black feminist critique of antidiscrimination doctrine, feminist theory and antiracist politics." In *Feminist legal theories*, 23–51. Routledge, 2013.

Crowder-Meyer, Melody. "Gendered recruitment without trying: How local party recruiters affect women's representation." *Politics & Gender* 9, no. 4 (2013): 390–413.

Dahl, Robert A. "The city in the future of democracy." *American Political Science Review* 61, no. 4 (1967): 953–970.

Daniels, Ashley. "Unlocking the power of the sister(hood) vote: Exploring the opinions and motivations of NPHC sorority Black women supporting Black women candidates." PhD diss., 2021.

Darcy, Robert, and Charles D Hadley. "Black women in politics: The puzzle of success." *Social Science Quarterly* 69, no. 3 (1988): 629.

Darcy, Robert, Susan Welch, and Janet Clark. *Women, elections, and representation*. 2nd ed. University of Nebraska Press, 1994.

Davis, Kathy. "Intersectionality as buzzword: A sociology of science perspective on what makes a feminist theory successful." *Feminist Theory* 9, no. 1 (2008): 67–85.

Dawson, Michael C. *Behind the mule*. Princeton University Press, 1994.

Dawson, Michael C. *Black visions: The roots of contemporary African-American political ideologies*. University of Chicago Press, 2003.

Demo, David H., and Michael Hughes. "Socialization and racial identity among Black Americans." *Social Psychology Quarterly* (1990): 364–374.

Deveaux, Monique. "Feminism and empowerment: A critical reading of Foucault." *Feminist Studies* 20, no. 2 (1994): 223–247.

Dittmar, Kelly. "Voices. Votes. Leadership. The status of Black women in American politics." Center for American Women and Politics, 2015. http://cawp.rutgers.edu/sites/default/files/resources/hh2015.pdf.

Dittmar, Kelly. "Unfinished business: Women running in 2018 and beyond." Center for American Women and Politics, 2019.

Dittmar, Kelly. "Urgency and ambition: The influence of political environment and emotion in spurring US women's candidacies in 2018." *European Journal of Politics and Gender* 3, no. 1 (2020): 143–160.

Dittmar, Kelly. "Reaching higher: Black women in American politics." Center for American Women in Politics, 2021.

Dittmar, Kelly, Glynda Carr, Maura Reilly, and Lisa Rabasca Roepe. "Kamala Harris' liability was not electability." *Ms. Magazine*, December 19, 2019. https://msmagazine.com/2019/12/19/kamala-harris-liability-was-not-electability/.

Dittmar, Kelly, Kira Sanbonmatsu, and Susan J. Carroll. *A seat at the table: Congresswomen's perspectives on why their presence matters*. Oxford University Press, 2018.

Dovi, Suzanne. "Theorizing women's representation in the United States." *Politics & Gender* 3, no. 3 (2007): 297–319.

Dowe, Pearl K. "Sister strength, Black women as candidates." Presentation at American Political Science Association Annual Meeting, 2018.

Dowe, Pearl K. Ford. "Resisting marginalization: Black women's political ambition and agency." *PS: Political Science & Politics* 53, no. 4 (2020): 697–702.

Dowe, Pearl K. "Kamala Harris and the stereotypes we place on Black women." *The Hill*, October 13, 2020. https://thehill.com/opinion/campaign/520884-kamala-harris-and-the-stereotypes-we-place-on-black-women/.

Drake, Saint C., and Horace R. Cayton. *Black metropolis: A study of Negro life in a northern city*. Vol. 1. University of Chicago Press, 1970.

Duerst-Lahti, Georgia, and Cathy Marie Johnson. "Gender and style in bureaucracy." *Women & Politics* 10, no. 4 (1991): 67–120.

DuMonthier, Asha, Chandra E. Childers, and Jessica Milli. "The status of Black women in the United States." Institute for Women's Policy Research, 2017.

Eagly, Alice H., and Steven J. Karau. "Role congruity theory of prejudice toward female leaders." *Psychological Review* 109, no. 3 (2002): 573.

Ebbert, Stephanie. "Women's groups band together to defend Kamala Harris." *Boston Globe*, October 9, 2020. https://www.bostonglobe.com/2020/10/09/metro/womens-groups-band-together-defend-kamala-harris/.

Elder, Laurel. "Why women don't run: Explaining women's underrepresentation in America's political institutions." *Women & Politics* 26, no. 2 (2004): 27–56.

Eligon, John, and Audra Burch. "Black voters helped deliver Biden a presidential victory. Now what?" *New York Times*, November 11, 2020. https://www.nytimes.com/2020/11/11/us/joe-biden-black-voters.html.

Enloe, Cynthia. "Wielding masculinity inside Abu Ghraib: Making feminist sense of an American military scandal." *Asian Journal of Women's Studies* 10, no. 3 (2004): 89–102.

Farris, Emily M., and Mirya R. Holman. "Social capital and solving the puzzle of Black women's political participation." *Politics, Groups, and Identities* 2, no. 3 (2014): 331–349.

Fenno, Richard F., Jr. *Homestyle: Members of Congress in their constituencies*. Little Brown and Company, 1978.

Flammang, Janet A. *Women's political voice: How women are transforming the practice and study of politics*. Temple University Press, 1997.

Fordham, Signithia, and John U. Ogbu. "Black students' school success: Coping with the 'burden of 'acting white.'" *The Urban Review* 18, no. 3 (1986): 176–206.

Fowlkes, Diane L., Jerry Perkins, and Sue Tolleson Rinehart. "Gender roles and party roles." *American Political Science Review* 73, no. 3 (1979): 772–780.

Fox, Richard L., and Jennifer L. Lawless. "If only they'd ask: Gender, recruitment, and political ambition." *The Journal of Politics* 72, no. 2 (2010): 310–326.

Fox, Richard L. "Congressional elections: Where are we on the road to gender parity?" In *Gender and elections: Shaping the future of American politics*, edited by Susan J. Carroll, and Richard L. Fox. Cambridge University Press, 2005.

Fraga, Luis Ricardo, Valerie Martinez-Ebers, Linda Lopez, and Ricardo Ramirez. "Strategic intersectionality: Gender, ethnicity and political incorporation." Presented at the Annual Meeting of the American Political Science Association, Washington DC, August 31–September 4, 2005.

Franklin, V. P., and Bettye Collier-Thomas. "For the race in general and Black women in particular." In *Sisters in the struggle: African American Women in the Civil Rights-Black Power Movement*, edited by Betty Collier-Thomas and V. P. Franklin, 21–41. New York University Press, 2001.

Frasure-Yokley, Lorrie. "Choosing the velvet glove: Women voters, ambivalent sexism, and vote choice in 2016." *Journal of Race, Ethnicity, and Politics* 3, no. 1 (2018): 3–25.

Frederick, Angela. "Bringing narrative in: Race-gender storytelling, political ambition, and women's paths to public office." *Journal of Women, Politics & Policy* 34, no. 2 (2013): 113–137.

Freeman, Jo. *A room at a time: How women entered party politics*. Rowman & Littlefield, 2000.

Frymer, Paul. *Uneasy alliances*. Princeton University Press, 1999.

Frymer, Paul. "Race, parties, and democratic inclusion." In *The Politics of Democratic Inclusion*, edited by Wolbrecht and Rodney E. Hero, 122–142. Temple University Press, 2005.

Frymer, Paul. *Uneasy alliances: Race and party competition in America*. Vol. 114. Princeton University Press, 2010.

Gaines, Kevin K. *Uplifting the race: Black leadership, politics, and culture in the twentieth century*. UNC Press Books, 1996.

Galloway, Jim. "Stacey Abrams: 'I will not concede because the erosion of our democracy is not right.'" *The Atlanta Journal-Constitution*, November 16, 2018. https://www.ajc.com/blog/politics/stacey-abrams-will-not-concede-because-the-erosion-our-democracy-not-right/JQqttbuF09NYkMQbIYx9BM/.

Gamble, Katrina. "Young, gifted Black and female: Why aren't there more Yvette Clarkes in Congress? In *Whose Black politics?: Cases in post-racial Black leadership*, edited by Andra Gillespie, 293–208. Routledge, 2010.

Garcia Bedolla, Lisa, Katherine Tate, and Janelle Wong. "Indelible effects: The impact of women of color in the US Congress." *Women and Elective Office: Past, Present, and Future* 2 (2005): 152–175.

Gaskins, Keesha, and Sundeep Iyer. "The challenge of obtaining voter identification." Brennan Center for Justice at New York University School of Law, 2012.

Gay, Claudine. "The effect of Black congressional representation on political participation." *American Political Science Review* (2001): 589–602.

Gay, Claudine. "Spirals of trust? The effect of descriptive representation on the relationship between citizens and their government." *American Journal of Political Science* 95, no. 3 (2002): 717-732.

Gay, Claudine, and Katherine Tate. "Doubly bound: The impact of gender and race on the politics of Black women." *Political Psychology* 19, no. 1 (1998): 169-184.

Giddings, Paula. *When and where I enter: The impact of Black women on race and sex in America.* William Fowlkes Morrow, 1984.

Giddings, Paula. *In search of sisterhood: Delta Sigma Theta and the challenge of the Black sorority movement.* William Morrow, 1988.

Gilens, Martin. "Race and poverty in America: Public misperceptions and the American news media." *Public Opinion Quarterly* 60, no. 4 (1996): 515-541.

Gilkes, Cheryl Townsend. "Successful rebellious professionals: The Black woman's professional identity and community commitment." *Psychology of Women Quarterly* 6, no. 3 (1982): 289-311.

Gilkes, Cheryl Townsend. "Building in many places: Multiple commitments and ideologies in Black women's community work." In *Women and the Politics of Empowerment*, edited by Ann Bookman and Sandra Morgen, 53-76. Temple University Press, 1988.

Gilkes, Cheryl Townsend. *" If it wasn't for the women . . .": Black women's experience and womanist culture in church and community.* Orbis Books, 2001.

Gill, LaVerne, McCaine. *African American women in Congress: Forming and transforming history.* Rutgers University Press. 1997.

Gillespie, Andra, and Nadia E. Brown. "#BlackGirlMagic Demystified." *Phylon* 56, no. 2 (2019): 37-58.

Givhan, Robin. "Kamala Harris grew up in a mostly white world, then she went to a Black university in a Black city." *Washington Post*, September 16, 2019. https://www.washingtonpost.com/politics/2019/09/16/kamala-harris-grew-up-mostly-white-world-then-she-went-black-university-black-city/.

Graham, Renee. "Biden must choose a Black woman for vice president." *The Boston Globe*, July 29, 2020. https://www.bostonglobe.com/2020/07/28/opinion/biden-must-choose-black-woman-vice-president/.

Grose, Christian R. "Disentangling constituency and legislator effects in legislative representation: Black legislators or Black districts?" *Social Science Quarterly* 86, no. 2 (2005): 427-443.

Gurin, Patricia. "Women's gender consciousness." *Public Opinion Quarterly* 49, no. 2 (1985): 143-163.

Guy-Sheftall, Beverly. *Words of fire: An anthology of African-American feminist thought.* New Press, 1995.

Hancock, Ange-Marie. "Intersectionality as a normative and empirical paradigm." *Politics & Gender* 3, no. 2 (2007): 248-254.

Hancock, Ange-Marie. "Bridging the feminist generation gap: Intersectional considerations." *Politics & Gender* 10, no. 2 (2014): 292-296.

Hardy-Fanta, Carol, Pei-te Lien, Dianne M. Pinderhughes, and Christine Marie Sierra. "Gender, race, and descriptive representation in the United States: Findings from the gender and multicultural leadership project." *Journal of Women, Politics & Policy* 28, no. 3-4 (2007): 7-41.

Hardy-Fanta, Carol, Dianne Pinderhughes, and Christine Marie Sierra. *Contested transformation.* Cambridge University Press, 2016.

Harris, Fredrick C., Valeria Sinclair-Chapman, and Brian D. McKenzie. *Countervailing forces in African-American civic activism, 1973-1994.* Cambridge University Press, 2005.

Harris-Lacewell, Melissa Victoria. *Barbershops, Bibles, and BET: Everyday talk and Black political thought.* Princeton University Press, 2004.

Harris-Perry, Melissa V. *Sister citizen: Shame, stereotypes, and Black women in America.* Yale University Press, 2011.

Hayes, Danny, and Jennifer L. Lawless. "A non-gendered lens? Media, voters, and female candidates in contemporary congressional elections." *Perspectives on Politics* 13, no. 1 (2015): 95-118.

Hayes, Danny, and Jennifer L. Lawless. *Women on the run: Gender, media, and political campaigns in a polarized era.* Cambridge University Press, 2016.

Heilman, Madeline E., and Melanie H. Stopeck. "Being attractive, advantage or disadvantage? Performance-based evaluations and recommended personnel actions as a function of appearance, sex, and job type." *Organizational Behavior and Human Decision Processes* 35, no. 2 (1985): 202-215.

Herndon, Astead W. "Georgia was a big win for Democrats. Black women did the groundwork." *New York Times,* December 3, 2020. https://www.nytimes.com/2020/12/03/us/politics/georgia-democrats-black-women.html.

Herrick, Rebekah, and Michael K. Moore. "Political ambition's effect on legislative behavior: Schlesinger's typology reconsidered and revisited." *The Journal of Politics* 55, no. 3 (1993): 765-776.

Higginbotham, Elizabeth. *Too much to ask: Black women in the era of integration.* University of North Carolina Press, 2001.

Higginbotham, Elizabeth, and Lynn Weber. "Moving up with kin and community: Upward social mobility for Black and white women." *Gender & Society* 6, no. 3 (1992): 416-440.

Higginbotham, Evelyn Brooks. *Righteous discontent: The women's movement in the Black Baptist Church, 1880-1920.* Harvard University Press, 1994.

Hill, Mark E. "Color differences in the socioeconomic status of African American men: Results of a longitudinal study." *Social Forces* 78, no. 4 (2000): 1437-1460.

Hine, Darlene C. "We specialize in the wholly impossible: The philanthropic work of Black women." In *Lady bountiful revisited: Women, philanthropy, and power,* edited by Kathleen McCarthy, 70-93. Rutgers University Press, 1990.

Hine, Darlene Clark. *Hine sight: Black women and the re-construction of American history.* Indiana University Press, 1997.

Hine, Darlene Clark, and Kathleen Thompson. *A shining thread of hope: The history of Black women in America*. Broadway Books, 1999.

Hobson, Janell. "The "batty" politic: Toward an aesthetic of the Black female body." *Hypatia* 18, no. 4 (2003): 87–105.

Holman, Mirya R., Jennifer L. Merolla, and Elizabeth J. Zechmeister. "Sex, stereotypes, and security: A study of the effects of terrorist threat on assessments of female leadership." *Journal of Women, Politics & Policy* 32, no. 3 (2011): 173–192.

Holman, Mirya R., and Monica C. Schneider. "Gender, race, and political ambition: How intersectionality and frames influence interest in political office." *Politics, Groups, and Identities* 6, no. 2 (2018): 264–280.

hooks, bell. *Ain't I a woman: Black women and feminism*. South End Press, 1981.

Huddy, Leonie, and Nayda Terkildsen. "Gender stereotypes and the perception of male and female candidates." *American Journal of Political Science* 37, no. 1 (1993): 119–147.

Hunter, Margaret L. "Colorstruck: Skin color stratification in the lives of African American women." *Sociological Inquiry* 68, no. 4 (1998): 517–535.

Hunter, Margaret. "The persistent problem of colorism: Skin tone, status, and inequality." *Sociology Compass* 1, no. 1 (2007): 237–254.

Hunter, Tera W. *To 'joy my freedom: Southern Black women's lives and labors after the Civil War*. Harvard University Press, 1998.

Jewell, Malcolm E., and Sarah M. Morehouse. *Political parties and elections in American states*. CQ Press, 2001.

Jones, Jacqueline. *Labor of love, labor of sorrow: Black women, work, and the family, from slavery to the present*. Basic Books, 1985.

Jones, Martha S. *Vanguard: How Black women broke barriers, won the vote, and insisted on equality for all*. Hachette UK, 2020.

Jones-Branch, Cherisse. *Better living by their own bootstraps: Black women's activism in rural Arkansas, 1914–1965*. University of Arkansas Press, 2021.

Jordan-Zachery, Julia S. "Am I a Black woman or a woman who is Black? A few thoughts on the meaning of intersectionality." *Politics & Gender* 3, no. 2 (2007): 254–263.

Junn, Jane. "The Trump majority: White womanhood and the making of female voters in the US." *Politics, Groups, and Identities* 5, no. 2 (2017): 343–352.

Junn, Jane, and Nadia Brown. "What revolution? Incorporating intersectionality in women and politics." In *Political Women and American Democracy 1st Edition*, edited by Christina Wolbrecht, Karen Beckwith and Lisa Baldez, 64–78. Cambridge University Press, 2008.

Kahn, Kim Fridkin. *The political consequences of being a woman: How stereotypes influence the conduct and consequences of political campaigns*. Columbia University Press, 1996.

Kathlene, Lyn. "Uncovering the political impacts of gender: An exploratory study." *Western Political Quarterly* 42, no. 2 (1989): 397–421.

Kathlene, Lyn. "Power and influence in state legislative policymaking: The interaction of gender and position in committee hearing debates." *American Political Science Review* 88, no. 3 (1994): 560–576.

Kelley, Robin D. G. *Freedom dreams: The Black radical imagination.* Beacon Press, 2003.

Khalid, Asma. "Pressure grows on Joe Biden to pick a Black woman as his running mate." NPR, June 12, 2020. https://www.npr.org/2020/06/12/875000650/pressure-grows-on-joe-biden-to-pick-a-black-woman-as-his-running-mate.

King, Deborah K. "Multiple jeopardy, multiple consciousness: The context of a Black feminist ideology." *Signs: Journal of Women in Culture and Society* 14, no. 1 (1988): 42–72.

King, Mae C. "The politics of sexual stereotypes." *The Black Scholar* 4, no. 6–7 (1973): 12–23.

King, Mae C. "Oppression and power: The unique status of the Black woman in the American political system." *Social Science Quarterly* 56, no. 1 (1975): 116–128.

Koenig, Anne M., Alice H. Eagly, Abigail A. Mitchell, and Tiina Ristikari. "Are leader stereotypes masculine? A meta-analysis of three research paradigms." *Psychological Bulletin* 137, no. 4 (2011): 616.

Korecki, Natasha, Christopher Cadelago, and Marc Caputo. "'She had no remorse': Why Kamala Harris isn't a lock for VP." *Politico*, July 27, 2020. https://www.politico.com/news/2020/07/27/kamala-harris-biden-vp-381829.

Kunda, Ziva, and Paul Thagard. "Forming impressions from stereotypes, traits, and behaviors: A parallel-constraint-satisfaction theory." *Psychological Review* 103, no. 2 (1996): 284.

Kurtzleben, Danielle. "What we mean when we talk about 'suburban women voters.'" NPR Weekend Edition, April 7, 2018.

Kuruvilla, Carol. "Southern Baptist pastors compare Kamala Harris to Bible's Queen Jezebel." HuffPost, February 9, 2021. https://www.huffpost.com/entry/kamala-harris-jezebel-pastors_n_601d967fc5b68e068fbe2c22.

Ladam, Christina, Jeffrey J. Harden, and Jason H. Windett. "Prominent role models: High-profile female politicians and the emergence of women as candidates for public office." *American Journal of Political Science* 62, no. 2 (2018): 369–381.

Landry, Bart. *Black working wives: Pioneers of the American family revolution.* University of California Press, 2002.

Lang-Takac, Esther, and Zahava Osterweil. "Separateness and connectedness: Differences between the genders." *Sex Roles* 27, no. 5 (1992): 277–289.

Lawless, Jennifer L. "Politics of presence? Congresswomen and symbolic representation." *Political Research Quarterly* 57, no. 1 (2004): 81–99.

Lawless, Jennifer L., and Richard L. Fox. *It takes a candidate: Why women don't run for office.* Cambridge University Press, 2005.

Lee, Chana Kai. *For freedom's sake: The life of Fannie Lou Hamer*. University of Illinois Press, 2000.

Lien, Pei-te, and Katie E. O. Swain. "Local executive leaders: At the intersection of race and gender." In *Women and Executive Office: Pathways and Performance*, edited by Melody Rose, 137–156. Lynne Rienner Publishers, 2013.

Lindsey, Treva B. *Colored no more: Reinventing Black womanhood in Washington, DC*. University of Illinois Press, 2017.

Littlefield, Marci Bounds. "The media as a system of racialization: Exploring images of African American women and the new racism." *American Behavioral Scientist* 51, no. 5 (2008): 675–685.

Locke, Mamie E. "From three-fifths to zero: Implications of the Constitution for African-American women, 1787–1870." *Women & Politics* 10, no. 2 (1990): 33–46.

Lockhart, P. R. "How Black women have continued the fight to vote 100 years after suffrage." NBCNews.com, August 18, 2020. https://www.nbcnews.com/news/nbcblk/how-black-women-have-continued-fight-vote-100-years-after-n1237032.

Maddox, Keith B., and Stephanie A. Gray. "Cognitive representations of Black Americans: Reexploring the role of skin tone." *Personality and Social Psychology Bulletin* 28, no. 2 (2002): 250–259.

Maestas, Cherie D., Sarah Fulton, L. Sandy Maisel, and Walter J. Stone. "When to risk it? Institutions, ambitions, and the decision to run for the US House." *American Political Science Review* 100, no. 2 (2006): 195–208.

Maestas, Cherie D., and Mary Jo Sheperd. *Candidate emergence and recruitment*. Oxford University Press, 2019.

Mansbridge, Jane. "Should Blacks represent Blacks and women represent women? A contingent 'yes.'" *The Journal of Politics* 61, no. 3 (1999): 628–657.

Mansbridge, Jane. "Rethinking representation." *American Political Science Review* 97, no. 4 (2003): 515–528.

Mansbridge, Jane, and Katherine Tate. "Race trumps gender: The Thomas nomination in the Black community." *PS: Political Science and Politics* 25, no. 3 (1992): 488–492.

Marley, Patrick. "Republican official draws outrage for post accusing Kamala Harris of using sex to advance her career." *Milwaukee Journal Sentinel*, October 8, 2020. https://www.jsonline.com/story/news/politics/elections/2020/10/07/gop-official-deletes-post-claiming-kamala-harris-used-sex-advance/5910790002/.

Matthews, Donald R. "Legislative recruitment and legislative careers." *Legislative Studies Quarterly* 9, no. 4 (1984): 547–585.

Maxwell, Angie, and Todd Shields. *The long southern strategy: How chasing white voters in the South changed American politics*. Oxford University Press, 2019.

McAdam, Doug, John D. McCarthy, and Mayer N. Zald, eds. *Comparative perspectives on social movements: Political opportunities, mobilizing structures, and cultural framings*. Cambridge University Press, 1996.

McCourt, Kathleen. *Working-class women and grass-roots politics*. Indiana University Press, 1977.

McDaniel, Eric L. "The Black church and defining the political." *Politics, Groups, and Identities* 1, no. 1 (2013): 93–97.

McRae, Mary, and D. Noumair. *Race and gender in group research: African American research perspectives*. Institute of Social Research, University of Michigan, 1997.

Means, Taneisha N. "Her honor: Black women judges' experiences with disrespect and recusal requests in the american judiciary." *Journal of Women, Politics & Policy* 43, no. 3 (2022): 310–327.

Miller, Arthur H., Patricia Gurin, Gerald Gurin, and Oksana Malanchuk. "Group consciousness and political participation." *American Journal of Political Science* 25, no. 3 (1981): 494–511.

Minta, Michael D. *Oversight: Representing the interests of Blacks and Latinos in Congress*. Princeton University Press, 2011.

Minta, Michael D., and Nadia E. Brown. "Intersecting interests: Gender, race, and congressional attention to women's issues." *Du Bois Review: Social Science Research on Race* 11, no. 2 (2014): 253–272.

Moncrief, Gary F., Peverill Squire, and Malcolm E. Jewell. *Who runs for the legislature?* Prentice Hall, 2001.

Moncrief, Gary, Joel Thompson, and Robert Schulmann. 1991. "Gender, race and the state legislature: A research note on the double disadvantage hypothesis." *Social Science Journal* 28: 481–487.

Montoya, Celeste. "The rhetoric and reality of LGBT rights in the European Union." *Politics, Groups, and Identities* 7, no. 2 (2019): 462–464.

Moore, Robert G. "Religion, race, and gender differences in political ambition." *Politics & Gender* 1, no. 4 (2005): 577.

Morris, Monique. *Pushout: The criminalization of Black girls in schools*. New Press, 2016.

Morris, Tiyi Makeda. *Womanpower unlimited and the Black freedom struggle in Mississippi*. University of Georgia Press, 2015.

Morgen, Sandra. "'It's the whole power of the city against us!' The development of political consciousness in a women's health care coalition." In *Women and the politics of empowerment*, edited by Ann Bookman and Sandra Morgenm, 97–115. Temple University Press, 1988.

Morgen, Sandra, and Ann Bookman. "Rethinking women and politics: An introductory essay." In *Women and the politics of empowerment*, edited by Ann Bookman and Sandra Morgen. Temple University Press, 1988.

Moynihan, Daniel Patrick. "The Negro family: The case for national action." US Department of Labor, Office of Family Planning and Research, Washington, DC. 1965.

Mullings, Leith. "Resistance and resilience: The Sojourner syndrome and the social context of reproduction in Central Harlem." *Transforming Anthropology* 13, no. 2 (2005): 79.

Nadler, Ben. "Voting rights become a flashpoint in Georgia governor's race." Associated Press, October 9, 2018. https://apnews.com/article/fb011f39af3b40518b572c8cce6e906c.

Naples, Nancy A. "'Just what needed to be done': The political practice of women community workers in low-income neighborhoods." *Gender & Society* 5, no. 4 (1991): 478–494.

Naples, Nancy A. "Activist mothering: Cross-generational continuity in the community work of women from low-income urban neighborhoods." *Gender & Society* 6, no. 3 (1992): 441–463.

Nash, Jennifer C. "Intersectionality and its discontents." *American Quarterly* 69, no. 1 (2017): 117–129.

Naylor, Brian. "'Black votes matter': African-Americans propel Jones to Alabama win." NPR, December 13, 2017. https://www.npr.org/2017/12/13/570531505/black-votes-matter-african-americans-propel-jones-to-alabama-win.

NBC News. "Open letter to DNC Chair: 'There's too much at stake to ignore Black women.'" NBCNews.com, May 25, 2017. https://www.nbcnews.com/news/nbcblk/open-letter-dnc-chair-tom-perez-there-s-too-much-n764221.

Neal, Angela M., and Midge L. Wilson. "The role of skin color and features in the Black community: Implications for Black women and therapy." *Clinical Psychology Review* 9, no. 3 (1989): 323–333.

Nelson, Claudia. "Advocacy in action: 100 years of social action in Delta Sigma Theta Sorority, Inc." Delta Research and Education Foundation, Washington DC, 2013.

Niemann, Yolanda Flores, Elizabeth O'Connor, and Randall McClorie. "Intergroup stereotypes of working class Blacks and whites: Implications for stereotype threat." *The Western Journal of Black Studies* 22, no. 2 (1998): 103–104.

Niesse, Mark. "Battle over voter registrations set stage for Georgia governor's race." *The Atlanta Journal-Constitution*, August 17, 2018. https://www.ajc.com/news/state--regional-govt--politics/battle-over-voter-registrations-set-stage-for-georgia-governor-race/zaPRJHP5sY0AjUQ8b9RgTN/.

Niesse, Mark, and Nick Thieme. "Precinct closures harm voter turnout in Georgia, AJC analysis finds." *The Atlanta Journal-Constitution*, December 13, 2019. https://www.ajc.com/news/state--regional-govt--politics/precnct-closures-harm-voter-turnout-georgia-ajc-analysis-finds/11sVcLyQCHuQRC8qtZ6lYP/.

Niven, David. "Throwing your hat out of the ring: Negative recruitment and the gender imbalance in state legislative candidacy." *Politics & Gender* 2, no. 4 (2006): 473–489.

Nunnally, Shayla C. *Trust in Black America: Race, discrimination, and politics*. New York University Press, 2012.

Okazawa-Rey, Margo, Tracy Robinson, and Janie Victoria Ward. "Black women and the politics of skin color and hair." *Women & Therapy* 6, no. 1-2 (1987): 89-102.

Orey, Byron D'Andra. "Black legislative politics in Mississippi." *Journal of Black Studies* 30, no. 6 (2000): 791-814.

Orey, Byron D'Andrá, Wendy Smooth, Kimberly S. Adams, and Kisha Harris-Clark. "Race and gender matter: Refining models of legislative policy making in state legislatures." *Journal of Women, Politics & Policy* 28, no. 3-4 (2007): 97-119.

Orey, Byron D'Andra, and Yu Zhang. "Melanated millennials and the politics of Black hair." *Social Science Quarterly* 100, no. 6 (2019): 2458-2476.

Ortiz, Susan Y., and Vincent J. Roscigno. "Discrimination, women, and work: Processes and variations by race and class." *The Sociological Quarterly* 50, no. 2 (2009): 336-359.

Padilla, M. "Student wins $725,000 in lawsuit over 'troll storm' led by *The Daily Stormer*." *New York Times*, August 10, 2019. https://www. nytimes. com/ 2019/08/10/us/taylor-dumpson. html.

Pardo, Mary. *Mexican American women activists*. Temple University Press, 1998.

Parks, Sheri. *Fierce angels: Living with a legacy from the sacred dark feminine to the strong Black woman*. Chicago Review Press, 2013.

Payne, Charles. "Men led, but women organized: Movement participation of women in the Mississippi Delta." In *Women and Social Protest*, edited by Guida West and Rhoda Lois Blumberg, 156-165. Oxford University Press, 1990.

Phillips, Christian Dyogi. *Expansion and exclusion: Race, gender and immigration in American politics*. University of California, Berkeley, 2017.

Phillips, Christian Dyogi. *Nowhere to run: Race, gender, and immigration in American elections*. Oxford University Press, 2021.

Philpot, Tasha S., and Hanes Walton Jr. "One of our own: Black female candidates and the voters who support them." *American Journal of Political Science* 51, no. 1 (2007): 49-62.

Pinkney, Alphonso. *The myth of Black progress*. Cambridge University Press. 1984.

Pitkin, Hanna F. *The concept of representation*. University of California Press, 1967.

Prestage, Jewel L. "Black women state legislators: A profile." *A Portrait of Marginality: The Political Behavior of the American Woman*, edited by Marianne Githens and Jewel Limar Prestage, 401-418. Addison-Wesley Longman Press, 1977.

Prestage, Jewel L. "In quest of African American political woman." *The Annals of the American Academy of Political and Social Science* 515, no. 1 (1991): 88–103.

Price, Kimala. "What is reproductive justice? How women of color activists are redefining the pro-choice paradigm." *Meridians* 19, no. S1 (2020): 340–362.

Ransby, Barbara. *Ella Baker and the Black freedom movement: A radical democratic vision.* University of North Carolina Press, 2003.

Reflective Democracy Campaign. Confronting the Demographics of Power: American Cities, August 2020.

Reingold, Beth, and Adrienne R. Smith. "Welfare policymaking and intersections of race, ethnicity, and gender in US state legislatures." *American Journal of Political Science* 56, no. 1 (2012): 131–147.

Reston, Maeve. "Kamala Harris' secret weapon: The sisters of AKA." CNNPolitics. January 27, 2019. https://www.cnn.com/2019/01/24/politics/kamala-harris-sorority-sisters-south-carolina/index.html.

Robnett, Belinda. *How long? How long?: African American women in the struggle for civil rights.* Oxford University Press, 1997.

Rogo, Paula. "A GOP congressman tried to come for maxine waters so she corrected him quick, fast, and in a hurry." *Essence Magazine*, October 24, 2020. https://www.essence.com/news/gop-congressman-rep-maxine-waters-mike-kelly-takedown/.

Roper Center. "How groups voted in 2016." 2016. https://ropercenter.cornell.edu/how-groups-voted-2016.

Rosenthal, Alan. *The decline of representative democracy.* SAGE, 1998.

Rosenwasser, Shirley M., and Jana Seale. "Attitudes toward a hypothetical male or female presidential candidate: A research note." *Political Psychology* 9, no. 4 (1988): 591–598.

Rosenwasser, Shirley Miller, and Norma G. Dean. "Gender role and political office: Effects of perceived masculinity/femininity of candidate and political office." *Psychology of Women Quarterly* 13, no. 1 (1989): 77–85.

Rosette, Asleigh Shelby, and Tracy L. Dumas. "The hair dilemma: Conform to mainstream expectations or emphasize racial identity." *Duke Journal of Gender Law and Policy* 14 (2007): 407.

Rouse, Stella M. *Latinos in the legislative process: Interests and influence.* Cambridge University Press, 2013.

Rouse, Stella M., Michele Swers, and Michael Parrott. "Gender, race, and coalition building: Agenda setting as a mechanism for collaboration among minority groups in Congress." In *APSA 2013 Annual Meeting Paper, American Political Science Association 2013 Annual Meeting.* 2013.

Roux, Mathilde. "5 facts about Black women in the labor force." U.S. Department of Labor, Washington, DC, 2021. https://blog.dol.gov/2021/08/03/5-facts-about-black-women-in-the-labor-force.

Rucker, Philip. "Trump has a challenge with white women: 'You just want to smack him.'" *Washington Post*, October 1, 2016. https://www.washingtonp

ost.com/politics/trump-has-a-challenge-with-white-women-you-just-want-to-smack-him/2016/10/01/df08f9ee-875b-11e6-a3ef-f35afb41797f_story.html.

Sanbonmatsu, Kira. "Political parties and the recruitment of women to state legislatures." *The Journal of Politics* 64, no. 3 (2002): 791–809.

Sanbonmatsu, Kira. "Do parties know that "women win"? Party leader beliefs about women's electoral chances." *Politics & Gender* 2, no. 4 (2006): 431.

Sanbonmatsu, Kira. "State elections: Why do women fare differently across states?" In *Gender and elections: Shaping the future of American politics*, 2nd ed., 263–286. Cambridge University Press, 2013.

Sapiro, Virginia. "If US Senator Baker were a woman: An experimental study of candidate images." *Political Psychology* 3, no. 1/2 (1981): 61–83.

Schattschneider, E. E. "Partisan politics and administrative agencies." *The ANNALS of the American Academy of Political and Social Science* 221, no. 1 (1942): 29–32.

Schlesinger, Joseph A. *Ambition and politics: Political careers in the United States*. Rand McNally, 1966.

Schneider, Monica C., and Angela L. Bos. "Measuring stereotypes of female politicians." *Political Psychology* 35, no. 2 (2014): 245–266.

Schneider, Monica C., Mirya R. Holman, Amanda B. Diekman, and Thomas McAndrew. "Power, conflict, and community: How gendered views of political power influence women's political ambition." *Political Psychology* 37, no. 4 (2016): 515–531.

Schram, Sanford F., Joe Soss, Richard C. Fording, and Linda Houser. "Deciding to discipline: Race, choice, and punishment at the frontlines of welfare reform." *American Sociological Review* 74, no. 3 (2009): 398–422.

Scola, Becki. "Women of color in state legislatures: Gender, race, ethnicity and legislative office holding." *Journal of Women, Politics & Policy* 28, no. 3–4 (2007): 43–70.

Scott, Jamil, Nadia Brown, Lorrie Frasure, and Dianne Pinderhughes. "Destined to run? The role of political participation on Black women's decision to run for elected office." *National Review of Black Politics* 2, no. 1 (2021): 22–52.

Scruggs-Leftwich, Yvonne. "Significance of Black women's vote ignored." *Women's E-News*, November 15, 2000. http://www.womensnews.org/article.cfm/dyn/aid/341/context/archive.

Settles, Isis H. "Use of an intersectional framework to understand Black women's racial and gender identities." *Sex Roles* 54, no. 9 (2006): 589–601.

Shah, Paru, Jamil Scott, and Eric Gonzalez Juenke. "Women of color candidates: Examining emergence and success in state legislative elections." *Politics, Groups, and Identities* 7, no. 2 (2019): 429–443.

Shaw, Stephanie J. *What a woman ought to be and to do: Black professional women workers during the Jim Crow era*. University of Chicago Press, 1996.

Shingles, Richard D. "Black consciousness and political participation: The missing link." *American Political Science Review* 75, no. 1 (1981): 76–91.

Shorter-Gooden, Kumea, and N. Chanell Washington. "Young, Black, and female: The challenge of weaving an identity." *Journal of Adolescence* 19, no. 5 (1996): 465–475.

Silva, Andrea, and Carrie Skulley. "Always running: Candidate emergence among women of color over time." *Political Research Quarterly* 72, no. 2 (2019): 342–359.

Simien, Evelyn M. "Race, gender, and linked fate." *Journal of Black Studies* 35, no. 5 (2005): 529–550.

Simien, Evelyn M. "Doing intersectionality research: From conceptual issues to practical examples." *Politics & Gender* 3, no. 2 (2007): 264–271.

Simien, Evelyn M. *Black feminist voices in politics.* State University of New York Press, 2012.

Simien, Evelyn M., and Rosalee A. Clawson. "The intersection of race and gender: An examination of Black feminist consciousness, race consciousness, and policy attitudes." *Social Science Quarterly* 85, no. 3 (2004): 793–810.

Simpson, Andrea Y. *The Tie that binds: Identity and political attitudes in the post-civil rights generation.* New York University Press, 1998.

Simpson, Andrea Y. "Public hazard, personal peril: The impact of non-governmental organizations in the environmental justice movement." *Rich. Journal of Law & Public Interest Law Review* 18 (2014): 515.

Sinclair-Chapman, Valeria. "Symbols and substance: How Black constituents are collectively represented in the United States Congress through roll-call voting and bill sponsorship." PhD diss., Ohio State University, 2002.

Singh, Robert S. *The Congressional Black Caucus: Racial politics in the United States Congress.* SAGE, 1998.

Sisters Lead Sisters Vote. "Open Letter to Joseph Biden." April 24, 2020.

Smooth, Wendy G. "African American women state legislators: The impact of gender and race on legislative influence." University of Maryland, College Park, 2001.

Smooth, Wendy. "Intersectionality in electoral politics: A mess worth making." *Politics & Gender* 2, no. 3 (2006): 400–414.

Smooth, Wendy. "Standing for women? Which women? The substantive representation of women's interests and the research imperative of intersectionality." *Politics & Gender* 7, no. 3 (2011): 436–441.

Smooth, Wendy. "African American women and electoral politics: Translating voting power into office-holding." In *Gender and elections: Shaping the future of American politics*, edited by Susan J. Carroll and Richard L. Fox, 167–189. Cambridge University Press, 2014.

Smooth, Wendy. "Black women's politics pre-dating the age of Trump." Presented at the 2019 National Conference of Black Political Scientists (NCOBPS) Annual Meeting, Baton Roughe, Louisiana, 2019.

Smooth, Wendy, and Elaine Richardson. "Role models matter: Black girls and political leadership possibilities." *The Black Girlhood Studies Collection*, edited by Aria S. Halliday, 131–156. Canadian Scholars Press, 2019.

Sonenshein, Raphael J. "Can Black candidates win statewide elections?" *Political Science Quarterly* 105, no. 2 (1990): 219–241.

Sparks, Holloway. "Dissident citizenship: Democratic theory, political courage." *Hypatia* 12, no. 4 (1997): 4.

Stack, Carol B. "Sex roles and survival strategies in an urban Black community." In *Woman, Culture and Society*, edited by Michelle Zimbalist Rosaldo and Louise Lamhere, 112–128. Stanford University Press, 1974.

Stack, Carol B., and Linda M. Burton. "Kinscripts." *Journal of Comparative Family Studies* 24, no. 2 (1993): 157–170.

Stephan, Walter G., and David Rosenfield. "Racial and ethnic stereotypes." In *The Eye of the Beholder: Contemporary Issues in Stereotyping*, edited by Arthur G. Miller, 92–136. Praeger Publishers, 1982.

Sterling, Dorothy, ed. *We are your sisters: Black women in the nineteenth century*. W. W. Norton, 1997.

Stewart, Abigail J., Isis H. Settles, and Nicholas J. G. Winter. "Women and the social movements of the 1960s: Activists, engaged observers, and nonparticipants." *Political Psychology* 19, no. 1 (1998): 63–94.

Stokes-Brown, Atiya Kai, and Kathleen Dolan. "Race, gender, and symbolic representation: African American female candidates as mobilizing agents." *Journal of Elections, Public Opinion and Parties* 20, no. 4 (2010): 473–494.

Stone, Pauline Terrelonge. "The limitation of reformist feminism." *The Black Scholar* 10, nos. 8/9 (1979): 24–27.

Stout, Christopher T., Kelsy Kretschmer, and Leah Ruppanner. "Gender linked fate, race/ethnicity, and the marriage gap in American politics." *Political Research Quarterly* 70, no. 3 (2017): 509–522.

Streeter, Leslie Gray. "'A dog whistle and a Lie': Black parents on the critical race theory debate." *Washington Post*, December 8, 2021. https://www.washingtonpost.com/parenting/2021/12/07/black-parents-crt-race/.

Sudarkasa, Niara. "Interpreting the African heritage in Afro-American family organization." *Families in the US: Kinship and Domestic Politics*, edited by Harriette Pipes McAdoo, 91–104. Sage Publications, 1998.

Swain, Carol Miller. *Black faces, Black interests: The representation of African Americans in Congress*. Harvard University Press, 1995.

Sweet-Cushman, Jennie. "Where does the pipeline get leaky? The progressive ambition of school board members and personal and political network recruitment." *Politics, Groups, and Identities* 8, no. 4 (2018).

Swers, Michele L. "Transforming the agenda: Analyzing gender differences in women's issue bill sponsorship." In *Women transforming congress*, 260–283. University of Oklahoma Press, 2002.

Tate, Katherine. "Black political participation in the 1984 and 1988 presidential elections." *American Political Science Review* 85, no. 4 (1991): 1159–1176.

Tate, Katherine. *Black faces in the mirror: African Americans and their representatives in the US Congress*. Princeton University Press, 2003.

Terborg-Penn, Rosalyn. *African American women in the struggle for the vote, 1850–1920*. Indiana University Press, 1998.

The Combahee River Collective Statement. United States, 2015. Web Archive. https://www.loc.gov/item/lcwaN0028151/.

Thielemann, Gregory S. "Minority legislators and institutional influence." *The Social Science Journal* 29, no. 4 (1992): 411–421.

Thomas, Anita Jones, and Constance T. King. "Gendered racial socialization of African American mothers and daughters." *The Family Journal* 15, no. 2 (2007): 137–142.

Thomas, Anita Jones, and Suzette L. Speight. "Racial identity and racial socialization attitudes of African American parents." *Journal of Black Psychology* 25, no. 2 (1999): 152–170.

Thomas, Sue. "The impact of women on state legislative policies." *The Journal of Politics* 53, no. 4 (1991): 958–976.

Thomas, Sue. "Introduction." In *Women and elective office: Past, present and future*, edited by Sue Thomas and Clyde Wilcox. 2nd ed., 3–25. Oxford University Press, 2005.

Thornton, Michael C., Linda M. Chatters, Robert Joseph Taylor, and Walter R. Allen. "Sociodemographic and environmental correlates of racial socialization by Black parents." *Child Development* 61, no. 2 (1990): 401–409.

Tien, Charles. "The racial gap in voting among women: White women, racial resentment, and support for Trump." *New Political Science* 39, no. 4 (2017): 651–669.

Tilly, Louise A., and Patricia Gurin, eds. *Women, politics and change*. Russell Sage Foundation, 1990.

Verba, Sidney, and Norman H. Nie. *Participation in America: Political democracy and social equality*. University of Chicago Press, 1987.

Walton, Hanes. *Black politics: A theoretical and structural analysis*. Lippincott, 1972.

Walton, Hanes, Robert C. Smith, and Sherri L. Wallace. *American politics and the African American quest for universal freedom*. Routledge, 2017.

Ward, Orlanda. "Seeing double: Race, gender, and coverage of minority women's campaigns for the U.S. House of Representatives." *Politics & Gender* 12, no. 2 (2016): 317–343.

Weaver, Vesla M. "The electoral consequences of skin color: The "hidden" side of race in politics." *Political Behavior* 34, no. 1 (2012): 159–192.

Weitz, Rose, and Leonard Gordon. "Images of Black women among Anglo college students." *Sex Roles* 28, no. 1 (1993): 19–34.

Welch, Susan. "Women as political animals? A test of some explanations for male-female political participation differences." *American Journal of Political Science* 21, no. 4 (1977): 711–730.

White, Deborah Gray. *Too heavy a load: Black women in defense of themselves, 1894–1994*. W. W. Norton, 1999.

White, Ismail K., and Chryl N. Laird. *Steadfast democrats: How social forces shape Black political behavior*. Vol. 19. Princeton University Press, 2020.

Wilhite, Al, and John Theilmann. "Campaign contributions by political parties ideology vs. winning." *Atlantic Economic Journal* 17, no. 2 (1989): 11.

Williams, Linda Faye. "The civil rights–Black Power legacy." In *Sisters in the Struggle: African American Women in the Civil Rights-Black Power Movement*, edited by Betty Collier-Thomas and V. P. Franklin, 306–332. New York University Press, 2001.

Wilson, Walter Clark. "Latino congressional staffers and policy responsiveness: An analysis of Latino interest agenda-setting." *Politics, Groups, and Identities* 1, no. 2 (2013): 164–180.

Wilson, William Julius. "The declining significance of race." *Society* 15, no. 2 (1978): 56–62.

Zhou, Li. "The push for Joe Biden to choose a Black woman as his running mate, explained." Vox, May 1, 2020. https://www.vox.com/2020/5/1/21239006/joe-biden-vice-president.

Index

For the benefit of digital users, indexed terms that span two pages (e.g., 52–53) may, on occasion, appear on only one of those pages.

401(c)4 organizations, 32
2008 election, 38, 65–66
2016 election, 16, 38–39, 85, 90–91, 148–49, 175n.7, 176n.16
2018 election, 32
   Black women candidates in, 8–9, 16–17, 56–57
   Brian Kemp's voter disenfranchisement in, 10–11, 175n.5
   Stacey Abrams' campaign, 8–9, 10–12
2020 election, 11–12
   Black voters in, 38, 70, 103, 176n.17
   Black women candidates in, 7, 17, 67
   Kamala Harris vice presidential campaign in, 32, 35–36, 89–93

abortion, 121–22, 149–51, 152
Abrams, Stacey, 8–10, 112
   2018 campaign, 8–9, 10–12, 40
aggression (of Black women) stereotype, 28, 90, 91, 92, 94, 96, 108, 149
Aird, Lashrecse, 73–74, 77, 78, 104–5
Akbari, Raumesh, 131–32, 142
Alaska, 164–65
   Anchorage, 122–23, 140–41
Alaska Budget and Legislative Services Office, 122–23
Alaska Energy Railbelt Authority, 122–23
Alaska Municipal Light and Power, 122–23
Alaska State Senate, 122–23
Alcindor, Yamiche, 34–35
Alexander, Joni, 128–29
Alexander-Floyd, Nikol, 164

Alpha Kappa Alpha Sorority, Inc. (AKA), 34, 59, 75, 123–24, 125–26
   IvyPAC, 32
   and Kamala Harris, 32
   Non-Partisan Lobby for Economic and Democratic Rights, 32
Alpha Phi Alpha Fraternity, Inc., 177n.7
Alsobrook, Connie, 76, 99–100, 105–6
Alston, Vernetta, 105
ambition on the margins, 4, 14, 30, 41, 43, 50–51, 114–15, 119–20, 143–44, 164, 165
ambition theory, 14, 18–19, 27–28, 34, 119, 143
American University, 34, 177n.1
Anchorage Assembly, 140, 141
angry Black woman stereotype, 16, 44, 89, 94, 101–2
Anthony, Sarah, 66, 75, 107–8
antislavery activism, 23–24
   See also Emancipation
appearance, politics of, 94–98, 101–2
Arkansas, 59–60, 73
   Des Arc, 112
   Little Rock, 128
   Pine Buff, 128–29
Arkansas Bureau of Legislative Research, 128
Arkansas House of Representatives Legislative Black Caucus, 110, 128
Asian Americans, 117–18, 141–42
Associated Press, 11
Atkins, Tameika, 9–10
Atlanta Journal-Constitution, 11, 83–84

autonomy (of Black women), 28–31, 47–48, 52, 145
  collective, 30–31

backlash, 24
Back to Africa movement, 45–46
Baker, Ella, 7, 9, 163
Barnes, Riché J. Daniel, 29–30, 48–49
Barr, Bill, 91
Baxter, Sandra, 23
Beatty, Joyce, 35–36
Bejarano, Christina E., 24
Benicia African American Moms Group, 142–43
Benicia Arts and Culture Commission, 63–64
Benicia Unified School District, 63–64
Biden, Joe, 175n.1
  and Kamala Harris, 11–12, 38, 89–92, 103, 145
Black, Gordon S., 18–19
Black boys, 50, 141–42
Black church, 23–24, 31, 76–77
  See also church auxiliaries; religion
Black girls, 10, 30, 58, 59–60, 68, 83, 159
  socialization of, 49–50, 56, 59, 79
Black Greek letter organizations (BGLOs), 27, 31, 32, 71–76, 177n.7
  See also Alpha Kappa Alpha Sorority, Inc. (AKA); Delta Sigma Theta Sorority, Inc.; Sigma Gamma Rho Sorority, Inc.; sororities; Zeta Phi Beta Sorority, Inc.
Black Lives Matter, 17
Black men, 26–27, 45–46, 53, 131, 145
  and candidate recruitment, 36–37
  and employment, 47–48
  and sexism, 25, 69–70, 159
Black political culture, 2–3
Black political elites, 65
Black political women, 1, 14–15, 133
#BlackWomen, 145
Black women "saving democracy," 145–46
Black Women's Political Ethos, 146
Black Women's Roundtable, 39, 40–41, 70, 89–90
Blue Wave, 16
Bottoms, Keisha Lance, 16, 72

Bowser, Muriel, 157
Bradford, Karen Bradford, 112
Brady, Henry E., 3
Brailey, Carla, 83–84, 96–97, 129–30
bridge leadership, 25
Brooks, Deborah Jordan, 90
Brown, Elsa Barkley, 30–31
Brown, James, 34–35
Brown, Nadia, 164
Brown, Ruth Nicole, 50
Bryant, Kristin, 62–63
Bryner, Sarah, 20–21
Bureau for Consumer Financial Protections, 116
Bush, Cori, 17, 176n.17
Butler, Helen, 9–10

Caldwell-Johnson, Teree, 59, 125–27, 141–42
California, 63–64, 90–91, 117–18, 142–43, 164–65
  Oakland, 133
  San Francisco, 16, 148, 155
California Association of African American Administrators and School Superintendents, 142–43
Calloway, Sheila, 68–69, 76
Campbell, Melanie, 70, 89–90
candidate emergence, 3, 19, 42, 143, 146, 165–66, 167–68
  community work predicting, 69, 79–80
  party support's effect on, 109–10
  and the radical imagination, 50–53
  recruitment's effect on, 43
candidate nominations, 7–8, 13–14, 16, 35–36, 37
candidate recruitment, 18–20, 84–85, 104–5, 109–10, 113, 114–15, 129
  by community members, 65, 79–81, 82, 103–4, 165–66
  by Democratic Party, 39, 109
  effects of, 50–51, 62, 65, 103–4
  lack of, 36–38, 43–44, 103–4, 105, 109
  and majority-minority districts, 21
  networks enabling, 27
  and party leadership, 37–38
  See also party recruitment
Cantrell, LaToya, 16

INDEX

Capitol Hill, 35–36
caregiving, 22–23, 26
　See also children; motherhood; parenting
Carroll, Susan J., 37–38, 43, 50–51, 103–4
Carter, Jimmy, 10, 175n.5
Center for American Women in Politics, 53–54
Center for Popular Democracy, 74–75
children, 26, 32, 34–35, 60–61, 62–63, 67–68, 80, 113, 121, 125–27, 142–43, 152, 153
　childcare, 70–71, 131
　political participation of, 58–59
　and racist stereotypes, 84–85
　socialization of, 4, 26, 46
　and strong Black woman stereotype, 49–50
　See also Black boys; Black girls
Chisholm, Shirley, 9, 13–14
church auxiliaries, 23–24, 27, 51
Citizen Political Ambition Study, 19
civic duty, 24–25
civic empowerment, 31
civic engagement, 2, 3, 15–16, 31–32, 40–41, 70, 78–79
civic organizations, 23–24, 27, 51, 59, 73–74, 81, 118–19, 123–24
Civil Rights Movement, 25, 31, 38, 70, 87
Civil War, 30–31
Clark, Septima, 9, 133
class, 4–5, 24–25, 29–30, 31, 48–49, 77, 94
　class oppression, 25
　and household/community responsibilities, 42–43
　and labor, 44–46
　and voting rights, 7
classism, 45–46
Clay, William Lacy, 17
Clinton, Hillary, 38, 62–63, 85
clubs, 15–16, 23–24, 27, 30, 51, 67, 70, 71, 148, 159
Cohen, Cathy, 33
collective wisdom, 83–84
Collins, Patricia Hill, 13–14, 23

Colorado, 40
Colored Women's Club Movement, 71
Combahee River Collective, 52, 145, 163
communal goals, 17–18
communal socialization, 48–49
community commitment, 2–3, 77, 143–44, 160
　racialized, 45
　and running for office, 59, 68
　See also motivation; service
community development, 5
community expectations, 6, 25, 78, 155–56, 158, 159, 160, 162
community organizations, 4, 5, 61, 81, 165–67
Confederacy, 58
confidence, 22–23, 28, 51, 53, 57, 62, 63–64, 138
Connecticut, 21
conservative politics, 91, 149–52, 161–62
controlling images, 87
Cooper, Anna Julia, 9, 26, 46
COVID-19 pandemic, 35–36, 122, 134–35, 145–46
critical Black consciousness, 13–14
critical race theory (CRT), 84–85
CROWN Act, 141
cultural expectations, 46

Daniels, Ashley, 146
Davis, Angela, 116, 163
Dawkins-Haigler, Dee, 58, 97, 98
Dawson, Michael C., 82–83
Delaware, 125
　Black women legislators from, 175n.7
　Wilmington, 87, 124, 137
Delta Sigma Theta Sorority, Inc., 32, 67, 71–72, 73, 74–75, 125
　D4Women in Action, 32
　Delta Days in the Nation's Capital, 55–56, 176–77n.4
　National Vigilance Committee, 32
Demessie, Menna, 111, 112
Demings, Val, 175n.7
democracy, 10, 14, 74–75, 108, 140
　Black women saving, 145–46
Democratic National Committee, 38–39, 111

204 INDEX

Democratic Party, 15–16, 58, 65–66, 70, 74–75, 123–24, 132–33, 145–46, 147, 176n.14
    and campaign funding, 176n.1
    candidate recruitment by, 39, 109
    Democratic Party of Arkansas, 112
    gendered support for, 88–89, 103
    and Kamala Harris, 7–8, 32, 89–93
    lack of support for Black women, 37, 38–41, 102–13
    and Maxine Waters, 35
    Michigan Democratic Party, 109
    nominations by, 7–8, 13–14, 17, 32, 35, 89–93
    Rockingham County Democrats, 66
    role of Black voters in, 1, 9–12, 38, 90–91, 103, 108
    role of Black women in, 38–40
    and Stacey Abrams, 9–12
    Texas Democratic Party, 83, 96, 129–30
Democratic Party of Arkansas, 112
descriptive representation, 13–14, 139–40, 147–48
desegregation, 12–13
Des Moines School Board, 59, 125–26, 141–42
DiLorenzo, Charlotte, 65–66, 100–1
discrimination, 14–15, 20–21, 42–43, 51, 116–17, 149, 167
    antidiscrimination law, 141
    colorist, 97
    in labor, 12–13, 45–46
    racially gendered, 23–24, 30–31, 41, 47, 49–50, 81
    resistance to, 9
disenfranchisement, 7, 145–46
    in 2018 election, 10–11, 175n.5
    See also voter suppression
dissident citizenship, 51, 53
Dittmar, Kelly, 16, 136–37
DMV area, 148, 155–56
Dodd, Chris, 91–92
double jeopardy, 24
doubly bound status, 24, 33
DREAMers, 141–42
dual-minority identity, 56
DuBois, W. E. B., 45–46
Dumpson, Taylor, 34
DuPont Company, 124, 125

educational groups, 23–24
egalitarianism, 50
electability, 37–38, 43–44, 103–4
election monitoring, 10
Emancipation, 23–24, 30–31
emasculation, 28, 98–99
Emerge America, 110–11
EMILY's List, 176n.1, 176n.17
empowerment, 5–6, 12, 13, 17, 31, 61, 79, 133, 149–50, 163
endorsements, 40, 66, 74
engaged citizenship, 52
environmental justice, 70
ESPN, 177n.1
Essence Magazine, 38–39
excellence, 43, 44–45, 46, 47–48, 60–61, 79, 81
extroversion, 28

Facebook, 53–54, 72
Fair Fight, 11–12
femininity, 36, 84, 90, 95, 98
feminism, 26, 46, 52, 88–89, 146
Fenty, Anthony, 129–30
Fife, Carroll, 135–36
Flammang, Janet A., 28
Florida, 54–55, 56, 57, 148, 150–51, 175n.7
    Jacksonville, 94
    Miami, 93–94, 148
    Tallahassee, 75, 76–77, 106, 148, 151
Flowers, Vivian, 59–60, 110–11, 112–13, 128
Floyd, George, 132
Fox, Richard L., 19, 28
Fox News, 34–35
Fraga, Luis Ricardo, 24
freedom, 7, 8, 42–43, 163
Frymer, Paul, 108
Fudge, Marcia, 17
fundraising, 28, 53–54, 68, 71, 111, 136, 166–67
    and candidate recruitment, 43–44, 104–5
    challenges to, 20–21, 37–38, 40, 43–44, 60–61, 90–91, 99–100, 103–5, 106, 107–8, 166
    early, 176n.1
    networks enabling, 4, 20, 27, 31, 32, 53, 65, 73–74, 75–76, 82, 109, 165
    and social capital, 4, 27, 31

INDEX

Gamble, Katrina, 19
Garvey, Marcus, 45–46
Garza, Alicia, 9
gatekeeping, 36–37, 43, 160, 165–66
gendered racial identity, 4, 22–27, 41, 131, 158
gender gap, 38, 103
gender identity, 4, 22–27, 41, 152, 158
gender roles, 25, 28, 46
gender socialization, 22–23, 27–28, 47
Georgia, 9, 21, 40, 58, 97, 103, 145–46, 175n.5
   in 2018 election, 8–12
   Atlanta, 16, 58, 61–62, 72, 94, 148, 150
   Conyers, 99, 105–6, 138
   Covington, 76
   Fairburn, 61
   Macon, 154
   Milledgeville, 16
   Rockdale County, 67, 97–98
   Savannah, 1
Georgia Coalition for the People's Agenda, 9–10
Georgia House of Representatives, 9
Georgia Stand Up, 9–10
Georgia State Senate, 9
Gilkes, Cheryl Townsend, 24–25, 31, 92
Gilmore, Brenda, 17–18, 68, 80, 132–33
Glaize, Lydia, 61–62
Gray, Freddie, 155–56
Gray-Jackson, Elvi, 122–23, 127, 140–41
group consciousness, 33, 46, 82–83, 167

Haley, Grace, 20–21
Hamer, Fannie Lou, 1, 9, 163
Harris, Kamala, 112
   in 2020 election, 7–8, 11–12, 40, 89–93, 145, 175n.2
   Alpha Kappa Alpha membership, 32
   racist attacks on, 35–36, 89–93, 166
   in the Senate, 17, 175n.7
Harris-Perry, Melissa V., 101–2
Hayes, Jahana, 21, 176n.17
healthcare, 70, 121–22, 131, 132, 142, 146, 153, 161
   See also abortion
Height, Dorothy I., 42
Higher Heights for America, 31–32, 40–41
Hill, Jamelle, 177n.1

Historically Black Colleges and Universities (HBCUs), 2, 23–24, 31, 70–71, 77, 121, 125–26, 177n.7
home socialization, 47–48
hostility, 34–36
housewives, 28–29, 47
Howard University, 96, 177n.7
Hurston, Zora Neale, 102
hypervisibility, 41, 47

identity politics, 13–14
Illinois, 21, 54–55
   Chicago, 70, 72, 148, 150
immigration policy, 35, 123–24
incumbents, 16–17, 18–19, 40, 139, 176n.17
   See also re-election
intergenerationality, 26, 46
intersectionality, 5, 19–20, 25
   and Black women's identity, 22–23, 86, 114
invisibility, 22–23, 34, 41, 47, 81
Iowa, 7–8, 164–65
   Des Moines, 59, 125–26, 141–42
Iowa Solid Waste Authority, 125–26

Jack and Jill of America, Inc., 2, 125–26
Janey, Kim, 16
Jasmine, 56, 155
Jean-Pierre, Karine, 175n.1
Jenkins, Andrea, 16
Jenkins, Angie, 62, 64–65, 100, 121–23, 133–35, 137–38, 141
Jenkins, Shawnette, 141
Jewell, Malcolm E., 37
Jewish people, 145–46
jezebel stereotype, 87, 92
Jim Crow, 96
Joi, 155, 159
Jones, Doug, 103, 145
Jones, Tishaura, 16, 55–56, 60, 68, 74–75, 177n.5
Jones-Potter, Velda, 87–88, 124–25, 135, 137
Jordan, Barbara, 9, 143–44
Jordan, June, 82, 163
Jordan-Zachery, Julia, 164
justice, 5–6, 8, 42–43, 55–56, 58, 68, 70–71, 113, 131, 146, 163–64
   racial, 32
   reproductive, 70

Kansas
  Salina, 59
Kappa Alpha Psi Fraternity, Inc., 177n.7
Karrie, 73
Kavanaugh, Brett, 91
Kelley, Robin D. G., 8
Kelly, 151–52, 154
Kelly, Mike, 116–18
Kemp, Brian
  voter disenfranchisement in 2018 election, 10–11, 175n.5
Kennedy, Florynce, 9
King, Mae, 3, 34, 164
Kunda, Ziva, 90

labor activism, 70
labor participation, 28–29, 48
lady, racially gendered, 45, 113
Lansing, Marjorie, 23
Latinos, 7, 24, 38, 103, 117–18, 139–40, 141–42
Lawless, Jennifer L., 19, 28
Lawson-Rowe, Meredith, 58, 59, 62–63, 100, 141
Leadership Conference on Civil and Human Rights, 123–24
leadership development, 21–22, 31, 42, 118–19, 125–26, 143, 165
leadership skills, 5–6, 49–50, 56, 75–76, 118–19, 120–21, 124
liberal politics, 77, 88–89, 91, 149–54, 161–62
Links, Inc., 2, 31, 59, 73–74
Local Progress, 74–75
Locke, Mamie, 3, 164
Louisiana, 121
  New Orleans, 16
Lyles, Vi, 16

Maine, 40
majority Black districts, 4–5, 15, 53–55, 164–65
majority-minority districts, 15, 21
  See also majority Black districts
Malcom, Ellen, 176n.1
mammy stereotype, 87, 89, 92

marginalization, 54–55, 60–61, 122, 140, 164, 167
  and ambition on the margins, 4, 12–13, 41
  and community support, 21–22
  and dissident citizenship, 51
  and motivations to run, 19–20, 55–56
  and networks, 31, 78–79, 82–83, 118–19
  within political parties, 36–40
  and racialized gender, 25, 33–34
  and radical imagination, 8–9
  resisting, 82–115
  and Stacey Abrams, 12
  and stereotypes, 5–6, 34
Markell, Jack, 125
marriage, 29–30, 48–49, 85, 113, 150, 151–52
Maryland, 54–55, 123–24, 148, 152
  Baltimore, 155–56
  See also DMV area
Maryland House of Delegates, 138
masculinity, 28, 88–89, 117
Massachusetts
  Boston, 16
  Framingham, 16, 175n.8
matriarchs, 13, 87, 98–99
McBath, Lucy, 21, 176n.17
McClintock, Tom, 116–17
Means, Tenesha, 101
Medicaid, 142
mentoring, 51, 53, 55, 74, 83–84, 104–5, 112–13, 128, 143
methodology of book, 13, 53–55, 148–49
Metro Nashville Council, 17–18
Michigan Democratic Party, 109
Michigan House of Representatives, 66, 75, 107, 109
middle-class people, 1, 2, 4–5, 27, 45–46, 49–50, 127, 161, 166–67
Miller, Arthur H., 82–83
Minneapolis City Council, 16
Minnesota, 21
  Minneapolis, 16
misogynoir, 92
Mississippi
  Gulfport, 9

Missouri, 121
  St. Louis, 16, 55–56, 68, 155
Mitchell, Tia, 83–84
Moncrief, Gary F., 37
Moore, Michael K., 19
Moore, Vonda Searcy, 72
More, Roy, 145
Morris, Tiyi Makeda, 25
Mosby, Marilyn, 155–56
Mosley Braun, Carol, 60–61, 102
Moss, Gethsemane, 63–64, 65, 142–43
motherhood, 24, 29–30, 45–46, 48–49, 123–24, 153
  and political role models, 58–59, 60–61
  and political socialization, 47–48
  racialized, 84–85, 98–99
  and racial socialization, 26
  strategic, 48–49
motivation, 4, 16, 17, 19–20, 26–27, 41, 47, 52, 53–54, 56, 60–61, 67, 122–23, 152, 166
  networks/community providing, 2, 4–5, 8, 14–51, 53, 59, 68, 69, 80, 126–27, 139
  See also community commitment
Motley, Constance Baker, 9
Mullings, Leith, 42–43
multiple jeopardy, 24
Murray, Pauli, 9

NAACP, 31–32, 67
nascent ambition, 50–51
Nash, Diane, 163
National Association of Black Social Workers, 176n.10
National Association of Colored Women (NACW), 70–71
National Black Nurses Association, 176n.10
National Coalition of 100 Black Women, 125
National Coalition on Black Civic Participation, 31–32, 40–41
National Council of Negro Women, 31–32
The Negro Family: The Case for National Action (Moynihan Report), 98–99

neo-Nazis, 34
networks, 4, 5, 13, 21–22, 40–41, 51, 52, 70, 72, 73, 77, 80–81, 97, 127, 143
  and candidate recruitment, 27, 36–37, 53
  and Democratic Party, 102–13
  and fundraising, 4, 20–21, 27, 31, 32, 53, 65, 73–76, 79–80, 82–83, 99–100, 109, 165
  and legislative office, 128, 131, 138
  and marginalization, 31, 33, 78–79, 82–83, 118–19
  and motivation, 2, 4–5, 8, 14–51, 53, 59, 68, 69, 80, 126–27, 139
  and parenting, 142–43
  and radical imagination, 8
  and resisting marginalization, 5–6
  and social capital, 24–25, 42, 160
  and socialization, 30–32, 44, 47–48, 55, 79, 118–19, 143–44, 165–67
  and Stacey Abrams, 8–9
  and volunteering, 55, 67–68, 165–66
  See also Black church; Black Greek letter organizations (BGLOs); church auxiliaries; civic organizations; clubs; Historically Black Colleges and Universities (HBCUs); social organizations; sororities
New DEAL Leaders, 74–75
New Georgia Project, 9–12
New Hampshire, 65–66, 100–1, 164–65
  Hampton, 66
New Hampshire House of Representatives, 65–66, 100–1
New York City, 148
  Brooklyn, 149
  Harlem, 42–43
New York State, 175n.9
Nicole, 152, 157
Niven, David, 37
non-incumbents, 16, 21, 175n.7
non-majority-minority districts, 15, 21, 175n.7
nonprofits, 5–6, 70, 86, 120–21, 123–24, 126, 127, 130, 166–67
nontraditional forms of participation, 15–16, 23–24, 27, 30–31, 51, 52–53, 55–56

North Carolina, 105
  Charlotte, 16, 154
North Carolina House of
  Representatives, 105
NPR, 92–93
Nunnally, Shayla C., 26, 46

Obama, Barack, 38, 62–63, 65–66
Ohio, 164–65
  Reynoldsburg, 58, 62–63, 64, 67, 100–
    1, 121, 137–38, 141
Ohio Attorney General's Office, 121
Ohio Department of Health, 121–22
Ohio Information Technology Office, 121
Omar, Ilhan, 21
one-drop rule, 97
on-the-job training, 120–27
oppression, 11–12, 16, 23–25, 29–30, 48–
    49, 86–87, 145–46, 163
  See also classism; patriarchy; racism;
    sexism; white supremacy
O'Reilly, Bill, 34–35
Othering, 34–36

Pacific Islander Americans, 141
paradox of participation, 30–31,
    130, 167–68
parenting, 28–29, 48, 84–85, 142–43
  See also children; motherhood
Parham-Copeland, Mary, 16
Parks, Rosa, 7, 163
partisanship, 18–19, 32, 122–23, 127, 128,
    131, 136
  See also Democratic Party;
    Republican Party
party leadership, 37–39, 40, 43–44, 90–
    91, 103–4
party politics, 19, 109–10
party recruitment, 18–19, 37–38
  See also candidate recruitment
party support, 37–38, 103–4, 106–10
patriarchy, 69–70, 87
Pelosi, Nancy, 35, 176n.14
Pennsylvania, 116, 164–65
  Winchester, 104
Perez, Tom, 38–39
Pitkin, Hannah, 147–58
Planned Parenthood, 152

police violence, 12–13, 132, 155–56, 160
policy development, 5–6, 166–67
political ambition socialization
    model, 28
political conditions, 18–19
political efficacy, 24–25
political ideology, 46
political pipelines, 19
political science, 2–3, 78–79, 164
political socialization, 4, 22, 23–24,
    27–30, 31, 34, 47–48, 49–50, 55,
    78–79, 167–68
poverty, 70, 87, 98–99, 128–29
Pratt, Sharon, 52–53, 87
Pressley, Ayanna, 176n.17
Prestage, Jewel, 3, 164
privilege, 19–20
Pro Georgia, 9–10
progressive politics, 13–14, 38, 74–75,
    103, 131, 147–48
property, 23–24
public speaking, 53, 65
public sphere, 101–2

queerness, 141, 149–50, 151–52
Quest Scholars Network, 74

race identification, 46
race roles, 46
racial/community uplift, 13, 31, 44–46,
    66, 71, 95, 154
racial identity, 4, 22–27, 41, 46, 95, 97, 158
racial pride, 50
racism, 4, 16, 23, 83–84
  attacks on Kamala Harris, 35–36,
    89–93, 166
  and children, 84–85
  by Donald Trump, 34–36, 92
  resisting, 26, 70, 77, 79–80, 131
  and sexism, 4, 23, 45, 48–50, 60–61, 69,
    71, 79–80, 87, 93
  systemic, 64, 70, 83–84, 108
  by white women, 25, 69–70
  See also aggression (of Black women)
    stereotype; angry Black woman
    stereotype; jezebel stereotype;
    mammy stereotype; sapphire
    stereotype; stereotypes; strong Black

woman stereotype; welfare queen stereotype; white supremacy
radical imagination, definition, 8, 12–15
Rascoe, Ayesha, 92
rational choice model, 18–19
rebellious professionalism, 31
rebuke, 34–36, 83–84, 98–102, 116–18
redistricting, 15
re-election, 66, 67, 129
  See also incumbents
religion, 12–13, 15–16, 27, 51, 70, 118–19, 150–51, 152
  See also Black church; church auxiliaries
representation (political), 15
reproductive justice, 70
Republican Party (GOP), 9, 15–16, 17, 35, 102, 104, 116, 142, 145, 175n.5, 176n.14
  white women's support for, 1, 38, 85, 102, 103
resilience, 49–50
respectability politics, 45–46, 98
Reynoldsburg City Council, 58, 62–63, 64, 67, 100, 121, 137–38, 141
Richardson, Elaine, 49–50
Robinson, Jo Ann, 9
Robnett, Belinda, 25
Rochester, Lisa Blunt, 175n.7
Rockingham County Democrats, 66
role models, 29–30, 48, 59, 73
Ryan, April, 34–35

Sanbonmatsu, Kira, 37–38, 43, 50–51, 103–4
Sanders, Symone, 175n.1
Sanders, Willa Black, 128
sapphire stereotype, 87
Savannah State University, 2
Schlesinger, Joseph A., 18–19
Schlozman, Kay Lehman, 3
Schumer, Chuck, 35
Scott, Deborah, 9–10, 164
Scott, Elsie, 39
Scott, Jamil, 164
segregation, 33, 98–99, 161
  See also desegregation
self-determination, 45–46

self-promotion, 28
self-reliance, 29–30
service, 3, 54–55, 60, 62, 81, 87, 104–5, 117–19, 124–25, 131
  and ambition on the margins, 42–43
  and the Black Church, 76
  and Black sororities, 71, 75–76, 123–24
  to the community, 17–18, 65–66, 121, 139–43
  expectations of, 29–30, 111
  and motivation to run, 2–3, 52–53, 67–68
  and networks, 53
  and socialization, 27–28, 55–56, 57–58, 59, 79, 82
  See also community commitment
sexism, 4, 12–13, 45–46, 51, 97–98
  by Black men, 25, 69–70, 159
  by Donald Trump, 34–36, 92
  and racism, 4, 23, 45, 48–50, 60–61, 69, 71, 79–80, 87, 93
sexuality, 50, 99, 151
sexual violence, 45, 60, 145, 152
  by Donald Trump, 85
shaming, 12–13, 36, 83–84, 86–87, 93, 94, 98–102, 112, 114
  by Donald Trump, 34–35
Shelby v. Holder (2013), 10–11
Shingles, Richard, 33–34
Sigma Gamma Rho Sorority, Inc., 32
Simien, Evelyn M., 164–65
sisterhood, 51, 75
skin color, 96–97
slavery, 7, 36, 92, 98–99, 143
  See also antislavery activism; Emancipation
Smith, Beverly Evans, 71–72
Smith, Valyncia, 99–100, 106, 138–39
Smooth, Wendy, 49–50, 130, 164, 167–68
soccer mom stereotype, 84
social capital, 4, 24–25, 26–27, 29–31, 42, 48, 53, 93, 160
social justice, 58, 131, 146
social media, 34–35, 90, 92, 95, 106, 128, 137–38, 145
  See also Facebook; Twitter
social organizations, 2, 4, 59, 73–74, 81, 118–19

social science, 2–3, 95
solidarity, 24–25, 69–70
sororities, 1–2, 31–32, 72–73, 77, 123–24, 125–26, 155
　and political support, 32, 55–56, 71–72, 74–76
　and social capital, 27
　See also Alpha Kappa Alpha Sorority, Inc. (AKA); Black Greek letter organizations (BGLOs); Delta Sigma Theta Sorority, Inc.; Sigma Gamma Rho Sorority, Inc.; Zeta Phi Beta Sorority, Inc.
Soul Food, 13
South Carolina, 58
　Lexington County, 58
South Korea, 128–29
Sparks, Holloway, 51
Speight, Suzette L., 50
Spelman College, 9, 125–26
Spicer, Yvonne, 16
Squire, Peverill, 37
stereotypes, 5–6, 18–19, 24–25, 34, 36, 41, 82–84, 86–89, 93–96, 98, 99, 101, 108, 109–10, 145–46, 149, 150, 166, 177n.1
　aggression stereotype, 28, 90, 91, 92, 94, 96, 108, 149
　angry Black woman stereotype, 16, 44, 89, 94, 101–2
　jezebel stereotype, 87, 92
　and Kamala Harris, 89–93
　mammy stereotype, 87, 89, 92
　sapphire stereotype, 87
　soccer mom stereotype, 84
　strong Black woman stereotype, 49–50, 101–2
　suburban mom stereotype, 84
　welfare queen stereotype, 84, 98–99
stigma, 24–25, 33, 94, 177n.1
Strickland, Shanette, 60–61, 62–63, 67, 100
strong Black woman stereotype, 49–50, 101–2
student activism, 70
substantive representation, 13–14, 147–48, 155–56, 159, 160
suburban mom stereotype, 84

suffrage movement, 25
　and Black women candidates, 175n.9
sunshine laws, 100
super joiners, 2
survival, 42–43, 48, 69–70, 83–84, 113
symbolic representation, 147, 159

talented tenth, 45–46
Taylor, Ivy, 85–86
temperance organizations, 23–24
TennCare, 142
Tennessee, 80, 131–33, 142
　Nashville, 17–18, 68
　Tennessee House of Representatives, 132–33
　Tennessee State Senate, 13, 17–18, 131–32
Terrell, Mary Church, 9
Texas, 9, 54–55, 56, 83, 96, 129–30
　Dallas, 148, 155
　Houston, 148, 150, 151, 158
　San Antonio, 85
Texas Democratic Party, 83, 96, 129–30
Thagard, Paul, 90
#ThankYouBlackWomen, 145
Thomas, Anita Jones, 50
Top Ladies of Distinction Incorporated, 2, 31
transferrable skills, 5–6, 52–53, 68, 118–20
trans women, 16
Trump, Donald, 16, 35, 90–91, 114, 116
　racist sexism of, 34–36, 92
　sexual assaults by, 85
　white women's support of, 38, 85
Truth, Sojourner, 9
Tubman, Harriet, 9
Twitter, 34–35, 95
two-party system, 108

Underwood, Lauren, 21
University of Texas at Austin, 9
US Attorney's Office, 60–61
US Congress, 15, 17–18, 21, 32, 136–37
　117th, 31–32
　Congressional Black Caucus, 35–36
　House Financial Services Committee, 116–18

House of Representatives, 9, 16–17, 34–35, 116–18, 175n.7
  Senate, 17, 35, 39–40, 90–91, 103, 145–46, 175n.7
  Senate Judiciary Committee, 91
US Constitution, 23–24, 35
US Department of Housing and Urban Development, 17
US Department of Justice, 10–11
US Midwest, 53–54
US Northeast, 53–54
US South, 1, 10–11, 30–31, 53–54, 75, 103, 150–51, 164–65
US Supreme Court, 91
US West Coast, 53–54

Verba, Sidney, 3
Virginia, 73–74, 77, 104–5, 128–29, 148, 151
  See also DMV area
Virginia House of Delegates, 73–74, 77, 104–5
Virginia State University, 77
visionary dreams, 8
voluntary apartheid, 61–62
volunteer work, 5, 51, 53, 62–63, 65–66, 69, 70–71, 74–76, 79–80, 124, 136, 163–64
  and networks, 55, 67–68, 165–66
voter education, 11–12, 26, 31
Voter Empowerment Collaborative, 61
voter mobilization, 4, 7, 27, 32, 38–39, 70, 90–91, 103, 111
voter participation, 11–12, 26–27, 53
voter registration, 9–10, 11–12, 32
  exact match screening process, 10–11
voter suppression, 8–9, 11–12
  by Brian Kemp's in 2018 election, 10–11, 175n.5
  See also disenfranchisement
voting rights, 7, 10–11, 12–13, 25, 71
  See also suffrage movement
Voting Rights Act (1965), 7, 10–11, 12–13

Washington, Booker T., 45–46
Washington, DC, 38–39, 52–53, 54–55, 83–84, 87, 94, 148, 152, 155–56, 157

  See also DMV area
Washington, DC Public Service Commission, 129–30
Washington, DC Sports Commission, 129–30
Washington, Sherri, 67, 97–98
Waters, Maxine, 34–35, 177n.1
  "No, I will not yield," 116–18
welfare queen stereotype, 84, 98–99
Whitaker, Nicole, 104
White House, 34–35, 145
white men, 20, 22, 37–38, 63–64, 85, 91, 92–93, 107, 161, 164
white supremacy, 58, 60
  See also racism
white women, 1, 15, 19, 20, 21, 26–27, 28–30, 44, 45, 48–49, 53, 89, 112, 156
  and the Democratic Party, 112–13
  and the gender gap, 38
  and labor participation, 36, 48
  motivation to run, 16
  political ambition of, 2–3, 14, 78–79, 114
  political participation of, 3
  and the politics of appearance, 95, 149
  racism by, 25, 69–70
  support for Donald Trump, 38, 85
  support for progressive politics, 147–48
  support for Republican Party, 1, 38, 85, 102, 103
  white womanhood, 84, 85, 165–66
Wilkins, Jheanelle, 123–24, 138
Williams, Linda, 46
Williams-Cox, Diane, 75, 76, 106–7
Wilson, Erin, 175n.1
women's conventions, 23–24
"women's issues," 131
working-class people, 1, 45

Xavier University, 121

Yale University, 86
  Law School, 9
Yancey, Tenisha, 66, 109
YMCA, 68

Zeta Phi Beta Sorority, Inc., 32, 72